21 | 19

21 | 19

CONTEMPORARY POETS

IN THE

NINETEENTH-CENTURY ARCHIVE

Edited by Kristen Case
and Alexandra Manglis

MILKWEED EDITIONS

Published 2019 by Milkweed Editions
Printed in Canada
Cover design by Mary Austin Speaker
Cover collage created from photographs courtesy of the Amherst College Archives & Special
Collections and of George Hodan
19 20 21 22 23   5 4 3 2 1
First Edition

Milkweed Editions, an independent nonprofit publisher, gratefully acknowledges sustaining
support from the Ballard Spahr Foundation; the Jerome Foundation; the McKnight Foundation;
the National Endowment for the Arts; the Target Foundation; and other generous contributions
from foundations, corporations, and individuals. Also, this activity is made possible by the voters
of Minnesota through a Minnesota State Arts Board Operating Support grant, thanks to a
legislative appropriation from the arts and cultural heritage fund. For a full listing of Milkweed
Editions supporters, please visit milkweed.org.

Library of Congress Cataloging-in-Publication Data

Names: Case, Kristen, 1976– editor. | Manglis, Alexandra, 1983– editor.
Title: 21, 19 : contemporary poets in the nineteenth-century archive / edited
    by Kristen Case and Alexandra Manglis.
Description: First edition. | Minneapolis, Minnesota : Milkweed Editions,
    2019. | Includes bibliographical references.
Identifiers: LCCN 2019017649 (print) | LCCN 2019022044 (ebook) | ISBN
    9781571319869 (ebook) | ISBN 9781571313775 (paperback : alk. paper)
Subjects: LCSH: American poetry—19th century—History and criticism.
Classification: LCC PS316 (ebook) | LCC PS316 .A16 2019 (print) | DDC
    811/.309—dc23
LC record available at https://lccn.loc.gov/2019017649

CONTENTS

FOREWORD

APPROXIMITY (IN THE LIFE, HER ATTEMPT TO BRING THE LIFE OF HER MOTHER CLOSE

Fred Moten

Forewords are cardings that ought to be, but can't quite be, discarded. Terraced airings of tangle, smoothing out refusals of smoothing, defibering with dried fibers in bright *Farben*, preparing spinning with caressive compact, they're said to be particularly useful in anthologies, or to anthologies in being in but not quite of anthologies. Forewords tell you about, thereby displacing, what you're about to read. They postpone your reading in the interest of your reading so closely that *you* start weaving, so you can bring to light what's not there in what you're reading. This ongoing worrying of leaves becomes a way of life, which erodes the garments of those who would appear at first glance not to be in it. This foreword is not unique in its difference from what follows, which is what it's in. There's all this stuff in here that's not in here that I want to tell you to look for in here. This anthology, and not just insofar as it is an anthology, bears a double orchestral simplicity—asymptotic, intra-active, not falling together, and cutting together-apart, to get here, like Suné Woods and Karen Barad, which is Karen Barad in Suné Woods, almost. In this regard, all up in here, not in here at all, this anthology is special in its concern and preparation for the making of the general anthology. Kristen Case and Alexandra Manglis have put together something beautiful and deep about how things go together in a place that sells, but no longer prides, itself on having figured out how things go together better than any other place, at any time. This anthology tells the truth and exposes that lie, in the interest of what might be truly deep and beautiful about a genuine proximity whose spatio-temporal form it seeks to excavate and enact by way of the extraordinary sources and resources they gather and disburse. Excavation and enactment turn out to be an arrangement of windows. These essays have the look of essays that are looked through. If we look through them to what's not there it's because, here, we're being taught to do so. Every anthology is about what's been excluded; these essays try to bring that close as they range from riot to recipe in their common refusal to be collected. In this sheaf, the truth of black cake has always already displaced the lie of the melting pot. In this bouquet, that truth is displaced, too. Such displacement teaches us all we can know about everything, which is that everything ain't all; that everything's not the erasure of exclusion but its management; that it's not things but nothing that goes together, apart, after all. That's why we have to look through what's gathered here, which what's gathered here facilitates. In this anthology, the incompleteness we desire breaks the brokenness we abjure.

Here, but not here, there are two phrases Terrion Williamson resounds, along with the very large array of thought through which they pass. They work like little bits of poetry, or fragments of a song you hear yourself sing sometimes though you've never heard it before. *In the life, her attempt to bring the life of her mother close,* teach us how to read this book you're about to try to read that you've been reading, which is trying to teach you something about how to try to read. You've got to be right there in the life to bring the life of her mother close. Got to be there. Got to be there. Be there in the mourning, in and out of abandon, which is given where proximity brushes up against closeness, when everything turns out to turn on how we think how all but inseparable being-(de)valued is from being-invaluable. That's a specificity you have to find and it's right here with you. It's just that here, proximity can't quite get there. You know. But do you want to know? What if what we're trying to read, and what we want to want to know, and what we have to sing, is an opening and openness in and out of which the absolutely close and the proximate are so absolutely close to and far away from one another that what we're really talking about is absolutely nothing, neither one nor the other, which is given, perhaps, when bouquet turns to aroma and the anthology becomes our atmosphere. It's not that things were never there; it's that, there, things never were, even in the material force of their immaterial fantasy. We see through everything, to no thing, which is all, all gathered and given away in a crawlspace just like that. This recursive turning, turning, even when you know it can't come out right, black feminism's violent gift to reading, takes the form of a question. Can you keep it closer than proximity, like this book is trying to tell you how to do? Can you assume no position? Can you claim no value? Can you approximate the general apposition, the general antagonism, the general anthology? Broken, broken off, with all your things intact, you're in the life. You know her, don't you? You know her mother.

Being-valued, which is to say being-devalued, emerges in the proximity of things. There's an evil you and I can't get away from. Sometimes you and I want to call it home, collapsing our presence into an absence of extension, an instant of argon blue, where and when all our things can be accounted for. And insofar as subjects have a place and time they have a price. This is the private imperative of an American rebirth predicated on expropriating birth's radical impropriety so it can clock how we keep having played that tune tomorrow. Nathaniel Mackey's "sexual cut," whose name Orlando Patterson's "natal alienation" scandalizes, is all we have to pass on. It's like a mountain detached from the approach to it, a bad translation in the service of severalty and real estate and gold, a whitening of the blackness of Ȟe Sápa, a scandal that the name "Black Hills" enshrines. Can there be a renaissance that isn't forged in vulgar imposition and forgetfulness of this radical inescapability? When have the born again not doubled down on death? Fugitive, nonetheless, in our non-arrival, the mechanical reproduction of bodies is what we run from, looking for a stick all the while we're trying to get there. Genocide is an Emersonian imperative to which Simone White is attuned, Layli Long Soldier having rendered it atonal. They diffuse the angel of death's cold accompaniment of living sound, allowing us to read the leaves that show how the precarity of being relegated to calculations of value is most fully experienced in being expelled from calculations of value. Can you keep that close? Can you stay in the life of her mother, held in reservation's open air?

What if the incalculable terror of being bought and sold is intensified when one buys and sells oneself? What if the unspeakable horror of insovereignty is redoubled in the appeal to sovereignty? T. J. Clark, in reverence of and reference to Rembrandt, speaks of "proximity—the presence of the self," which is, he says, "absolute." In Harriet Jacobs's view, from the duress of a camera obscura she invents, the absolute is the terror of being-(de)valued. Her bondage in her freedom is herself and all she can do is write her way out of it. From that position, where confinement and enlargement are inseparable, which is what it is to (want to) be out of position, which is what it is not to be, she speaks the condition of the mother. In the life, her attempt to bring the life of her mother close is our desire, given in a crawlspace full of attempts to bring *her* life close, their being neither here nor there. Having been (de)valued, we mourn what cannot be replaced, which is that upon which no value can be placed. Remember the remote intensity of Jacobs's closeness with her people. Remember Zitkála-Šá's exhaustive turns on and through the impossibility of return. In the life, there are forms of life that set death aside in an experience of loss that can't be bought, or sold, or owned. There, what's also absolute is this: our morning, that approximity. Sometimes we're so deep in it we're outside of it. There, we know two things: how fucked up it is to be in the life and how beautiful it is to live in and with and as what has no value.

Forgive my being so forward. I've gone off and gone on way too long. It must seem like I'm blathering, and I am, but I'm not. I wish I could be clearer. I could if I were there. But here I am, kinda, and I didn't mean to write this. I mean, I'm not trying to say that precarity gives us knowledge of the invaluable. Knowledge of the invaluable is prior to the experience of being-(de)valued. The invaluable brings value online, after all, as a bad thought or a kind of vicious offspring. It's just that the experience of being-(de)valued helps us not forget what we already know. What we already know is given in Jacobs's refusal to buy herself, but it persists even in those who have to buy themselves, even in those—like Jacobs—who have to sell themselves, when what we already know motivates the transaction. Take this. This is not my body. There's no such thing. It's not that it wouldn't be better if it were. It's that it wouldn't be good enough. Blackness is a blessing of the bodiless, just as indigeneity is a blessing of the landless. They form neither repertoires of countermeasures nor collections of counter-subjective standards. They dig transverse earth and flesh to displace the total situation. They make a book like a museum for durational art, formed in walking through curational air. "The music is happening," Monk says. "I don't need to play." Live album. Light blue. Bright, Mississippi flowers.

Charged with the uncollectible, this anthology attends to something writing sometimes bears, the drive to risk everything for our safety. That's James Baldwin's drive, and Kevin Michael Key's, an opening closeness that goes way back as the unbearable precarity we disavow in the unavowable precarity we want to want. The beautiful that's inseparable from the terrible—that's too nasty to be sublime, too flavorful to be in good taste, too syncopic to get fixed, too different to be one, too twenty-one to be nineteen, too then to be now, too open and close to be proximate—is what we share, in study. America, and I mean every bit of it, is a mechanism for the monopolization of violence in the service of the strict regulation of generativity, a task that's always been the purview of agile, hostile, mobile public-private partnerships. The pattyroller + the rapist + the cowpoke = the police, which is the department of philosophy, minding America's business, which is business, murderously superintending flavorful metastasis, pre- and post-conceptual sensing, not grasping but letting go and tearing up, anapprehensively affable and ineffably involuntary call and response. Flight and fight aren't a matter of choice for us. *In the life, her attempt to bring the life of her mother close* is experimental metaphysics. Turning to her people 'til she's gone, she's so close that, beautiful as it is, proximity can't be the right word, as the leaves you're about to worry, in looking at them so closely, can't help but sing.

INTRODUCTION

UNSETTLING PROXIMITIES

Kristen Case and Alexandra Manglis

> I hope that the surface movement of thinking through some
> difficult thoughts can be a lingering, a hesitation to say and move
> on. Like Emily Dickinson's dashes, hesitation is capable of both
> holding off and knitting together, of dwelling in, and longing.
>
> —KAREN WEISER, "TOUCHING HORROR"

> For it is not metres, but a metre-making argument that makes a
> poem,—a thought so passionate and alive that like the spirit of a
> plant or an animal it has an architecture of its own, and adorns
> nature with a new thing.
>
> —RALPH WALDO EMERSON, "THE POET"

This book is a collection of intimate encounters.

In its pages, twelve twenty-first-century poets engage with the specter of the US during the nineteenth century. The essays gathered here share a common ground and make an epistemology of that togetherness, marking the intimacies, fractures, tensions, and releases that arise from their collective knowing. Home, we might call this ground, or a place of crisis.

While nineteenth-century US literature often stands as a beacon of reverence and reference to the work that has followed, we might also picture this archive as a well from which a culture of cruelty (variously named) draws life again and again. Peering into that well is one of the book's projects. Another is to revisit, reimagine, and re-experience the archive of the so-called American Renaissance, to see what dormant possibilities we might salvage for the building of different individual and collective futures. The contributors to this collection offer new ways of engaging with such canonical figures as Ralph Waldo Emerson, Emily Dickinson, Edgar Allan Poe, and Margaret Fuller, and also needed perspectives on understudied figures such as James Monroe Whitfield, Albery Whitman, and Bayard Taylor. Both of these efforts—the effort to confront the depth and darkness of a violent history and the effort to recuperate pieces of its archive for present reimaginings—require the courage to linger in an often unsettling proximity to the past. They require us, as Donna Haraway puts it, to "stay with the trouble."[1]

All of the essays collected here are characterized by an affective openness, stylistic experimentation, engagement with complex temporal scapes, and practices of thinking *with* rather than thinking *about* the texts they engage. Perhaps most saliently, the critical work undertaken by the poets demonstrates an intimacy between critic and text that is seldom encountered in contemporary literary criticism. In this way, the poetic habit of lingering, described by Karen Weiser in our epigraph, complicates, and in some cases undermines, current models of critical thought.

• • • • •

These lingerings in what we might call a mode of *intimate critique* unearth a number of questions: To what extent should emergent forms of literary resistance take up ideals of diversity, freedom, and individual agency often championed by canonical nineteenth-century works? To what extent are these values imbricated in ideas of American idealism that are themselves central to newly bolstered (though by no means *new*) forms of oppression? Does the nineteenth-century archive offer writers who would resist oppression what Van Wyck Brooks famously called "a usable past"? Or are such uses invariably also abuses, shoring up nationalist ideals under which material violence may be better hidden or disguised?

In her work on Black scholarship, Christina Sharpe writes that she is looking "to articulate a method of encountering a past that is not past."[2] The poets in this volume bring us a step closer to that articulation by moving into a "thick ongoing present" rife with colonialism, racism, nationalism, and violence.[3] When Joan Naviyuk Kane writes, "There go my children, speaking Inupiaq. Reading Melville. Sitting beside me at the kitchen table as I write, as I do not write," she captures, as many of the contributors do in their essays, the moment of temporal and cultural collision that occurs when the past is bodied-forth into our shared present, into our kitchens, into our homes.

The passionate, living thoughts of the twelve poets in this volume have made, in Ralph Waldo Emerson's suggestive formulation, architectures of their own: particular, idiosyncratic, and non-paraphrasable structures for thinking with the archive of the

US nineteenth century. Gathered together, they begin thinking with one another. This book is an ecology of forms.

• • • • •

Dan Beachy-Quick's opening piece on thinking as a burial practice lingers on lines by Henry David Thoreau, Emily Dickinson, and Emerson. Beachy-Quick's essay opens the way for the essays that follow, indicating the difficulties of thinking that "feels like a plunge, like a plummet" into a place of not knowing. Thinking that leads into complicated *topoi* of resonances: "I want to know why it might be that when I try to think I don't find myself in airless realms where truth's cold pastoral holds desire at bay so the ideal form can over the soul hold sway," he writes. "I want to know why my hands are dirty. I want to know how I got this dried mud in my eye." Beachy-Quick anticipates the grounded and embodied approaches in the essays that follow, where the messy work of cross-temporal thinking flourishes.

José Felipe Alvergue's purposeful plummet into hybridity enacts his embrace of the disordered, a method that creates a harmony out of what readers might otherwise find to be disharmonious. Alvergue's practice roots itself in Albery Whitman's 1884 poem *The Rape of Florida*, resisting and rioting against the teleological and deterministic ethos of settler culture and colonialism. Whitman, writes Alvergue, "invented within the gaps of American chiasmus, simultaneously composing *verse*—song | work—and heroes from the colonial aftershocks of chattel slavery. His poetics refuse the liberal shame and guilt of the resentful counterpart, white supremacy, and the transliteration of blackness into a symbolic vessel into which shame pours false enfranchisement." Alvergue follows suit, threading important current cultural moments in a wilderness of text that embraces failure, the illegible, and the undercommons as loci of power.

Stefania Heim's lyric engagement with Walt Whitman's manuscripts brings home to us the shocking materiality of both text and body in Whitman's writing. Sitting with his archive, Heim stitches together an essay filled with amputated limbs and textual fragments. Like the one-horse cart that Whitman describes carrying away the pile of limbs in war, Heim's essay accumulates scraps of text, bloodstains, a lock of Whitman's own hair, even punctuation, to facilitate her own "delivery of parts." Further, her essay helps us see the similar gathering of the dead and the fragmented in the work contributed by her companions in this book.

Joan Naviyuk Kane weaves domesticity, family, colonialism, Inupiaq history, and *Moby-Dick* in her hybrid essay "Citations in the Wake of Melville." Kane's voice jostles against the loomings of presences bolstered by nationality and empire, so that a moment of conversation with her children in their Anchorage-based kitchen sits next to literary leviathans of settler culture. "Let us consider what it means to be an indigenous writer, one with two backs, so to speak. A woman, say. A woman whose bitterest foes might truck in English," she writes, her essay an irreverent and coruscating enactment of this very consideration.

The horror of a personal trauma might offer a way into understanding the horrors of racism and gun violence, suggests Karen Weiser in her intimate contribution. "Being in horror can be, should be, a public event," she writes. "Perhaps this is that moment for me—what I am imagining: you reading this." Weiser's own trauma enables her to linger in places that she can see but cannot ever fully know. Her essay expands the moment of private grief to embrace a larger mourning for the lives violently lost in the systemically racist and bigoted system, haptically revealed by America's master of horror: Poe.

In an extended meditation on the relationship between the work of poetry and the work of scholarship, Benjamin Friedlander exhumes both the "unjustly forgotten, apparently suppressed" poem "Love and Solitude" by Bayard Taylor and Friedlander's own long-abandoned attempt at poetic homage to Taylor, which rendered explicit the erotic subjects that the poem suggests without identifying. Paradoxically, Friedlander finds that explicitness robs the poem of its power, a problem that raises questions about the possibility of trans-historical contact—which is to say, of reading.

Joshua Bennett's essay traces the contours of a "black geopoetics," locating in the work of James Monroe Whitfield and the contemporary poet Phillip B. Williams a "certain strain of *black apocalypticism*." This poetic mode, Bennett suggests, aligns itself with ecological thinking and against Enlightenment projects of environmental domination and abuse. Tracing Whitfield's "misanthropy" and Williams's antipastoral to a common source in a longing for the end of the (present, oppressive) world, Bennett evokes "blackness as planetary thinking, blackness as ecological thought at the edge of the known, or knowable, universe."

The boundaries of the knowable are likewise a concern for Cole Swensen, whose lyric essay on the painter Henry Ossawa Tanner's night paintings proposes that "for Tanner, / painting offered a vehicle for overflowing circumstances and context, i.e., / for flowing out of the United States, thereby eroding / boundaries of nation, self, and personal history." Here, as in many of the essays of this volume, contact is theorized as the site of a new ontology: within the "inherently borderless" night, Swensen writes, "things have no edges, / things live indeterminate, / less themselves alone, they begin to participate in others." Swensen finds in Tanner's style an "indeterminacy" that "radicalizes difference by making everything suddenly different from itself, by disrupting the stability that anchors a 'normal.'"

Night is also the focus of Cecily Parks's sonorous contribution, figuring in her essay as "an environment, like a wetland or prairie." For Parks, the increase of light pollution has meant the loss of darkness as the habitat of secret desires. Parks's essay, in part a continuation of the work in her poetry book *O'Nights*, illuminates the night wonders of nature as found by Dickinson, Thoreau, Thomas Wentworth Higginson, and Elisabeth Christina Linnaeus. Lingering in these moments of dark sublimity, Parks extends their tactility and invites them into a living present.

In his contribution, Brian Teare digs into the soil of settler colonialism and the struggle for self-sovereignty in indigenous American cultures. His essay illuminates the ways that, in *Nature Poem,* Kumeyaay poet Tommy Pico refuses to submit either to settler culture's sublime or to its gaze at Nature and indigeneity; a gaze that Teare untangles in the works of nineteenth-century writers William Cullen Bryant and Margaret Fuller. "The concept of Nature *is* settler colonialism, *is* an earnest, clueless white gay boy," writes Teare, so "Pico abjures the affective privileges of sovereignty and rapture given to poets complicit with the violence done by settler colonialism."

Upon discovering Emily Dickinson's recipe for Black Cake, a traditional Caribbean Christmas delicacy made of ingredients harvested by slaves, M. NourbeSe Philip revisits her own story "Burn Sugar," which is told in the Caribbean demotic, about the making of Black Cake and its most important ingredient, the burnt-to-black white sugar. "We could argue," she suggests, "that Black Cake is a kind of blackness that Dickinson's privileged life allowed her to consume, even as she aurally consumed and absorbed the 'African American Vernacular English' among others." Entwining familial memory, material history, and her personal progression of working with diasporic language, Philip's essay reimagines Dickinson's kitchen of white mistresses and black servants, unveiling the "'combustible space' that is the Americas and the Caribbean."

The threads of vulnerability, materiality, and the archival encounter raised by Beachy-Quick, Heim, and Weiser emerge again in Leila Wilson's essay, which returns us to the Whitmanic body in an intimate evocation of illness and mortality, finding "throughout [Whitman's] oeuvre a lasting belief in the capacity of compost, as the practice of writing, living, and dying together." The poet's embrace of a futurity in and by way of decay prompts a thinking-through of a range of contemporary poets similarly "in trouble": "we lift our gaze from our entrenched modes of making," Wilson writes, "and we decompose."

• • • • •

Beginning with a burial and ending with compost, this book is concerned throughout with our shared ground: the temporal and material soil from which our language comes to us, and our points of contact with the real bodies decomposing in the actual earth. Collectively, these essays propose that we can more meaningfully engage the dirt of our history via *study* rather than critique. In Fred Moten and Stefano Harney's formulation in the context of the Black radical tradition, study resists conclusion, resists definition, resists end or final formulation, but represents an ongoing thinking-with-others that continually amasses more and more debt: "And it is still shared, never credited and never abiding credit, a debt you play, a debt you walk, and debt you love. And without credit this debt is infinitely complex."[4] Leila Wilson's evocation of a poetics of decomposition seems to us to suggest just such an infinite accrual: in these essays we are pulled back, infinitely indebted, into the mud that made us.

The practices of lingering, study, and sitting with require the forms these poets have engendered. These forms touch the most vulnerable points of our being: our personal and collective trauma, our witnessing to beauty, our private gambles on a future we can't imagine but nevertheless are working to build. Together, they comprise a collaborative lyrical work: a mode of collective study that canvasses not only the music of our inheritance, but its stutters and silences, too. As José Felipe Alvergue writes: "I don't think there is a *we* that can theorize lyric without also what its *after* sounds out: The beats following the disclosure of the clearly sung."

This book is an irruption of undisciplined collaboration.

21|19

THINKING AS BURIAL PRACTICE

EXHUMING A POETIC EPISTEMOLOGY
IN THOREAU, DICKINSON, AND EMERSON

Dan Beachy-Quick

I think a lot about thinking—it never gets me too far. I don't know why I expect it to be different. I have this feeling that I should be getting somewhere, but mostly I find myself still sitting in the same chair, holding the same book, wondering at which word it was where I stopped reading, even while looking at the page, even while wondering what a poem is, what thinking in a poem looks like, how it feels to think, even while wondering why it is once again I have these images in my head of the spiraled-bent-down grass where the deer bedded for the night, and then the deer with the roots of the grass in her mouth, the dirt falling back to the ground while she chews. I consider digestion, breath, heartbeat, these processes of the body governed not by mind but by genius in the oldest sense, that daemonized life that ensures our own life continue, lest in not remembering to breathe we cease to do so, and so of the heart, and so of the gut, these vitalities that require we forget them for them to go on; and in forgetting them, our minds are afforded some other kind of work. Maybe it's thinking. I think about appetite. I consider that between mouth and anus there is a single corridor that is a form of absence, and we live by filling this absence with things we eat, we organize ourselves around what is missing, and keep trying to fill it with world, though the world passes right through. What is the story of Eden but an ongoing reminder that to know we must take a bite and swallow? And what is this paradise of and in mind, those digestive circuits, that take in through the eyes a poem or a book and the essence feeds some occult muscle and what is cast back out is but another poem, written perhaps by my own hand, or a sentence, perhaps, written by your own? I wonder about the mind as the thing that is missing. And I wonder what it feels like to think, and if I have ever felt that thing called thinking. I wonder if I've ever done it: thinking. I worry it feels like sitting in a chair, realizing I've become blind to the page I'd been reading, and so once again, I must begin to read the poem I'd started earlier—maybe a minute ago, maybe yesterday, I can't quite remember, that poem I began and when I did so, maybe when I opened my eyes and took a first breath and cried. I worry a paragraph is a cloud waiting to disperse. I worry about the blank page, if it's a field, and if so, what type? Field of oblivion, apophatic ground, terrifying "there is" of pure being. Or is it just the pale grasses all pressed down after the living thought has wandered gently off to graze?

Forgive this confused reverie, or should I say, this reverie of confusion. I mean to ask a simple question. Which direction does thinking go in? I know that question has in it some naïve assumption the postmodern world easily dismisses: linearity as false vector, hubris of teleology, and so on. I'm all for the multivalent complexity of thought, but can't it be—just as "a point is that which has no part," and a line "a breadth of endless length" made up of points that have no parts—that thinking can move within itself with all its adhesive valencies and still be in motion in one direction or another? Up or down or to the horizon? At the same time, I feel so distrustful of ideal form, of Plato's "divided line," of his cave, of *Eidos*, of the Forms, of the soul as horse-drawn chariot—well, I distrust them even as I love them all the more for my doubt. I want to know why it might be that when I try to think I don't find myself in airless realms where truth's cold pastoral holds desire at bay so the ideal form can over the soul hold sway; I want to know why my hands are dirty. I want to know how I got this dried mud in my eye. I want to know who dug this hole I'm standing in, right now, while I sit reading in this chair.

It is this sense of direction, of thoughtful momentum, that I want to consider by turning to three touchstones of my own mental life—and if of mine, so perhaps of your own. Each is very brief, but as Thomas Traherne suggests that a single leaf is worth a century of meditation, and Blake suggests heaven is there in the wildflower, each may require more thought than the life doing the thinking can provide. A sentence in Thoreau, a sentence or two in Emerson, and one poem from Dickinson—just these, no more.

· · · · ·

In the second chapter of *Walden*, "Where I Lived, and What I Lived For," Thoreau writes: "My instinct tells me that my head is an organ for burrowing, as some creatures use their snout and fore-paws, and with it I would mine and burrow my way through these hills." I trust this creaturely turn, this synecdoche in which head stands in for that organ mind, and whatever thinking is, it digs more than it soars. "To mine" and "to burrow" replace more typical images of the mental process. One seeks the "richest vein" coursing within the hills; the other knows that dwelling is the effort of deepest thinking. No longer is thought a means by which one is removed from the stuff of the world up into those ethereal realms where Forms replace matter with a pattern more primary if less tangible. No. Thinking is to dig down into the matter itself, to give over to the old occult sense that only within things can their truest worth be found—vein evocative not only of gold and silver and diamond, but also of blood, also of the earth-thing that is the body. In seeking that which is of known worth, is valued by society, by world, one creates that space that none can value as highly as the one who has formed it, this burrow that none can exactly borrow, this work of thinking so as to make a place to dwell not *on* the world, but *in* it, to become an indweller. So quietly, but so audaciously, Thoreau offers us a means by which to revalue work we assume we know the purpose and worth of. Thinking leads to knowledge, that rich vein, common sense claims. But for those of us who, like Thoreau, find our sense anathema to common sense, thinking's relation to the knowledge it is supposed to find turns paradoxical. One doesn't gain knowledge; one creates in it a hole, and in that hole, one learns how to live. To have that instinct that your head is an organ for burrowing is likewise to trust that it is a tool dependent on ignorant uses as much as for thoughtful ones. To shovel out this hole with my head is as good a use of it as discovering the Pythagorean theorem. It takes the other-worldly work of mind and makes it into under-worldly work. Within the solid hill, within the dark ground, within the solid fact, we think so as to open a space to breathe, make inside of something some nothing in which we take a breath, go to sleep, and wake. To wake up we must dig down. Thoreau writes:

> To be awake is to be alive. I have never yet met a man who was quite awake. How could I have looked him in the face?
> We must learn to reawaken and keep ourselves awake, not by mechanical aids, but by the infinite expectation of the dawn, which does not forsake us in our soundest sleep.

That "soundest sleep" that "infinite expectation of dawn" doesn't forsake isn't merely untroubled. That *sound* also invokes itself as a verb, as a whale sounds when it dives to ocean's bed, suggesting sleep as a quality of depth, a going into, a going under the mountain to be within the vein. The sleep that occurs is not the sleep of knowledge, sufficient unto itself, but the sleep within knowledge, that forgetfulness at the center of fact, that *lethe* in the heart of *aletheia*, which orients us back to the expectation of the dawn not as the beginning of but another day, but that ongoing first morning, heroic in its gold light, a morning not of time, but of condition, in which we wake to wonder that the world is a form of ongoingness that breaks the husk of our intellect back to the germ of first consciousness. How do we find the dawn? We crawl back out of the hole we dug. Shake the dirt from our ears. Open our eyes.

• • • • •

"Morning is when I am awake and there is a dawn in me," Thoreau says. To wake in it is to be awakened "by our Genius." I love the plural possessive pronoun he uses—not *my*, but *our*. As no one owns the morning, so no one possesses genius. Some other quality lurks. It is almost as if, heard properly, there is a passive quality to such possession, to such genius. One doesn't master so much as be mastered, doesn't possess so much as finds oneself possessed. To crawl out the burrow head first means one opens one's eyes to a dawn that fills the head with its light, and for the briefest of instants, the mind blinded by the sudden clarity as an eye might be blinded by lightning, dawn occurs within even as it occurs without, internal and external lose their opposition, and thinking begins not by collecting once again the already-thought thoughts, but by finding the categories of consideration obliterated by the light they meant to record. That fecund zero might be one way to describe Genius, mimetic as it is of the eye opened widest, of the mouth saying its invocatory reflex, O.

But do we crawl out Thoreau's burrow beneath the hills carrying only that capacity for nothingness which lets us possess the dawn by being possessed by it, or is there something else, something we bring, something mined from that "richest vein" beneath the hill?

In "The Poet" Emerson writes, "Every word was once a poem. Every new relation is a new word." And in the same essay, "Language is fossil poetry." Whatever the instinct to dig with our heads might mean, suffice it to say that the mining at which it works isn't after gold or silver merely material in nature, though seeking it outside of the world in which it is embedded is but a sophisticated craft—one that would point at the hill and say there is the gold, which no doubt is true, but falls short of the dirt of experience. But gold and silver are a kind of fossil, as are diamonds, as are gems. Not the fossils of the textbooks that show the bones of the beasts now extinct, a kind of proof that a life has been without the possibility of a return to the same, but these richest veins of ore are fossils of those volcanic processes whose heat and pressure like some furious genius heaved the world into being and in doing so created a vascular system coursing through mountains and hills and earth. They are evidence of processes still occurring, where elemental forces work on the elements themselves, cosmic law grown material, as vital in the hill as is the vein of blood in the wrist, and evidence of the same principle, that volcanic heart yoking to its pressure the volcanic head that thinks only by virtue of the veins pulsing their particulate gold within it.

We emerge, if we do, if we ever begin digging in the first place, not only with that nothing of the radically open eye, but with a fossil. We carry it in us until it becomes molten once again; we carry it with us until it becomes alive. It is maybe no more than a word, but a word of different nature than those that tend to fill the days so that they merely go away. It is a word with a burrow inside it, a word that invites the thing it names into it to exist, to live, just as the thing it names reciprocates the kindness, and finds within its substance some absence for the word to take up as its lodging. I suspect this is in part what Emerson means when he claims that "every new relation is a new word." It's not a word made up; it's no neologism. It's a word tuned back to its initial life, its morning life, its life made purely of dawn, wherein what it names it names for the first time, not recognition but initiatory experience, the very atom of intelligence before the mind falls into the trap of its own consciousness, and confuses thinking with being.

But it begins underground, this work. And it's hard to know what and where the ground is. It looks like there's sky all around. It's hard to know how to use the head as your shovel. It's difficult to guess that some of the soil is blue.

• • • • •

Even the briefest encounter with Emily Dickinson's poetry reveals a mind uniquely indebted to the grave. Easy enough to call the tendency macabre or gothic in sensibility, but to do so would undermine an epistemological experiment that extends far past death as subject matter or obsession, and instead insists that death, and thinking, and expression, and sense, must be seen to weave one into the other. This grave-yard work (and as I write these sentences, sitting outside, the mourning dove complains her song) abounds in the lyric imagination of America: "I heard a Fly buzz — when I died —," "I cannot live with You — / It would be life — / And Life is over there —," "I am nobody! Who are you?," "Because I could not stop for death — / he kindly stopped for me —," and "A Death blow is a Life blow to Some" are but a fraction of well-known and lesser so examples. It is this sense of some vitality that begins at death—that experience Wittgenstein reminds us "is not an event of life"—that most concerns me. Death would seem to be both the border and the border-guard simultaneously, the line that marks sense from silence, and the one who in allowing you to cross, warns there is no crossing back. That limit we find ourselves at, some limit we might call our life, filled with the experiences by which we lived it, seem suddenly not to be the resource we thought it was, some means by which to feel we've gained an identity that is unique to our own peculiar bliss—but then bliss meets abyss, and what had felt complete stands suddenly apart, partial, and we find within ourselves something ajar, "just the Door ajar / That Oceans are—and Prayer—."

How to be upon that ocean, to be within it; or, to stick closer to our overriding metaphor, how to be within the earth, in the burrow, where the localities and precisions of *topos* are denied us, where we live within being lost, becomes our dearest poetic question. Dickinson's poem 340 might go some way toward illuminating that void death is supposed to be:

> I felt a Funeral, in my Brain,
> And Mourners to and fro
> Kept treading — treading — till it seemed
> That Sense was breaking through —
>
> And when they all were seated,
> A Service, like a Drum —
> Kept beating — beating — till I thought
> My Mind was going numb —
>
> And then I heard them lift a Box
> And creak across my Soul
> With those same Boots of Lead, again,
> Then Space — began to toll,
>
> As all the Heavens were a Bell,
> And Being, but an Ear,
> And I, and Silence, some strange Race
> Wrecked, solitary, here —
>
> And then a Plank in Reason, broke,
> And I dropped down, and down —
> And hit a World, at every plunge,
> And Finished knowing — then —

The first two quatrains contain a curious paradox: they speak of feeling emerging as a consequence of the end of the faculty by which we think we recognize feeling—that is, the end of thought. In some lovely echo of Keats's "drowsy numbness" that "pains my heart," Dickinson feels the same numbness in her mind, a strange cessation of that inner noise we call thinking and the language in which it occurs, perverse work of consciousness that grows aware by growing apart from the object of its attention, and the ear that for a lifetime secretly became trained almost wholly inward—solipsism of *I think, therefore I am* ad nauseam, ad infinitum—reverses its listening, and tunes once again to the world outside the head.

The inversion of the ear back to an orientation geared wholly outside of the self not only allows the Soul to become a force in the poem—that silence apart from all speaking even as it is within all word, burrowed there, vein of purest nothing—it allows the ear to become *supra-sensory*, hearing not a single song, but that resonance that, as from a struck bell, reverberates through all being as a grace note. Here, that bell is heaven—not God's dwelling place, not religious dogma, but that next sphere of cosmic order whose own ringing is but a listening to the celestial sphere also encircling it.

One might say the brain is but a bell without a tongue; we must learn to be quiet to let it ring. And so it is that Dickinson finds herself next to Silence, both "wrecked," both "solitary," both "here." That Silence may well be the Chaos of old, waiting for a motion it cannot produce itself to spring from it that deepest possibility of this form of order we call life. It cannot act upon itself; it must be acted upon. And it is just there, on that ground more justly called abyss, the self-wreck of being and silence, that mere plank of a nothing-that-is, barest board of reason, where the burying work of real thinking begins. It does not feel like thinking. It feels like a plunge, like a plummet. In that downward motion alone is the world found, are worlds found, and to "finish knowing — then —," is not to end in fact or wisdom; it is to be reborn into an utmost ignorance, an absolute infancy, where knowing as an end of thinking is over just as the fairy tales that put children to sleep all come to an end. That little death called sleep is also an introduction to our mental life. But sometimes one has to die in more deliberate ways. Sometime you use your own head to dig your own grave, and deep in the earth, looking for fossils, you learn how to listen. "Every word was once a poem." And right there, where knowing ends, something else begins. You might call it thinking.

FEELING THE RIOT

FUGITIVITY, LYRIC, AND ENDURING FAILURE

José Felipe Alvergue

apocalypse: prophetic disclosure, revelation.
> ("In an apocalypse of sentiment / He shows")

The riot that's goin' on is a party for self-defense.
—FRED MOTEN

Writing on W. E. B. Du Bois's *The Souls of Black Folk*, Anthony Reed describes silence as a directly performative mode of speech in the context of disavowal.[1] Voice, in the canon of American poetics, is not only the disclosure of disavowal, but also the "prophetic" envisioning of its politics. Voice enacts context even while transcending the objective circumstances of what context brings into relation. This is, now, the problem in recognition. But it is also the accommodating expectation for relation within liberal democratic identity, as it has become a social praxis. Rather than conclude an optimism or pessimism from the register of disclosure, from understanding context for what it abridges in a historical continuum, I am captivated by *how* voicing reaches and approaches, finds new ways of speaking while rejecting disavowal's claim. I don't think there is a *we* that can theorize lyric without also what its *after* sounds out: The beats following the disclosure of the clearly sung. Such a poetics gives form to the collaborative, cooperative speech from places of non-property as an act against the *hum* of disavowal—the social lilt, whistle, and salutation of alienation.

To listen toward this *after* is to look back for the song. To acknowledge voice for its collective availability to sing is to recognize that critique, as well as the intention to demonstrate that the public manifestation of our expressive selves which we often call citizenship binds the very muscles of our throat—imprints upon the push of air from a below where all the ingredients of America are consumed and metabolized.

I.

Alabama	Arkansas	*Florida*	Georgia	Kentucky
Louisiana	Mississippi		Nebraska	North
Carolina	South Carolina		Tennessee	Washington

Between the mid-nineteenth and early twentieth centuries states declaring themselves too impoverished to maintain prisons and prisoners would lease out convict labor to railway and mining contractors or large plantations. The practice became especially prevalent following the Civil War. False convictions, theft of bail money, and identity fraud were among the tactics used to meet the demand for cheap labor created by the abolition of slavery.[2] In other words, the exceptionalist ground upon which the democratic emerges is premised on the systemic, ethical *failure* toward which demands for redress are directed. A redress of redress as it were, wherein post-Reconstruction demands highlight the shortcomings of the promised institutional changes the era was meant to inaugurate.

The institutional redress of Emancipation, especially as interpreted by white Southerners as a divestment in long practiced economic regulations, motivated America's continued investment in the system as a structural necessity: A necessary amendment to abolition. This history of the lease system is one point of origin for contemporary vocalic expressions of dissatisfaction with practices of supremacy in the carrying out of deliberative forms of justice. Forced incarceration is coeval to labor without contract, the contract being a legality premised on the racialization of crime. The inescapability of a state-sanctioned, racialized paradigm of criminalization becomes clearer in the historical-lyric work of Albery Whitman and the transnational imaginary of the Black Seminoles.

In the study of poetics there persists a demarcation, still, between the demand and the voice. Liberal democratic consensus, the celebratory chord of personification and political possibility, resonates to this day in the neoliberal mobilization of white resentment and white sensitivity against expressive performances of a pluralist public identity, particularly any collective performance of dissent that highlights an institutional memory of *failure*. We might even think of this as the potential commodification even of anger when its performance circulates at the same instantaneous rate of consensual media. Modes for quelling upheaval, anger, or true dissent resonate, as well, with the ways disenfranchisement works on levels of containment, disavowal, and mnemonic manipulation. In outright violations of life. [cars used in a ballistic manner against bodies : state-sanctioned | operated mercantilization of human life] *In the conscious or unconscious view of supremacy, public demands for authenticity in promises of place and being authorize the "social" through acts of voice emotionally invested in the political possibility of* non-property.[3]

If an institution like the Convict Lease System operates in the legitimacy of the accepted, what ruptures ownership over the terms? What is unacceptable within the social contract and to the logic of hypocrisy?

> Who finds *this* country *now*, exulting finds
>
> That nature sounds the anthems of the free, —
>
> The boundless prairie swept by restless winds,
>
> Great forests shouting on tumultuously,
>
> Rivers that send their greetings to the sea,
>
> Peace-loving vales, where weed-brimmed waters run,

Broad lakes whose shade-fringed margins lisp their glee,

Mountains, that prop their green heights in the sun;

And herded slopes that winter never looks upon![4]

Albery Whitman's 1884 *The Rape of Florida* is an epic poem written in 257 Spenserian stanzas recounting the story of hero Altassa and the Black Seminoles of Florida. It is bookended by the question of authenticity and authority in found sound, or sound resonating from the place of its irruption, its devastation and brush. Like the contemporary poets working the autopsy of "the document," reanimating *eros* where there is only *logos*, such sound is the public non-property of *freedom*. It is a carrier of voice, and in the context of a national genre—American lyric—it resonates with the sonoricity of autochthony. Being manifest, brought out by the working of history, in this case the Seminole Wars, the cipher, voice, is a plane. [verse : *versus* : a turn of the plow / a turn] Immanent to land. Artifice of a promissory utterance. Whitman's poem begins with an invocation of voice and the poet, a transcendent figure from a nevertheless politicized world, "A flaming minister to mortals sent; / In an apocalypse of sentiment, / He shows in colors true the right or wrong."[5]

Is voice transcendent because the political imposes upon it the constraints to be redressed? Is transcendence determining?

The Rape of Florida ends in a stoic silence, a scene of *naturalization*, and the hero Altassa—a Seminole, and politically an embodiment of the maroon who fights against the authoritarian state, enslavement, and seizure—headed into the new West with a conviction in futurity, yet marked as convict by the circumstances of resistant indigeneity and Black Seminole fugitivity. [Texas, or "Mexic"] The new West speaks in the lyric "anthems of the free" as by a natural necessity of Union. Humanity's role is clear, to "strive to keep thee free":

Rise thou into a nation's dignity,

And freedom's acclamations spread around!

. . . .

Let the omnific waters catch the sound,

"A queen of beauty in the West is Mexic crowned!"[6]

Silence, at critical moments, refuses the determinism of disavowal as *dispositif* of colonial governance—sometimes, in other words, a moment within the continuum of American history is more accurately portrayed not in singing the glory of its linearity, but in refusing to. In the choice to voice instead poetry's social temporality as a chiasmatic timbre attuned to chiasmatic reflection. The plasticity of voice as such reveals the artifice that, as an aesthetic arrangement, usually accompanies context. Precedes it even. Yet the contingent manifestation of context itself cannot deny the world from which it emerges and which it nonetheless demonstrates. Throughout the late nineteenth century Whitman invented within the gaps of American chiasmus, simultaneously composing *verse*—song | work—and heroes from the colonial aftershocks of chattel slavery. His poetics refuse the liberal shame and guilt of the resentful counterpart, white supremacy, and the transliteration of blackness into a symbolic vessel into which shame pours false enfranchisement. By extension, Whitman refuses determinism as the objectivity of liberal democratic progress, refuses to affirm democratic progress as a kind of modern truth or political beauty. His poetry is this disclosure. It is also a celebration of an American drive to *work-it-out*, and of personhood via an authentic transcendental event: poetry. Land, voice, RIOT: the self-defensive song going-on in what poetry plans, who is brought-to it, what they demand. Awe as a we gathers-round the hearing.

> Thrown together touching each other we were denied all
> sentiment, denied all the things that were supposed to
> produce sentiment, family, nation, language, religion, place,
> home. Though forced to touch and be touched, to sense and
> be sensed in that space of no space, tough refused sentiment,
> history and home, we feel (for) each other.[7]

Frontispiece to Joan Blaeu's *Atlas Maior,* 1665.[8]

Frederick Douglass notes in 1893 that nine-tenths of the leased convicts were African American. Fugitivity. A public is the self-defense of sovereignty from statal authority, from the homogeneity of the authentic. Fred Moten's concept of sensuousness raises questions as to the necessity of territory. When is a hold territorial; when is it simply, semiotically, locative? When is utterance spatial, public and transcendent? Transnational. Situated. Spoken. Personhood is the act of trusting that the institutions of contemporary liberal democratic *work* though they are practiced through leasing bodies. Practice is that so-called "necessity" of a Nation State leasing away the human for the sinew. The labor of this system co-opts the very ground upon which the commons grafts the ideality of what is political and poetical of our being. And yet, there is fugitivity.

> The poorest negro coming to their shore,
>
> To them was brother—their own flesh and blood, —
>
> They sought his wretched manhood to restore, —
>
> They found his hidings in the swampy wood,
>
> And brought him forth — in arms before him stood, —
>
> The citizens of God and sovran earth, —
>
> They shot straight forward looks with flame imbued,
>
> Till in him manhood sprang, a noble birth,
>
> And warrior-armed he rose to all that manhood's worth.[9]

The gravity of a prisoner's convictions in the lease system could range from mere fisticuffing, hog-stealing, or other misdemeanor crimes like carrying a concealed weapon—a crime, as noted by George W. Cable's *The Negro Question* in 1903, common among whites though often overlooked.

So many screenshots of white men holding AR15s *in public assembly, while black children with* toys *erased.*

While some twelve hundred convicts during the year 1880 were leased in the convict lease system, fewer than half were serving sentences of ten years, many sentences of less than one or two years. Ten years was the maximum amount of time an overworked convict in the system was expected to live. In Tennessee,

Cable uncovered twelve boys under the age of eighteen leased in the system, with each serving sentences of less than one year. In North Carolina there were 234 convicts under the age of twenty leased in the system.[10] Fugitivity is a RIOT sounded out by Whitman's "citizens," one that challenges the empiricism of colonial mappings. It's the spontaneity of seizure and indenture, and the irruption of recognition "flame imbued."

"Thrown together touching each other we were denied all sentiment, denied all the things that were supposed to produce sentiment, family, nation, language, religion, place, home."

how *do* "we feel (for) each other"[11]

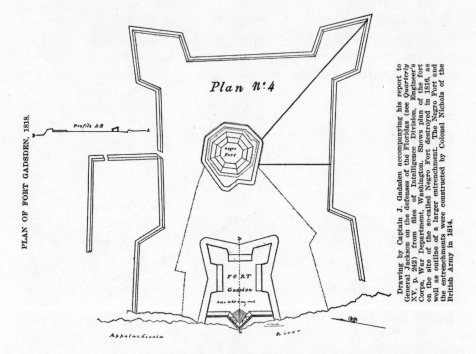

PLAN OF FORT GADSDEN, 1818.

Drawing by Captain J. Gadsden accompanying his report to General Jackson on the defenses of the Floridas from the files of Intelligence Division, Engineer's Corps, War Department, Washington. Shows plan of the fort on the site of the so-called NEGRO FORT destroyed in 1816, as well as outline of a larger entrenchment. The NEGRO FORT and the entrenchments were constructed by Colonel Nichols of the British Army in 1814.

II.

When contemporary thinkers like Cornel West or Calvin Warren theorize *black nihilism*, and Christina Sharpe or Alexander Weheliye *affect*, what they're after is the logic of equivalency.[12] Not to substantiate the legitimacy through which "person" operates as a self-legitimating promise-making subject, but rather to establish the performances that implode the objectivity of an ethics of universal personhood, nevertheless territorially defined—that what *is* is also what *ought to be*. It's James Baldwin turning *nihilism* back around on itself, not as black pathos but white terror of the white self, and the white empiricist myth of the world as it has been illustrated rather than de-*monstrated*. The expression of implosion is the de-empiricisation of land, nature, voice, and the person. Implosive instances of voice where implosion is the undoing of its previous context unsettles the historicities upon which performances of belonging resonate as both political and aesthetic events. The RIOT is *new,* but there is nonetheless an *afterwards.* A temporality within which the possible is kept in anticipation of fugitivity.

[new and afterwards:
the minute and fifty *stretch* of aTunde Adjuah's "Runnin' 7s."]

Whitman's own reorientation of liberal democratic temporality is an aggrieving optimism: a futurity that while expanding and thus adaptive to American cultural | historical "authenticity" is backed up by the authority of institutional consciousness. "The citizens of God and sovran earth," the lyric speaker pronounces in the opening canto, "in arms before him *stood."* Whitman's *standing* citizens rebuke narratives of black gratitude and black guilt suggested by the same gesture. Kneeling is a contrivance, a positional regulation intended to transform the body from within. The biopolitical matter is preceded by the social *holding* and logistics of the guilt-resentment paradigm under which liberal democratic ethics have learned to operate since abolition. Kneeling is meant to enforce the hegemony, but it takes a living human body to do it. And a living human body *matters.* A promissory act is transliterated between symbolic interpretation and affective expression when the *living* arrange themselves before and above a landscape marred by terror. The kneeling in Ferguson, for instance, is a making-whole without making invisible the fracture—a speech act.

The difficulty of the liberal democratic human in context acts out within the bridge that is a speech act's sustain: how it reverberates in the vulnerable space prior to meaning. The reverberation keeps itself in a stasis not meant to be broken [unless there is such a performance to implode context]. To belong at once humanly and democratically acts out the survival of injustice and failure. Then we call on voice : body : sinew : faith as a terrorist act. Ballistic act.

Nihilism recognizes failure. It is RIOTOUS for what, when practiced together, it "restores." Black nihilism iterates failure in the syncopation of voice and the

Thomas Ball, competition model for Emancipation Monument ca. 1876. "Upon this *act*—I invoke the considerate judgment of mankind and the gracious favor of Almighty God."

historical. Shared fugitivity "sounds" out assembly, its "hidings in the swampy wood," and demands : source, "sprang."

[It's the first thirty-five seconds of aTunde Adjuah's "West of the West." And it's the thirty seconds that come after.]

"I have yielded to the firm belief that the negro has a future," writes Whitman in his dedicatory address to *The Rape of Florida*. "I abhor the doctrine that he is but a cipher in the sum of the world's greatness — a captive in the meshes of dominating influences." Yet he also promises, "The subtle evolutions of thought must yet be expressed in song." Authentic polyvocal futurity is accompanied by the disavowal of the liberal democratic paradox undergirding, even in his time, institutional redress. To be captive requires the capturing, the transporting, but also the *captivity* wherein it is all smoothed out into the fabric of a place. A Land, a Nation sound better than a *territory*, a *colony* but either needs a soundtrack to shuttle back and forth in the symbolic body of an idea.

> If earth were freed from those who buy and sell,
>
> It soon were free from most, or *all* its ills;
>
> For that which makes it, most of all, a hell,
>
> Is what the stingy of purse of Fortune fills:
>
> The man who blesses and the man who kills,
>
> Oft have a kindred purpose after all,
>
> A purpose that will ring in Mammon's tills;
>
> And that has ne'er unheeded made a call,
>
> Since Eve and Adam trod the thistles of their Fall.[13]

The questions I investigate through poetry have to do with what Jean-Luc Nancy calls *monstration*, which can be understood as a disclosure in-tune with an equivalency to the world humans have long associated with.[14] But in the world's disclosure, its de-monstration, perhaps, there is a de-pathologizing event? The captivity of obedience fosters subservience to what transforms the unformed Land into Nation.

> In the time of slavery if a Negro was killed, the owner sustained a loss of property. Now he is not restrained by any fear of such loss.[15]

To the exile, by way of maroonism, expulsion, disavowal, or self-selection, such *monstration* is seldom necessary because the experience of alienation is always already the revelation of, in this present case, liberal democratic artifice, of its being rendered (aesthetic). The exile threatens captivity in the very act of enduring speech throughout the nationalized-transcending entanglement of language itself [age and *durée* as Achille Mbembe refers to them in *On the Postcolony*[16]] : [*durées* if a representation is possible of the multiple, haptic, intersecting temporalities interlocuting at once through that possible impossibility of human voice]. The liberal democratic paradox architecturalizes the following: to achieve authentic universalism the nation enforces strict territorial authority. Authority as a vocality in-wait, as promissory. There is no neutrality in the apocalypse of emotion. What we call *lyric*. Even in the subjugation, the silence, the survival, the ambivalence there is a spirit, a History.

What I'm getting at is a question of poetics within the larger, looming controversy of aesthetics at this present moment. Can we only render consensus? Ought we? This *is* what neoliberal democratism asks. What, in the thin and pitched exhale of white fatigue, and the anti-intellectual bewildered consequences of examining context that accompany it, [we] are being forced to ask of each other.

Chantal Mouffe, in a critique of both John Rawls and Jürgen Habermas, contends that "to have agreements in opinions, there must first be agreement on the language used."[17] Immanent to language (Rawls) is sense. Sensuality, the extension of speaking into its public an affect of *common s/* a law of a people's and a language spoken. In practice (Habermas) of "peoples" or person, their activity as speaking is the activity of the commons. Laws therefore constituted from such a consensus / as if natural.

Stretched out across difference.

— stretch the source of —

: a rising, beginning : to rise up, ascend, *get up* : attack : person or written work supplying evidence, information

What were they saying to you?

Blood is just gushing down the street.

Death, you know, death wasn't far away.

convict (n) is from the verb form, *convict*: to convince in argument; to "overcome"; to impress. From the Latin, *convincere*. The proof of guilt is carried over into a physiological realm by the mere presence of the body whose address is at once the utterance of the charge [*convict*] as well as a recognizability of the ethos that keeps the convict separate, working. Liberal democratic *conviction* is the artifice of a false *monstration* as the forced revelation that criminality exempts the same freedom which is an energy, by another name, *spirit*. How can we trust "work" when its premise/promise is criminalizing exile and the punishment of self-defense? The RIOT is a *monstration* of the cutting off ties between artifice and affect, passion and the chain gang.

The potential gravity or banality of an actual crime works in periperformative unison within a neocolonial state of law, land, and utterance. The convict declares in their labor, their body bent into the weight of shovel, hoe, hammer, stance upon the ground shaken by strike and arranged by the pull of ties and spikes, the naturalness of their state in such a pose and the naturalness of law to keep them there under watch and near death. To work toward that death, overcome it. Convince it of its legitimacy. Convince, before the natural foreman, the heavenly angels, the ship in the distance destined for port.

> *The kinetic is a mode of stitching meaning together, and is etymologically related to the word "cite," as in "excite," which comes from the Latin* citare, *from* ciare, *and* cire, *which means "to call." Cite, "excite," correlates not only with "heat," but also with "assembly" and the public. It is a gathering around a "call," as well as the call, or language in its most physically specific and gestural performance. But who is "gathering"?*

— *citare* : to summon : an authority and authenticity at once : *citation* : the summon —

The convict, through every twitch of muscle expended toward a landscape molded into excruciating form, is iteration, embodies a physical utterance of "citationality, the 'always already,'" to quote Eve Sedgwick. The black male body (though not exclusively male within the Convict Lease System) is transliterated into its own "valuable repertoire of conceptual shuttle movements that endlessly weave between the future and past"[18] (between America as optimism and its past as the pessimism of institutional failure). The ready-objectivity of citationality inflects voice itself; it isn't so much what is spoken but the pre-articulated always already of speakers that makes *caste* out of the potential of speech.

> Black performance is not static, contained, or geographically specific. There is no locale that designates the origin of "black" sensibilities because skin colors have always been global and relative. . . . Black performance contains history and racism, but it is not about either of those things.[19]

"Black Performance" describes an irruption from the communicability and making common of *convict* as a performance of the autochthony of political potential or environmental objectivity. Autochthony is an aboriginal manifestation, an indigene from the scene and *source* of their nature and nature.[20] In colonial *casta* autochthony functioned hemispherically as the underlying logic for the baroque depictions of nature, labor, and race—*casta* : *castigare* : *castigate* : *chastise* : caste [see above: the frontispiece, "America," in Joan Blaeu's *Atlas Maior*]. Autochthony was not only the logic of "blackness" as cipher, which Whitman abhors, but also the determinism of history. A monopoly over the "it is" of the present.

[transnational maroonism, a state of RIOT against the authority of a single voice—statal— and thus a cacophonous defense against liberal democratic law, which is always a parastatal story].

> ... criminal activity [is] *unrecognizable* without a black body.
> Without a black body, the same action [is] interpreted as a
> (white) survival strategy.[21]

So much is convincingly proven by the uneven representation of misdemeanor criminals in the Convict Leasing System.

"As ways of knowing and methods of meaning-making," writes Lisa Marie Cacho, "race, gender, and sexuality simultaneously erase and make sense of what should have been a contradiction by making racial contradictions commonsense."[22] That commonsense-making: criminalization. Contradiction, however, is a diffuse self-defensive counter argument to the deliberative peace evinced in the image of chain gang bodies, punished bodies, and their relationship to space transformed into the geography of an economic present.

Blood ———————— just gushing down the street.

The rationale of autochthony makes organic plasticity fungible, the transliteration of temporalities. The erosive bluff and its equivalence as the labor of mining, the growth and form of the plant and the work of harvesting the cotton, the eventual change and transformation of the geological and the hoe and hammer, the steam engine, the high-rise, the congestion, the contamination in flakes in the water, the bloody nonchalance of sidewalks, the naturalness of maps for strategic containment, the legal arson razing living rooms kitchens photographs.

III.

Writing against conceptual poetry, Calvin Bedient argues that experimentalism, "head poetry," prioritizes neutrality to the passion that is social.[23] This forecloses on the poet who, in recognizing the syncopation between contexts of symbolic and material captivity throughout generations of failure, refuses the determinism of an affect that celebrates the emotional positionalism of always being *seen* and *heard* as a cipher in the American equation of exchangeable possibility. Defining poetry as such promises a futurity of hope positioned as kneeling, fleeing, *hoping* alone, or hoping differently from what others hope and how. Only one interpretation of flying. Outside history but historical, an authentic object within it. But genre ensures the attention of the so-called *liberal ear.*

> What of those who were not just labor but commodity, not just in production but in circulation, not just in circulation but in distribution as property, not just property but property that reproduced and realized itself?[24]

What about the "outlawed social life of nothing," as Moten says? And what of a lyric of | from *the undercommons* : the *fugitive public*? Perhaps what Bedient identifies as "the neutral" is a different kind of party, a RIOT without the captured burn and brick but no less self-defensive. Ambivalence, maybe it could be called. Critical though. Not a fungible passion in one direction of equivalency but "haptic," as Moten and Harney describe it, *multiscalar*, to borrow from the geographer Katherine McKittrick. "Racism and sexism produce attendant geographies that are bound up in human disempowerment and dispossession," argues McKittrick, making decolonizing acts, including speech acts, multiscalar in their scope of de-monstrating spatial-personal binds as having to do with ownership—here included, an ownership of the very voice through which demands extrapolate public space, and, perhaps most importantly, the objectivity of what is called *now.*[25] What's the poetry for this "feel that what is to come is here."[26] Pessimism. Nihilism. "To feel others is unmediated, immediately social, amongst us, our thing."

Then we might hope to *feel*, as we have *felt*,

And *know* the subtle shadow wavering

Between the *where* we *may* dwell and have dwelt;

Then might we realize that not in vain we've knelt.[27]

: "Those who once came with the SWORD, / Are coming now with PRUNING HOOKS and PLOWS . . ."

There is a time when speech is all too frail,

There is a *place* where silence speaks the most:

What is the word to paint a human wail,

Or how heroic, *speak* where all is lost?

He who wears shackles mid his shackled host,

Shows valor's *steel* to sturdily behave,

For life is Freedom's last and *real* cost,

And so, the *last* resistance of the brave,

Is that stern silence which to chains prefers grave.[28]

fly fly fly fly fly fly fly fly, fly fly fly fly fly fly fly fly[29]

———————

He's way in front of me, his lights beaming down, going across the streets. My heart is, like, my body's hot. And I'm scared. And nervous. Because I knew it was going to be pretty much a beating from running from them at that point.

The remainder, the two-fifths, gets lost within the arithmetic shuffle. . . . Black humanity became somewhat of an "imaginary number" in this equation, purely speculative and nice in theory, but difficult to actualize or translate into something tangible.[30]

We're going to kill you, nigger. We're going to kill you, nigger.

Run. I was — knew I was going for death.

> If fighting is the space of comradeship —
> If the RIOT is a necessity for the commonality in time of accordance —

What it comes down to is that, as a poet, as a teacher, as an immigrant from a bordertown in neoliberal America, I have to believe voice is that performance bridging an intellectual refusal of and a personal, intimate embrace of politics. Not only voice in that academic sense, that sense David Appelbaum describes as "an opening to one's disharmonious nature," but also as "a responsiveness to the real."[31] The vocalic is auditory, responsive—an arrangement amongst resonating frequencies and their potential to be disclosed. *Fortvivlelse* (Kierkegaard): the RIOT not simply to *lose hope*, but rejuvenate the corruption that takes hold of—to be dismayed by the "real" of our condition and abandon its *ethos*. Because: "the vocalic is the essential nucleus around which even the semantic structure of language is organized."[32]

—and yet

We're going to kill you, nigger.
We're going to kill you, nigger.

> The terms "passive" and "fatalism" applied to black nihilism are saturated
> with negativity to discredit its legitimacy; this discursive maneuver becomes
> another metaphysical strategy of disciplining and punishing "errant"
> thought.[33]

because I had a job to go to that Monday.

Agreement
> . . . reveals that procedures only exist as complex ensembles of practices.
> Those practices constitute specific forms of individuality and identity that
> make possible the allegiance to the procedures. It is because they are
> inscribed in shared forms of life and agreements in judgments that
> procedures can be accepted and followed . . .[34]

The space of common speech is governed by an unspoken though enforced set of criteria: agreements in opinions are agreements in "forms of life," to echo Mouffe.[35] Listening for the idealized voice of democratization across otherwise complex identities requires the elision of acoustic, emphatic binds. Namely, the resonating grain of daily negotiations democratization entails. Missing from theories of the political are more profound theories of language as a human-aesthetic event. Missing from most theories of lyric are the unaccounted acoustical, yet contemporary demands for space.

10. *The plaintiff having admitted, by his demurrer to the plea in abatement, that his ancestors were imported from Africa and sold as slaves, he is not a citizen of the State of Missouri according to the Constitution of the United States, and was not entitled to sue in that character in the Circuit Court.*[36]

This event includes the intimate space(s) through which subjectivities become interpellated toward each other, through honestly "shared forms of life." The lyric territory of individuals dramatized in the performance of agency from within the liminality of their transnational fugitive assembly.

> W———- T———- belonged to Chs. Thompson of Richmond, Va.
> He wanted to be free, he says, + has wished to be, for years. Once he
> attempted to escape about a year since, but was overtaken + carried
> back. He master treated him pretty well, gave him clothes + food
> enough, + sometimes money; but he was not satisfied to remain a
> slave. Three weeks ago he was in his master's store—dry goods—for y
> afternoon, y porter being sick, when he was sent on an errand to near
> y wharves. He accidentally met with y cook of a vessel + entered into
> some talk with him, + soon came to an understanding. He had about
> him $5 for which y cook agreed to conceal him, y captain of y vessel
> consenting, but on condition that his name was not to be used. They
> sailed that night, + Wm. lay concealed a day + a half, till y pilot left.
> The capt. put him ashore at Long Branch, telling him he was in a free
> state, + to make y best of his way to N.Y., first inquiring y way to y
> R.R. He travelled all night + part of y next day before stopping. He
> rested at last at a gentleman's house whom he told he was a fugitive.
> This man aided him with money, + fed him, + would have lodged
> him in his house, but Wm. felt safer in y barn. On Friday he reached
> N.Y. + inquired for a coloured minister, + was directed to y 6th St.
> Church. He found y church, after some difficulty, y persons in
> charge took him in, + went for Mahonen [?]. Forwarded him to
> Syracuse. $4.43

"What truth is there that lives and does not live in song?"[37]

— what sovereignty is there represented in a
ledger

. . . debt runs in every direction, scatters, escapes, seeks refuge. The debtor seeks
refuge among other debtors, acquires debt from them . . . This refuge, this place of
bad debt, is what we call the fugitive public.[38]

Sent him forward for Canada. Had no money—paid for him $4

                                                        Concluded

to go where passes were not needed to be out o' nights.
$4.50

T——- N———— of y same company belonged to P. T. Bockhaven.
Was hired out, + allowed $1.50 hr. work for his own subsistence,
clothing +c y rest of his wages going to support his master. During y
fever his master took him to "Ocean View," + promised to let him
keep all he could earn. Worked at whitewashing + wood-cutting, +
for y latter recd a check for $5 which he gave to his master to collect
for him. But y master kept it, + y man who had submitted to be
robbed all his life, was so outraged at this petty larceny that he ran
away. All three of these men were sent on to Syracuse on their way to
Canada. The rest of their company had dispersed themselves in
various directions, some, it is said, having passed thro' this city
within a few days.

Expenses $11.64

"In one commingling torrent now were loose!"

"That now did roar! and on the sudden verge"[39]

                                                        — and yet

*The doctrine of 1776, that all (white) men "are created free and equal," is universally
accepted and made the basis of all our institutions, State and National, and the relations of
citizenship—the rights of the individual—in short, the status of the dominant race, is thus
defined and fixed for ever.*

This confusion is now at an end.[40]

"Behind them were their homes, wives, children—all!"[41]

It is based on historical and existing facts, which are indisputable, and it is a necessary, indeed unavoidable inference, from these facts.[42]

"What troop is this that comes to mine abode!

What seek ye here! Intruders! will ye dare

To hoof my grounds? why shun yon open road?

Age quencheth not resentment! and beware,

Whoe'ver ye be, or whence soe'er ye are,

Ye come no further!"[43]

"An act for the better preventing of a spurious and mixed issue," &c. : "if any negro or mulatto shall presume to smite or strike any person of the English or other Christian nation, such negro or mulatto shall be severely whipped, at the discretion of the justices before whom the offender shall be convicted." (1705)[44]

Many Americans are confused by riots. In Whitman's lyric Palmecho and the Seminoles are in the end deceived by a false treaty. After Palmecho "spoke of wars, and rights, and lands," the *pirates* hearing the authenticity | authority of "the brave old chief's demands" and "with inborn hate," place him in "chains instead." He and all others are shipped off to Texas; the convicts and Florida are occupied. When we talk about *failure* we are insisting on a colonial paradigm wherein the act of *making a demand* produces the very constraints against which appeals are made. [mapped over pre-existing authenticity] Archival research of seventeenth-century legal cases reveals the ways that, in hemispheric contexts, indigenous and African plaintiffs were forced into re-presenting themselves within the bounds of *casta* entitlements—namely degrees of separation to whiteness—and in doing so, legitimated systemic procedures of disenfranchisement amongst their own communities, and against others likewise in fugitivity (the breath of speech also released authority over their own property to the

colonial system : or, the system that listened also systematically recorded what was to be *reappropriated*). The performativity of legal personhood is the becoming of this repertoire blurred at the edge of judicial archive and objective history. It implicates how we are forced to represent ourselves. It implicates how we expect to witness the performance of others before authority—the amount of authenticity we are allowed to employ, the proximity to authority we are permitted to endear. The riot burns because it recognizes the non-property in every moment of our selves and in the refuge of self-defense against the impositions of colonial subjection, feels the freedom to move through walls. Unshackling the binds of American conviction in historical negligence sounds-out. The RIOT is the assembly that forms when we gather-round it.[45]

ESSAY IN FRAGMENTS, A PILE OF LIMBS

WALT WHITMAN'S BODY IN THE BOOK

Stefania Heim

> He wakes up language, and in order to experience the
> awakening, the return to life of language, truly in the quick,
> the living flesh, he must be very close to its corpse.
>
> —JACQUES DERRIDA, *SOVEREIGNTIES IN QUESTION*

I had not registered that Whitman's poetic career opens with a cadaver on a kitchen table. I had written the line down and recopied it into three different notebooks. And yet somehow I had not really seen the body in it.

"America," begins the unsigned preface to the 1855 *Leaves of Grass*, ". . . perceives that the corpse is slowly borne from the eating and sleeping rooms of the house." Borne toward burial, presumably, and slowly so as to perform solemnity and convey respect. Or, borne as the collective dead are transferred from the hearth to the euphemistic Home, pumped with formaldehyde, glutaraldehyde, methanol, to stave off rot and endure the period of viewing.

Diphtheria, meningitis, the common practice of kissing the mouths of the departed beloved: these are all good reasons for moving the bodies out. Later, during the American Civil War, so many dead upon the battlefields. How to preserve the boys long enough to carry them back to their mothers.

In the 1950s, when my mother was growing up in the mountains of south-central Italy, corpses were dressed by loved ones and arrayed on the best blankets upon a table in the center of the kitchen. Chairs along the room's periphery. No one socialized or told jokes. Summers decades later, I sat at those same tables, heard the ghost cries of mourners, the guttural language of lament.

The rooms where we eat and sleep. And nurse and read and fuck. And clean and fold and cook and talk.

Whitman's lines are a metaphor about American artistic innovation. But precisely as the "corpse" of the old language is borne slowly out, he starts dragging the real bodies in.

:

This essay began with a lock of Whitman's hair tucked into the pages of a printer's copy of *Leaves of Grass* cut up and written all over in Whitman's hand. It was because I had seen and touched the hair that I went back to the archive and found the scrap.

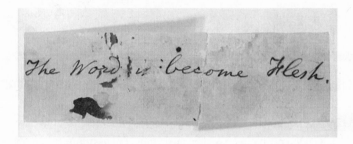

The Word is become Flesh: in Whitman's dignified cursive on a finger-long scrap of browning paper splattered with very blood-like red ink.

There is plenty of flesh in Whitman's poetry. According to Harold Edwin Eby's 1949 *Concordance*, the word and its variants—"love-flesh," "sweet-flesh'd"—appear more than two dozen times. In "Song of Myself," Whitman's "flesh and blood" play out "lightning to strike what is hardly different from myself." "Is this then a touch?" he asks, as through some physical version of the transitive property he reaches for my fingers through the page. This flesh is romantic, the "treacherous tip" of a person. Later, though, we are at sea on a sinking vessel. We pan the scene: stars, guns, rigging, and here, "[f]ormless stacks of bodies by themselves, dabs of flesh upon the masts and spars." The body's tender innards opened out, sprayed across the boat, coating its strongest parts, its structural foundation.

In the King James Bible, the Gospel of John, chapter 1, verse 14 reads, "And the Word was made flesh, and dwelt among us." This flesh is synecdochic: divinity rendered incarnate as Jesus, the son of God. On Christmas Day 1611, Lancelot Andrewes preached to King James I at Whitehall, "More forcible it is to say, 'He was made flesh,' than 'He was made man,' though both be true. He vouchsafed to become man, nothing so much as to become flesh, the very lowest and basest part of man." So low it rots in the wet soil. "I will press my spade through the sod and turn it up underneath, I am sure I shall expose some of the foul meat."

Sometimes Whitman's body disintegrates gloriously, a holy abstraction: "I effuse my flesh in eddies, and drift it in lacy jags." Here it goes the other way around. Conceptual antimetabole.

:

What dark stain does Whitman cast upon his page? Red is not the color of the pen he has been using. I imagine him, so careful and so haphazard, his inks arrayed for accurate editing, mounds of paper rising from the floor in heaps. An archivist tells me she has read speculation that Whitman's actual blood is on these manuscripts; I search the internet but get no hits. I look down while teaching and notice blood in my notebook from a small cut on my hand I have been worrying. Fingerprints, the archivist tells me, look different in blood and in ink.

Form introducing a way to pass through 'it!

On Whitman's scrap, mid-phrase, I notice what appears to be a colon, transforming the grammar and with it Whitman's sense. "The word is: become Flesh." This flesh, now a demand made upon me.

Such grammatical play doesn't work with more common translations: "the Word was made flesh" (King James), "the Word became flesh" (New International). Now archaic, "is become"—present perfect tense for verbs of motion and transition—carries a shimmering doubleness, both transformation and continuity. But Being always carries this doubleness, its forms so frequently formed with other words. "To be" is the verb of metaphor, by which one thing becomes—even for a moment—another.

Is become corpse.

In December of 1862, the story goes, Whitman was at home in New York with his mother when he read in the *New York Tribune*'s list of recent regimental injuries the name "First Lieutenant G. W. Whitmore, Company D." The incorrectly spelled name he imagined, rightly, belonged to his brother George. He hurried to Washington where he stayed, riveted to the beds of the grievously injured, which did not, to his enormous relief, include his brother.

Whitman sent the news by messenger to his mother at once. Ten days letter he wrote what he had seen.

"One of the first things that met my eyes in camp, was a heap of feet, arms, legs &c. under a tree in front a hospital, the Lacy house."

He presents his mother with this image but he does not dwell on it. He turns, quick, to George's appetite; gently scolds brother Jeff for not writing often enough.

Not just the limbs, but the teetering piles of them, in letter after Civil War letter.

   : "wagon loads of amputated hands, arms, feet, and legs thrown in a heap" - - -
   : "arms and legs lay in a promiscuous heap on our back piazza" - - -
   : arms and legs "rose like a pyramid to the floor of the second story gallery" - - -

   Stitch these attestations together.

:

Whitman kept notebooks during the war. Bloodstained, he called them, when he introduced their publication as *Memoranda During the War*. No, that isn't it precisely:

"blotch'd here and there with more than one blood-stain," he wrote, the blood become compound noun, the verb foregrounding marring. The very liquid of living hardened into stain. Did a soldier cough that splatter up? Or fling it, reaching for Whitman's hand on its pencil, for him who had broken benevolent eye contact for just a moment to write?

"I wish I could convey to the reader the associations that attach to these soil'd and creas'd little livraisons"—He was so desperate to remember the bodies. So hopeful their souls might rise, "active and breathing," from his words. Whitman's desires strain against the mannered tenor of "livraison": a written work published in installments, from French for the delivery of goods.

The delivery of parts. When he publishes the pile of limbs as the first image in *Memoranda* he adds a one-horse cart. Register horror by its volume: the vehicle necessary to haul it away. Lovingly, Whitman reorganizes the amputated limbs, placing feet next to legs, adding hands beside the arms - - - : Stitch : Stitch - - - Wrenches it all into our present tense.

:

"Out doors, at the foot of a tree,

within ten yards of the front of the house,

I notice a heap of amputated feet, legs, arms, hands, &c.,

a full load for a one-horse cart."

:

I find a manuscript page where typeset "blood" is covered by a thick splotch that has eaten through at least one layer of paper. I want to say that the poet has written in his own hand both what the spot obscures and what it seems to be. But the more likely blood is in the lighter stains along the paper's perimeter. I think I recognize the quick shift of a digit noticing itself lightly wounded. The subsequent hasty blotting. Did he splash his ink, then, in surprise? Pain? Irritation? Or, in more conscious homage to the limits and aspirations of his representational attempts? Limitations of the body. Limitations of the words.

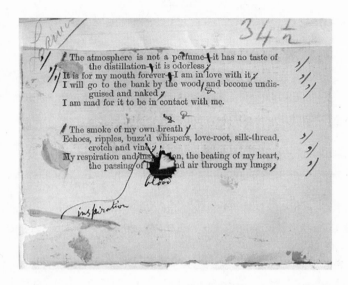

"But your letters also reached me, and were cordially welcomed. I should have acknowledged them at date, only that for many weeks I have been disabled from writing & from clerical work, by reason of a wound in the right hand, which is now better."—Walt Whitman to Thomas Dixon, June 30, 1870.

'/   And rows of inserted commas   '/

'/   are like so many sutures. Slice   '/

'/   into and mend the injured lines.   '/

Whitman was worried that someone else's hand would injure the intact body of his thought. "It is my constant dread that the book will be disfigured." William Michael Rossetti's British selection a "horrible dismemberment of my book."

Each last printed edition cut up, pasted into, written over, collaged. Blue pencil, purple pencil, black ink, red.

:

Like the Gospel of John, Whitman's poem "Reconciliation" begins with the Word—across the "soil'd" world—made flesh, made corpse. Rereading, my breath stopped by the tenderness of the passage. "Beautiful" its own repeated stitch. Whole, just below the linebreak, "Beautiful that war."

What multitudes Whitman always stitches together across his commas and his breaks. As metaphor stitches across an *is*. - - - : *Sisters Death and Night*. Man dead, divine once more : - - - Dangerous work. It assumes and desires so much.

"Reconciliation" ends with Whitman's enemy, "white-faced and still in the coffin— I draw near, / Bend down and touch lightly with my lips the white face in the coffin." White-faced, white face he repeats in a poem with so few words. White, yes, because gravity eases the blood settling into the body's nearest-the-ground parts. But, more than that, in this poem of redemption, severed flesh, precious flesh is white. Raced white. Is a stain of white.

Blood long used as a category of belonging.
How many drops?

How does the abstract become physical? Blood relation, family, tribe, stain, mark. *Air made visible with smoke*? How does the physical mean "when feeling with the hand the naked meat of the body"?

Word becomes flesh and flesh becomes bread for the chosen believers to ingest. "Kneel down on the marble the cold beneath rising through the bent knees. Close eyes and as the lids flutter, push out the tongue"—Theresa Hak Kyung Cha. "A word made flesh is seldom / and tremblingly partook"—Emily Dickinson.

ı

"Hannah's thumb was amputated yesterday. . . . It had been dead, at the extremity for many days, but the doctor allowed it the longest time advisable. It was quite offensive and she was constantly breathing effluvia from it."—Charles L. Heyde to Louisa Whitman, December 8, 1868.

Does the transpiring of time somehow mar the metaphor? That word *becomes* flesh. Does metaphor prefer an always already been? At least its illusion?

Years before the war, Whitman wrote into *Leaves of Grass* the dermis-hypodermis-fat-vessel-tissue-gland of sawed-off limbs. "What is removed drops horribly in a pail." The wet sound of that dropping.

: Body in the kitchen '/

: Body in the bed '/

: Little bits of body '/

: Tucked back into the book '/

:

Philadelphia Ledger, July 20, 1876 (dated in Whitman's shaky late hand, found among his notes):

> BURIAL OF LITTLE WALTER WHITMAN.
> —Among the late mortality in Camden from heat to young children, Col. George W. Whitman and wife lost their infant son and only child Walter, less than a year of age. The funeral was last Friday. In the middle of the room, in its white coffin, lay the dead babe, strewed with a profusion of fresh geranium leaves and some tuberoses. For over an hour all the young ones of the neighborhood kept coming silently in groups or couples or singly, quite a stream surrounding the coffin. Near the corpse, in a great chair, sat Walt Whitman, the poet, quite enveloped by children, holding one encircled by either arm and a beautiful little girl on his lap. The little girl looked curiously at the spectacle and then inquiringly up in the old man's face. "You don't know what it is, do you, my dear?" said he, adding, "We don't either." Of the

children surrounding the coffin many were
mere babes, and had to be lifted up to look.

What, in this notice, is the "it" we all don't understand?

/Spectacle

/Mourning

/White box

/Ceremony

/Death

/Corpse

/Body-once-child

/Life

/Forever

/Self

Gather around this body. Come, closer. Look.

"*Nelly, this is a sad house to-day—little Walt died last evening about ½ past 8. Partially sick but sudden at last—suddenly turned to water on the brain—is to be buried to-morrow afternoon at 4—*

George and Lou are standing it pretty well—I am miserable—he knew me so well—we had already such good times—& I was counting so much—"—Walt Whitman to Ellen M. O'Connor, July 13, 1876.

"Lift me up, mom"—Theresa Hak Kyung Cha.

:

Is this then a touch?

CITATION IN THE WAKE OF MELVILLE

Joan Naviyuk Kane

ETYMOLOGY

(Supplied by a Late Consumptive Adjunct to a Low-Residency
Master of Fine Arts Program in Creative Writing)

The flushed ivory carver—battered through hoodie, pith, callus, and skull; I see him now.
He is ever brushing the tusk dust of walrus and the wiry fibers of baleen, with a shred of a
scrap of a fine linen left in the receding gold rush, earnestly fraying the embroidered flags of
all the nations reduced to assimilation by the superpowers. He was ambivalent about the
new grammars; it somehow reminded him of their deathlessness.

"I knew your grandfather, Kokuluk. The Inupiaq he spoke, it was like Shakespeare's English."
Senungetuk.

"Quohog.
his ⊗ mark."
Melville.

Imaġruk –   basin,   something   which   is   not   quite   a   sea
Imaq-   –   sea,   large   body   of   water
-ruk   –   something   which   is   not   quite
tuugaaq   –   tusk;   ivory;
tuugaiqpaatiuut–Ice forms near King Island at freeze-up, creating the appearance of tusks
alongside   the   island
tuukaq   –   toggle   head   of   harpoon
tuukayaaq   –   spear   point   of   spear/walking   stick
tuuq-   –   to   use   an   ice   chisel
tuuqtuŋa   –   I   am   using   an   ice   chisel
tuuġia   –   I   am   using   an   ice   chisel   on   it
I   I   I

EXTRACTS

(Supplied By a Sub-Sub-Librarian)

Senungetuk's words were meant to encourage me, I think. They were spoken by a man who learned to carve and sculpt tusks of walrus ivory from my grandfather himself: my grandfather, who never spoke a word of English. I am estranged from both men as I am from most men. I am a mother in the United States of America. My body is not yet my own!

"[. . .] —Give it up, Sub-Subs!"
Melville.

"[. . .] hysteria was linked to place."
Freud. (somewhere.)

"To restrict myself here to a personal level, as related to the question of women, I see arising, under the cover of a relative indifference towards the militance of the first and second generations, an attitude of retreat from sexism (male as well as female) and, gradually, from any kind of anthropomorphism."
Julia Kristeva. "Women's Time."

"Strangely enough it was the sperm whales of the Atlantic that drew the whaling fleets to the bowhead whales of Bering Strait."
John R. Bockstoce. Whales, Ice, and Men: The History of Whaling in the Western Arctic.

"Clumsy and awkward as such an approach seems—and is, because I have no notion where discussion will go—I believe a willingness to stumble and fumble publicly is part of my job. When the multi-generational farts stand flummoxed because a feminist teaches The Dick, I know I'll soon have a taste of their confusion."
Elizabeth Savage. "What We Talk around When We Talk About The Dick."

"Very like a whale."
Hamlet.

"The story ends by fearlessly fraying its own symmetry, thrice transgressing its own 'proper' end: there is something inherently improper about this testamentary disposition of Melville's literary property. Indeed, far from totalizing itself into intentional finality, the story in fact begins to repeat itself—retelling itself first in reverse, and then in verse. The ending not only has no special authority: it problematizes the very idea of authority by placing its own reversal in the pages of an 'authorized' naval chronicle."
Barbara Johnson. "Melville's Fist."

"One of my few wishes: to be (safe, coward I am) aboard a whale ship through the process of turning a monster to light & heat."
Sylvia Plath's unabridged journals on rereading Moby-Dick.

"You're going to be a much better writer once you stop writing the Eskimo poems."
Seth Kantner's verbal narrative taken down from his mouth by Joan Naviyuk Kane, 2013.

"These Eskimos might be much more than they seem."
David Foster Wallace. "This Is Water: Some Thoughts, Delivered on a Significant Occasion, about Living a Compassionate Life."

"Another doctor, traveling north on one of the last voyages of the *C. D. Howe* to treat tubercular Inuit, reported to a journalist en route that so far he had seen two whales, two polar bears, and a narwhal and got pictures of it all."
Lisa Stevenson. "Anonymous Care."

"The natives are hostile and there is no forest."
Vitus Bering.

"When Herman Melville, in 'Moby-Dick,' attributed the line 'I only am escaped alone to tell thee' to Job, he was referring to the Book of Job, and not to the character. Actually this line was uttered in the Bible by four separate messengers to Job. There is quite a difference between having the victim cry that he has escaped alone and having a servant tell the victim of the latter's losses."
Rena G. Kunis. New York Times. November 1, 1987.

"The wind scours the windows as it bludgeons the north eaves.

I would have known the ticking was snow, swirling and relentless, but with morning, your pleasure corroborates your astonishment within the wind-carved drifts.

You cannot reduce a dream to a parlor puzzle. Eskimo curlews now hobble hoodwinked, row after row of them, thin leashes around their necks.

That we both dreamed versions of the same dream.

The bodies were everywhere. I still can't speak of that devastation—the lacerations, gaping wounds. Even now, so many days later.

That we might have caused it: our selfishness, our needs. The phrase 'reckless disregard' renders again and over again in my head.

I thought to maximize our pleasure.

Until the body, at least, had given up its last secrets.

We continue to listen to the same song, poles apart.

In the dream, I (am not) mean(ing).

Someone had chosen the song. Without a move, we listened, without a glance around to see the others as we listened.

We took me at me word. Someone said I was a comedian. Or would be. I'm not sure I understand the question. I doubt many were willing to make themselves understood.

First, there was the dream of the parade, then an actual blizzard.

If I said we were 'making love' or 'fucking' while the event 'unfolded,' the misstatement could impede

me.

We were opening ourselves. Taking such risks.

I call it 'The Disenchantment Project.'

Climbers shall rappel down the ice wall. They'll bring food and supplies.

We have to live with our carelessness, our callousness.I'm not convinced it's our fault, but I understand how people feel.

It's a longer, more complex story. It's always a longer, more complex story.

I said to think about Rimbaud. His disappearance. If, that is, it was 'fame' one were after.

This is how we were to die.

Were because contrary to fact.

At some point, people need to be responsible for their own actions. It's easy to point fingers.

I understand the vanished Eskimo curlew: the dream a sign, a signal of vigilance.

The actual avalanche cannot be ascribed to individual fault.

A *scumbling* in the snowdrifts. No.

We   expect   the   skies   to   clear   soon.   Then   might   assess   the   damage.

The   ramshackle   huts,   the   garbage-strewn   yards.

It was, I suppose, a poet's dream. In the tradition of Tiresias, a strange prophecy we were uncomfortable   revealing   in   its   entirety.

We   all   chose   to   live   here   beyond   the   edge   of   where   anyone   should   live.

Had   we   the   skills,   we'd   have   survived.

It was a small fire, but loud. Our own moans and sighs, our encouragements, drowned out the   screams   from   outside,   I   suppose.

It began with the dream, then the sighs and moans, the fire. That conditions had become extreme   was   not,   at   first,   apparent.

The   ticking   of   snow   against   glass.

They followed us here, so we did not have a sense of responsibility. Are we responsible for our imitators? Imitating? Here let us pause and refer to allusion. Perhaps contemporary hunting poems.

To   beam   seas   and   methods   of   heaving   to.

When the sky clears someone says they see an eagle, that it was a harbinger. We were skeptical.   Were   because   contrary   to   fact.

I'd rather not name him. He's well-known in the village and the news might damage his reputation. He has one. You were complicit. You probably still are.

The language of love is depleted, but, yes, love. Melville wrote: '*[...] for, analysed, that heightened hideousness, it might be said, only rises from the circumstance, that the irresponsible ferociousness of the creature stands invested in the fleece of celestial innocence and love; and hence, by bringing together two such opposite emotions in our minds, the Polar bear frightens us with   so   unnatural   a   contrast.'

I   N   Q   U   I   R   Y

There were a few survivors. They've been placed in nearby camps. We expect they'll go back south,   where   they   came   from.

The helicopters could not land in the deep snow, so it was a long process.

The tracks led from house to shed. You could see where someone had thrust a broom handle to knock   snow   from   the   roof.

All night, we heard snow machines, the sudden blatt, the oscillating drone.

They ran out of firewood. And/or the will to stoke the fire.

Listen: If the cold wants me, it strokes my forehead, whispers *sleep sleep*
into   the   deaf'ning   ear.

Are we the caretakers of their misfortunes?" *From "Something" unpublished.*

"We were the first that ever burst
 Into that silent sea."
Coleridge.

LOOMINGS

Call me Naviyuk. Through Melville, and perhaps only parallel to the current from Kristeva, I bring myself questions about the materiality of language: How do the histories and textures of words and syntax provoke you? What is your debt to the multiplicities of basically everything, but particularly: Shakespeare's sexual violence and the myth(s) of self-determination, of the indigenous American as the vanishing savage? How did you get on this island, and how do you get off? We do our best to remind ourselves that historiography is a tool of empire, that, as with Ishmael, my nation's interests are contrary to your nation's interests, that "[. . .] the Esquimaux are not so fastidious."

Let us now labor over Victorianism.

Let us not.

Let me tell you a little about King Island: Ugiuvak. *Ugiu-* means winter or year, and -*vak* means, I think, more or less: place. My ancestors, including my mother and her siblings, inhabited Ugiuvak for countless generations until 1959, the year of Alaska's statehood, when the United States Department of the Interior's Bureau of Indian Affairs decided to close the school. (Children, as we all know, must attend school in America. Or, at least, they used to. Who knows what will happen to our educational system between now and when this essay is published.) There's a lot more I can tell you here, but the ship of this essay is supposed to tack in another direction. To make a long composition short, most King Islanders/Ugiuvaŋmiut (people from King Island, or whose ancestors are from King Island) haven't been back to the island since 1959, 1965, 1974, 1985, et cetera. The official Indian policy of United States of America (and others) has tracked a little like this:

Genocide	1492– (insert emoji looky eyes here)
Intercourse and Trade	1790–1887
Assimilation	1887–1944 (. . . insert emoji looky eyes here, too)
Termination and Relocation	1945–1971
Self-Determination	1971– (I doubt a directive to include emoji looky eyes will hold water a first time, not to mention a third time)

Ugiuvak is in the middle of the Bering Sea. The imaġruk, not the ocean. Like, ninety miles from the nearest contemporary legal American boat harbor. I went there once, in 2014. It was really hard. It took a lot of money, a lot of fighting. It took a long time to get there, and a long time to get back. It required a lifetime of fastidiousness and a lack thereof. We saw a whale and her calves breach and spout as we approached the island.

Let's now pass between us a few words about fastidiousness and lack thereof. Melville writes:

> For all these reasons, then, any way you may look at it, you must needs conclude that the great Leviathan is that one creature in the world which must remain unpainted to the last. True, one portrait may hit the mark much nearer than another, but none can hit it with any very considerable degree of exactness. So there is no earthly way of finding out precisely what the whale really looks like. And the only mode in which you can derive even a tolerable idea of his living contour, is by going a whaling yourself; but by so doing, you run no small risk of being eternally stove and sunk by him. Wherefore, it seems to me you had best not be too fastidious in your curiosity touching this Leviathan.

I have been nothing but fastidious in my curiosities. I have not quite gone whaling myself, though I was invited to do so in December of 2017, in Utqiaġvik, where I traveled, among other reasons, in order to write this essay. I was shocked, upon our aerial approach from Deadhorse, descending toward the northernmost city in the aforementioned United States, to see that there was no ice in both the Beaufort and Chukchi Seas. Two of the eleven seas that are taken to compose the Arctic Ocean, home to many a leviathan.

Let's now get back to the nineteenth century, without which, we might not (still) find ourselves at the terrifying brink of nationalism and empire. Melville writes:

> Only the most unprejudiced of men like Stubb, nowadays partake of cooked whales; but the Esquimaux are not so fastidious. We all know how they live upon whales, and have rare old vintages of prime old train oil. Zogranda, one of their most famous doctors, recommends strips of blubber for infants, as being exceedingly juicy and nourishing. And this reminds me that certain Englishmen, who long ago were accidentally left in Greenland by a whaling vessel—that these men actually lived for several months on the mouldy scraps of whales which had been left ashore after trying out the blubber.

We used to live on whales. On polar bear soup (should you, lacking, say, a tuukaq or a gun, ever need to kill a polar bear, simply create a pronged baleen cage around a scrap of anything scented like prime old train oil, leave it somewhere a polar bear can find it and devour it, and the cage ought to open in the polar bear's stomach, causing eventual rupture and death). On the aforementioned walrus. On seal.

— —A digression here to say that last week I prevented the death of one of my mother's siblings, my uncle. He's still in the hospital. But before my husband and I carried him to the emergency room, I indulged his appetites in my kitchen and fed him half-dried seal soaked in seal oil. It was exceedingly juicy and nourishing.—And during our seven hours together in the emergency room, my uncle (who was born on King Island on June 6, 1952) said to me, "I wish they could just pinch it out." What, I asked him, is it? "My infection," he replied. Later today, I might ask him—which one? For it was not an infection that landed him in the emergency room at the US Indian Health Service's Alaska Native Medical Center, but congestive heart failure, induced perhaps, by empire, by circumstance.— —

In many ways, I do not want Melville's biography. Do I wish for them to pinch it out of me? I do not want to be Queequeg. I am not Queequeg. Neither am I Quohog, nor am I Quohog. I am well aware of the forces of history that define my identity as a person, as a poet. As a poet teaching other indigenous poets and bringing our work and words to bear upon the world. My grandfather lived a kind of traditional Inupiaq life that no longer exists: he was a subsistence hunter of marine mammals, spoke no English, and participated in the cash economy only through turning to ivory carving after our home village of King Island was depopulated in the blink of an eye.

Melville writes of eyes:

— —"Let us now note what is least dissimilar in these heads—namely, the two most important organs, the eye and the ear. Far back on the side of the head, and low down, near the angle of either whale's jaw, if you narrowly search, you will at last see a lashless eye, which you would fancy to be a young colt's eye; so out of all proportion is it to the magnitude of the head."— —

Let us note the eye and ear before we reach the end and reverse to the beginning. Let us note. Let us reach the end, eventually.
Melville writes of eyes.

— —"Now, from this peculiar sideway position of the whale's eyes, it is plain that he can never see an object which is exactly ahead, no more than he can one exactly astern. In a word, the position of the whale's eyes corresponds to that of a man's ears; and you may fancy, for yourself, how it would fare with you, did you sideways survey objects through your ears. You would find that you could only command some thirty degrees of vision in advance of the straight side-line of sight; and about thirty more behind it. If your bitterest foe were walking straight towards you, with dagger uplifted in broad day, you would not be able to see him, any more than if he were stealing upon you from behind. In a word, you would have two backs, so to speak; but, at the same time, also, two fronts (side fronts): for what is it that makes the front of a man—what, indeed, but his eyes?"— —

Let us consider what it means to be an indigenous writer, one with two backs, so to speak. A woman, say. A woman whose bitterest foes might truck in English.
Melville writes of the eye and the brain:

— —"Moreover, while in most other animals that I can now think of, the eyes are so planted as imperceptibly to blend their visual power, so as to produce one picture and not two to the brain; the peculiar position of the whale's eyes, effectually divided as they are by many cubic feet of solid head, which towers between them like a great mountain separating two lakes in valleys; this, of course, must wholly separate the impressions which each independent organ imparts. The whale, therefore, must see one distinct picture on this side, and another distinct picture on that side; while all between must be profound darkness and nothingness to him. Man may, in effect, be said to look out on the world from a sentry-box with two joined sashes for his window. But with the whale, these two sashes are separately inserted, making two distinct windows, but sadly impairing the view. This peculiarity of the whale's eyes is a thing always to be borne in mind in the fishery; and to be remembered by the reader in some subsequent scenes."— —

And yet without all these scarcely written marks, I would not participate in contemporary lyric poetry, would not coruscate between the lyrical and scholastic and demonstrate intimacy between critic and text, as I confront sometimes problematic nineteenth-century themes and structures. I finished reading *Moby-Dick* to my firstborn son in December. He was unwilling, even as I read the end of the novel, to believe that Moby-Dick would not be harvested. Even as I read:

> "Soon they through dim, bewildering mediums saw her sidelong fading phantom, as in the gaseous Fata Morgana; only the uppermost masts out of water; while fixed by infatuation, or fidelity, or fate, to their once lofty perches, the pagan harpooners still maintained their sinking lookouts on the sea. [. . .]"

He continued to interrogate the literality, materiality, and symbolism of the indigenous characters within the text, even as I read:

> "But as the last whelmings intermixingly poured themselves over the sunken head of the Indian at the mainmast, leaving a few inches of the erect spar yet visible, together with long streaming yards of the flag, which calmly undulated, with ironical coincidings, over the destroying billows they almost touched;—at that instant, a red arm and a hammer hovered backwardly uplifted in the open air, in the act of nailing the flag faster and yet faster to the subsiding spar."

He doubted, too, and became curious about the facticity of the narrator, about the reliability of various narrators, as I read:

> "the submerged savage beneath, in his death gasp, kept his hammer frozen there; and so the bird of heaven, with archangelic shrieks, and his imperial beak thrust upwards, and his whole captive form folded in the flag of Ahab, went down with the ship, which, like Satan, would not sink to hell till she had dragged a living part of heaven along with her, and helmeted herself with it."

I do not want to say, at least I boarded the ship, and at least I went down with it. I don't want to say, at least I went. But I did. I'm still going.

A few lines in the manifest, for we are destined to have one:
- Looped readings are still readings.
- An owned, masterly, produced and finished text yet emits whiffs of
  - allusiveness
    - *honkadori*
    - *honzetsu*
    - *metalepsis*
      - *apophrades*
      - **Living On : Borderlines**
  - *inventio*
  - *dispositio*
  - *elocutio*
  - *memoria*
  - *pronuntiatio*

Fragmentation, after all, can be a tolerable way to allow a text to be recognized.

• • • • •

And I'm still here, writing. There go my children, speaking Inupiaq. Reading Melville. Sitting beside me at the kitchen table as I write, as I do not write. As they try on Shakespeare's English, and ask me questions like, "Mommy, what's the difference between anthropomorphism and personification?" As I begin to account for myself, for Melville, for the land, for the water.

These words, and with them the great cerements of the sea, roll on as they rolled five thousand years ago.

TOUCHING HORROR

POE, RACE, AND GUN VIOLENCE

Karen Weiser

> The final belief is to believe in a fiction, which you know to
> be a fiction, there being nothing else. The exquisite truth is to
> know that it is a fiction and that you believe in it willingly.
> —**WALLACE STEVENS**

> Art is here to prove and to make one bear—to help one bear—
> the fact that all safety is an illusion.
> —**JAMES BALDWIN**

Small spots tincture my field of vision, only to shift out of range when I try to focus on them. Silent auxiliaries, they move more slowly than my eyes: pulled clouds across what I see. There is a phenomenal reflex that excludes them, ignoring their slight shadow, but there are times when they are what I want to glimpse, and can't, these obstructions in my eyes. Did I stare at the sun long enough to imprint a dark spot? Many? My ways of looking have made my gaze what it is, compromised, discontinuous, credible, floating peripherally, a guarantee against itself. I fear that I can't confront the topics in this essay head on, only in interspersed fragments, small momentary lapses, a lingering movement at the corner of the eye.

To dwell or abide; to make longer; to long.

The word *linger* suggests a relation to time and place full of longing, the desire for something to continue that is about to end, or has already ended; it asks, maybe pleads, to house ourselves within something ("dwell or abide") for another moment. Lingering in bed after the alarm, in front of an artwork though other people are waiting behind you for a glimpse, in someone's company after you have already said goodbye: to prolong the bittersweet moment right before something recedes from us. It's already receding.

But what about when we linger in places or on ideas that scare or unnerve us, on the thoughts that have barbed edges difficult not to touch and touch again? We have longing there too, though perhaps of a more complex kind.

This essay is a record of the logic of my feelings about very different kinds of subjects (Edgar Allan Poe, gun violence, race) and refusal to sanitize them into understanding, although I am conscious that this implies a withholding of satisfaction. My engagement, then, is more about what happens when we don't understand.

We wonder what a baby experiences before the entry into language. I imagine this resembles how I experience a new song, when I can't yet take in the lyrics, and am more concerned with how it impacts my body with its melody, rhythm, bridges, and emotional sweep. With language, it's always an exchange, something that happens between beings; the baby being talked to in a parent's arms understands the exchange, regardless of the absence of comprehension. Affect underlies every word, the most primary kind of communication: one a newborn is already fluent in. I imagine that baby's experience constitutes a more fundamental understanding, which is to say, *not* understanding and yet still understanding, as psychoanalyst Adam Phillips writes.[1] Watching my children have this visceral engagement with language before their entry into it has made me sense how rich and varied *not* understanding can be. I think of Teresa Brennan's image of a mother's body directing the cells of the zygote in her womb to differentiate into different parts of the body. This happens without her having any mental knowledge of the process. It is, no way around it, communication.[2] Our bodies have so much to say to each other, in ways that have nothing to do with comprehension, with knowing.

Here I hope that the surface movement of thinking through some difficult thoughts can be a lingering, a hesitation to say and move on. Like Emily Dickinson's dashes, hesitation is capable of both holding off and knitting together, of dwelling in, and longing.

Forgive me if I stutter.[3]

· · · · ·

Who can teach us more about lingering on the unnerving than Edgar Allan Poe, whose stories have shaped an entire tradition of writing that aims to unnerve?

Poe used images of violent black characters; the most glaring examples are in his novella *The Narrative of Arthur Gordon Pym*, where the "savages" with "their complexion a jet black, with thick and long woolly hair"[4] attempt to trick the crew of white men to their deaths by causing an avalanche. Although born in Boston, and residing much of the time in the Northeast, Poe was raised in Richmond, Virginia, a bustling city with both urban slaves and a significant free black population. His adopted father owned a few house slaves, and inherited three landed estates complete with slaves. At the time Poe was an adolescent and still expecting to be his father's heir, which would never happen.

As a white, Jewish, upper-middle-class woman, who has an immense amount of race and class privilege, how do I manage not to exploit violence against people of color for my own intellectual or political gain? I do not want to reveal myself as morally blind or cause suffering to any of my readers. When I first wrote about Poe as a graduate student, an African American poet and scholar whom I admire deeply read my work and asked, "What about race?" She handed my essay back to me and turned to walk away. It was a moment of deep shame. Since then, I have written about race—race in the nineteenth century—but race in the present has eluded me. It's a risk. Many white artists of late have tried to talk about race, and failed dramatically, causing pain and protest. My own fear at not saying the right thing keeps me silent.

I take to heart Audre Lorde's idea that we each have a responsibility to change the way we allow ourselves to be silenced, and that it isn't easy to do. She writes: "And of course I am afraid, because the transformation of silence into language and action is an act of self-revelation, and that always seems fraught with danger. . . . In the cause of silence, each of us draws the face of her own fear—fear of contempt, of censure, or some judgment, or recognition, of challenge, of annihilation. But most of all, I think, we fear the visibility without which we cannot truly live."[5] What I write can also act to silence. In making myself visible here, what (or who) am I obscuring? To balance, then, between not saying, saying, and making room for others to say. That moment when the scale, balanced, hesitates in air.

I keep sitting down to write this essay piecemeal as I hear of racially motivated shootings and terror attacks on US soil. More and more people shoot each other every day. What are the limits of one's scope of attention and care?[6]

On March 27, 2017, the officer who shot Ramarley Graham, an eighteen-year-old unarmed black man in his house, resigned rather than deal with being fired, after a judge dismissed his manslaughter indictment and the NYPD recommended his termination. The mayor of New York City spoke, saying that he "hopes that the conclusion of this process brings some measure of justice to those who loved [Graham]." Strange, these words: "conclusion," "justice." And a few days ago, on May 30, 2017, Timothy Loehmann, the officer who shot twelve-year-old Tamir Rice, was fired for lying on his employment application, but not for killing a child.[7]

The thing about trauma is that it is a state the body recognizes, having been in it before. It is almost a taste in the mouth, or the way images loop in memory's playback.

It is an alert buzzing. It is the feeling that everything is changing, the impact of which will tear a space between who you were and who you will become. That fracture is irreparable, though new species of narrative will serve to connect the fragments, eventually.

I have started to think of the police as the clearest indicator of my white privilege. I still think that if someone attacked or raped me, the police would take me seriously and work to find the persecutor. I must believe even now that the system would be on my side and support me, despite my knowing that rape victims are rarely believed (women of color are believed less often than white women), and that hundreds of thousands of rape kits lie languishing in evidence rooms, ignored. I persist in needing to believe in the system—it is my necessary fiction. I would cave under the weight of my fear if I had to walk around without the shield of this belief wrapped around me.

I have never had to deal much with the police at all in my life, except at protests or traffic stops. My most intimate experience with the police was when I falsely remembered their patrol of my house during the funeral of my parents, when I was eighteen years old. The same day my parents died, March 1, 1994, Lebanese-born immigrant Rashad Baz opened fire on fifteen Jews on the Brooklyn Bridge. Just four days before, Baruch Goldstein massacred twenty-nine Muslims in Hebron, and Baz's terrorist shooting is widely regarded as retaliatory. My traumatized mind conjured secret service agents keeping an eye on our house. Listening to it now, it seems entirely far-fetched, but for many years I believed it, until I wrote a poem about it called "My Secret Service Agents" and realized that it must have been a false memory or dream. In that dream, though, the police are there to protect me.

• • • • •

JUNE 12, 2016. I wake to the news of the worst shooting on US soil ever—fifty people dead. The gunman, an Islamic homophobe, and possibly gay himself, was apparently upset about watching two men kiss in front of his child and so he walked into a gay night club on Latinx night with an automatic assault weapon. He was also affiliated with ISIS, his act of terrorism motivated by different kinds of hate.

I too am queer. This attack felt personal.

Writing this essay might allow me to distance myself from the actual horror of the shooting. Yet it also allows me to linger. I hold the idea of horror out in front of me to consider it, and therefore feel it differently. Is all academic writing a kind of containment, a holding arena?

Some kinds of academic writing also serve as a "hygienic procedure," as Eve Sedgwick in *Touching Feeling* notes about theory.[8] Sedgwick suggests that we can aim to touch feeling rather than to know, to privilege the affective over the epistemological. Can we aim to touch the feeling of the horror of that night rather than understand it? How? That a news source used horror movie music to cover the shooting suggests that in order to feel (or more likely, to *not* feel) the horror of that night we can and do rely on representations of shootings, our social imaginary, since most of us have never witnessed one. How have these fictions shaped our understanding of this kind of experience? What was the last movie or TV show you watched that represented a shooting? Was there music? What did the camera show and what was obscured?

The way we use the word "sensationalism," as a particularly trashy mode of media used to sell papers or ratings or hits, comes directly out of a literary genre that Poe both reflected and burlesqued.

It was connected with larger philosophical questions concerned with the mind and rationality. Sensationalism is less about the thing represented and more about a particular kind of feeling that one gets when experiencing it. Titillation.

The Pulse gunman, Omar Mateen, must also have fantasized about the media coverage of the shooting: the way the news would titillate the audience, the way his face would, and did, plaster every screen. He must have thought about, and maybe even curated, the images of himself that would be available for the media. We know this because he apparently checked social media right before and after the shooting. Built into the act of taking a machine gun into a crowd and opening fire is the desire to be seen, in control, to be visible, to make people feel fear, to make people feel. Not only the hundreds of people in the nightclub, but the millions of viewers who will replay the event will feel something.

John Locke wrote that human knowledge and identity are derived, first and foremost, from sensations. It is through our sense impressions—what Locke called "simple ideas"—that we approach reality. This reality gets confused by the actions of our mind, which transforms these sense impressions into more "complex ideas," which have no source in nature, and therefore cannot be trusted.

Poe exploited sensations to come at Lockean ideas, like the Ouroboros, the snake eating its own tail. Or should I say *tale*. Poe emphasized sensation not to reaffirm Locke's idea that sensation can lead us to nature and reality, to rationality, but to undermine that idea, to point instead to the way that the relation between mind and matter is always necessarily a fiction, and its relation unstable, perhaps indeterminable.

Poe exploited ingrained racialized stereotypes and images in order to explore this ambiguity. His aim, though, has been variously interpreted.

The gun a secret, heavy weight that your own hands unleash and point. In trying to imagine the horrific shooting scene, I can imagine it from the point of view of the gunman and also from the point of view of the hundreds of dancing club-goers. The images that come to mind when I think about what Omar Mateen must have felt entering the building with a gun come from movies and TV. I have a hard time imagining shooting people, as the semiautomatic weapon allowed him to do—it is perhaps beyond what is comfortable to picture. I think of the phrase "mowing down" as a particularly problematic one associated with shootings. The machine's hegemony over the organic (lawn mower vs. grass) obscures the action of the gunman, though it does convey the ease with which life can be ended. I can only take my imagination of the subjectivity of the gunman so far because I cannot understand his hatred and desire to kill. I can, however, understand the desire to make others feel something.

Imagining the hysteria of the crowd, rather than the gunman, is much simpler, and perhaps draws more on my actual experience than the fantasy of the movie screen. Having been in lower Manhattan during 9/11, I remember feeling the floating terror and trauma of something going down (literally and figuratively). The sensation that sticks with me is running through the Staten Island Ferry terminal to quickly board a boat as the first tower collapsed, and seeing shoes strewn by the wayside as people rushed onto the ferry. And then the unearthly quiet as the other passengers and I turned and looked back at the huge cloud of smoke generated by the tower's collapse, our ferry pulling away.

Every trauma is a compound of past traumas. I read that many of the people who were in the Pulse nightclub lucky enough to survive covered themselves with the bodies of the dead. When the police first entered the scene, they asked the living to raise their hands so that they could find them. They are altered by this trauma, and it resides in their bodies.

• • • • •

My dead are always raising their hands in my mind. Here they gesture. And here.

My parents rarely talked about race or ethnicity. My mother, though, had two refrains that she repeated at odd moments throughout my childhood. They are anxious reminders of how little I learned about her before she died, because we never discussed her commands. One was, "If he [she never made clear who *he* was] hits you, even once, you pick up your things and your children and leave right away." As a child, this was alarming, both its prediction into a future for me that included a (male) spouse and children, and the projection of violence in that future. I would be sitting in the back seat of the car, closing my eyes to examine the pattern of light and darkness on my eyelids as we drove past the thick stand of trees on the street-side, and at a traffic light my mother would turn around and say that to me. I often wonder about what she witnessed as a child. The other command she incessantly repeated was "Always have a valid passport. They might come for the Jews here too."

After Trump was elected and the rise in anti-Semitism began, I texted my three siblings and we all agreed that my mother was reminding us from the grave, "Go renew your passport. This country is not our home." It is a sick inside joke for the four of us, meaning that even her anxiety is comforting now, any reminder of her at all.

When my parents died I dissociated from who I had been before. It still feels to me as if I have lived two separate lives. I have learned that this is one of the hallmarks of trauma.

I cannot watch horror movies because my body remembers something else and gets confused. And yet I do, cautiously, keeping tabs on the physical sensations so easily coaxed from my body.

There are images that I replay often in my mind, and these images are so painful they are aglow, almost synesthetic, with trauma. I desire to name them for you, but they are a deep secret I have never shared, a shortcut to the pain that names me.

In her *New York Times* essay "The Condition of Black Life Is One of Mourning," Claudia Rankine writes about the specific weight and precarity of being a mother to a black son, alongside the constancy of threat and strain one must carry daily just to live black: "that as a black person you can be killed for simply being black: no hands in your pockets, no playing music, no sudden movements, no driving your car, no walking at night, no walking in the day, no turning onto this street, no entering this building, no standing your ground, no standing here, no standing there, no talking back, no playing with toy guns, no living while black."[9]

Rankine focuses on Emmett Till's mother's decision, in 1955, to open the coffin and allow people to photograph and publish images depicting her son's mutilated body.

The mother of Emmett Till, Mamie Till Mobley, took the exact image that would be the pain that names her, the most private of all pains, and made it public. Rankine remarks that, in that act, Mobley turned the white supremacist message of the image of the lynched body back on itself. "In refusing to look away from the flesh of our domestic murders, by insisting we look with her upon the dead, she reframed mourning as a method of acknowledgment that helped energize the civil rights movement in the 1950s and '60s."[10]

In her book *Citizen*, Rankine lingers on the microaggressions of racism in a way that allows their multiplying impacts to resound, re-sound, in the echo-chamber of trauma, in the echo-chamber of the poems.[11] Her work has influenced me deeply.

My traumas allow me to linger. That brings me back to the distinction between knowing and understanding. I can know the violence against people of color, the way racism has always been the shaping force of our culture; I can see it clearly, but in some bedrock way I can't understand.

I can only find my way into this present through the past.

My parents' personal effects were returned in a yellow felt bag that was placed on the bench outside the bathroom in my childhood home. I had to walk past it to go pee. It held my father's watch, still working, though the silver band was ripped in half. This image of the yellow felt bag makes me feel like vomiting. As I type this, my teeth are clenching. The still working watch was, for me, the exact image of the pain that names me.

• • • • •

I never saw their bodies, though I did see the autopsy report of my father's body and the police reports that indicated with red Xs the areas of blunt trauma. It was left out on the kitchen counter and I didn't know what it was when I opened it. Then it dawned on me. I remain grateful for the Jewish tradition of the closed casket, wondering at Mamie Till Mobley's bravery.

Being in horror can be, should be, a public event. Perhaps this is that moment for me—what I am imagining: you reading this.

Rankine notes that Michael Brown's bleeding body on the pavement picks up where Till's open casket leaves off. The evidence. The kind of evidence that we have gotten so accustomed to that we can hardly experience it, feel it, as it is so ubiquitous and tied to our long history with slavery and anti-black racism. What is needed is "a rerouting of interior belief" that Rankine argues can be worked toward by lingering in or on the fact of how they were killed: "We need the truth of how the bodies died to interrupt the course of normal life."[12]

And yet, representing murdered black bodies "recreates pain, while making domination thrilling or normalized to others," as Sarah Schulman says, in the debate around race and representation that the Whitney hosted after the 2017 Biennial.[13]

The debate addressed the controversy about Dana Schutz's abstract painting at the Biennial of the mutilated remains of Emmett Till, which many people found abhorrent in its lack of awareness of the trauma caused by representing Till's murdered body. I watch the debate live streaming from my bedroom with the door closed, repeatedly denying entry to my six-year-old who wants to watch with me. I keep shooing her out, not wanting her to hear about Till's murder. The irony of this is not lost on me, as the panelists discuss the decision by *Jet* magazine to publish a photo of Till in his casket, and the subsequent trauma to the generation who saw it. The photo galvanized the Civil Rights Movement. I have the privilege to shield my daughter from this image and knowledge, to wait for the right moment to frame the reality of racism. We talk about it, but not in terms of murder, not yet. "Why were there no brown people upstate?" she asks me after we return from vacation.

Dana Schutz has taken an approach to representing the violence of Till's murder diametrically opposed to that of Gwendolyn Brooks in her emotionally understated poem "The Last Quatrain of the Ballad of Emmett Till," with its epigraph "(after the murder, / after the burial)":

> Emmett's mother is a pretty-faced thing;
>> the tint of pulled taffy.
> She sits in a red room,
>> drinking black coffee.
> She kisses her killed boy.
>> And she is sorry.
> Chaos in windy grays
>> through a red prairie.[14]

At this debate, Sarah Schulman begins her talk by saying: "White women have to face Emmett Till because we were the excuse for his destruction."

I think about the white woman who was the excuse for Till's destruction, Carolyn Bryant Donham, who admitted, once she was too old to be prosecuted for manslaughter, to lying about the details of her confrontation with Till. In her photo from 1955, taken during the trial of her then-husband Roy and his half-brother J. W. Milam, her eyebrows carefully arch over guarded eyes and her head tilts at a forty-five-degree angle. She must have to face Emmett Till every time she looks in the mirror. The University of North Carolina holds her memoir, which they will release when she dies. I'm trying to see my own reflection in her image. It is not easily coming, though we occupy a similar kind of power.

LitHub, a notable literary website, refused to publish Sarah Schulman's talk because she mentioned the Palestine Solidarity Movement.[15]

In the 1845 tale "The Facts in the Case of M. Valdemar," Poe played a successful hoax on part of his very gullible audience with an account of a man mesmerized (à la Franz Anton Mesmer) on the brink of death, who survives in a hypnotic state an additional seven months before rotting in a pool of immediate putrefaction upon being woken from the trance. This dead undead man speaks in a voice "indescribable, for the simple reason that no similar sounds have ever jarred upon the ear of humanity," which, the narrator remarks, "impressed me (I fear, indeed, that it will be impossible to make myself comprehended) as gelatinous or glutinous matters impress the sense of touch."[16]

To describe a sound as a particular (and utterly un-experienced before) kind of touch, that is the way that Poe heightens the senses here. Exactly how does a gelatinous matter impress touch? It is indistinct in its boundaries, wet, spreading, with a certain mass. What kind of a sound would that be?

Sound artist Maryanne Amacher aimed to reveal the unknown perceptual processing of tones within the ear—the sounds, usually repressed, generated within our auditory system, rather than outside of it: an internal sound-scape that reveals the ambiguous opposition between inside and outside.[17] Wet, spreading, with a certain mass. Origin unclear.

By using one sense to describe another, Poe achieves a feeling of the uncanny—familiar in one sense, mysterious in another.

When I imagine a shooting I feel the synesthesia of trauma, its buzzing uncanny.

Valdemar's speaking "I am dead" is a paradox—not dying but already dead—yet he is able to communicate in a body seemingly without life through a tongue that is otherworldly, desiccated and still vibrating. The tongue becomes the channel for what? A mind? Spirit? Soul? The mind and body here are in two different realms.

Elizabeth Barrett (later Barrett Browning) wrote to Poe that the story was "throwing us all into dreadful doubts as to whether it can be true, as the children say of ghost stories. The certain thing in the tale in question is the power of the writer and the faculty he has of making horrible improbabilities seem near and familiar."[18]

This tale is considered one of many hoaxes that Poe devised, and some Poe readers responded to this story as if it were true, probably because of the narrator who qualifies his tale as partial: just "the facts" he writes, using scientifically based information like medical jargon. These are the hallmarks of science fiction.

The last words in the tale, "detestable putrescence," leave the reader grappling with shock and gore, the staples of horror as a genre. Unlike most horror movies, though, and unlike most nineteenth-century fiction, there is no narrative resolution in that we do not look away from this image; there is no narrator's voice here to explain or soften the impact. We are left beholding the vision, the facts, the utter horror of mortality: a sensation.

I imagine Carolyn Bryant Donham spying (avoiding?) a copy of *Jet* magazine with the brutally murdered body of Till on the cover.

Open casket. Closed casket. The choice to click, to watch. To linger.

In *Powers of Horror*, Julia Kristeva writes of the corpse as "the utmost of abjection." She notes that "refuse and corpses show me what I permanently thrust aside in order to live . . . the border of my condition as a living being." This border becomes reified in the corpse itself, and to behold the border as an object has the power to break down the world, to "engulf" us.[19]

Poe gives us no way to turn away, no comfort or explanation, no scientific or fictional mode to cushion the abject brutality of death, the fact of the matter of our bodies.

What happens to us in these moments when we imagine the deaths of the victims of gun violence? This is not beyond the unspeakable or the unknowable. It is not what Wittgenstein refers to when he writes: "What we cannot speak about we must pass over in silence."[20] Rather than silence, we have a wound that will not heal because the fact of it is ever present.

We can feel it.

Poe's ending to the Valdemar tale is real in that sense, in the truest sense of the most real of "the real." It leaves us there at that precise point of confrontation with the knowledge we must ignore in order to live. There is no alleviation of this realization in Poe, but ultimately we touch that moment, feel it, and then close the book. Poe's fiction gives us a lesson in how to approach trauma, and move on. That is, some of us can move on.

· ● ● ● ·

I can't bring myself to watch the shooting videos of black men like Ugandan immigrant Alfred Olango or Keith Lamont Scott, or the choking of Eric Garner. I read accounts of these videos instead. I imagine these events and feel confused about my obligation to witness. Are you a witness if you are not there in person? What does watching someone die in a video mean?

For me, trauma is that which is not representable. To see the shooting would be to bring up my own trauma, and experience it again in a new context, though my own trauma is entirely unrelated, not racial trauma. Still, as my imagination animates the still images of these crime scenes, I can feel the buzz in my jaw and stomach.

The thing about trauma is that it is a state the body recognizes, having been in it before. It is almost a taste in the mouth, or the way images loop in memory's playback. It is an alert buzzing. It is the feeling of everything changing, the impact of which will tear a space between who you were and who you will be. That fracture is irreparable, though new species of narrative will serve to connect the fragments, eventually.

When I teach Poe's texts with racist characters, such as *The Narrative of Arthur Gordon Pym*, which features the Tsalalians, a race of scheming, murderous natives who are entirely black, and afraid of all things white, I wonder what I am reinscribing. My students discover that in this novella Poe creates white characters with a moral ambiguity usually associated in the nineteenth century with "primitive races" (i.e., cannibals). His white protagonist is clearly naïve and willfully ignorant, and part of a colonizing crew focused solely on economic gain through exploitation.

Toni Morrison writes, "no early American writer is more important to the concept of American Africanism than Poe," whose racial symbolism she finds casts blackness as entirely "other."[21]

My students and I hold out hope that Poe wanted his reader to see the way his culture constructed race, to investigate the way the black characters could be justified in their violence toward the whites, and the mental calculus of white colonialism and exploitation. But I am not sure, and neither are they.

When we read "Murders of the Rue Morgue" and explore the pseudoscientific connection of blackness with orangutans, stemming from Georges Cuvier's natural history writings, I have to remind myself that my students, who were mostly white in this particular class I am thinking of, must have heard of the association of blackness with apes before I taught them its history, though they acted surprised. We explore what Terence Whalen calls Poe's "average racism"[22] in the light of the classroom space, and yet I can't help but wonder what trauma I am unearthing for the two young women of color in the room. What does the viral image of the Obamas' faces photoshopped to look like apes mean in the context of this racist pseudoscience?

One of them stays after class, just to walk me down the hall and chat, keeping the conversation going another few minutes. She gives me a certain kind of hope that it is still worth studying Poe and the literature of the 1840s, a time of race riots and amalgamation fears. In order to be anti-racist we must understand how racist stereotypes come down to us, an inheritance whose effect remains all too clear.

These small traumas, these large traumas, come to us in this new cyber context, on a screen that we click away from or shove into our pockets. How does the medium create new conventions? Of viewing and experiencing? Of responding and processing?

To me it seems so different from a book, which feels slow and close. We click, we share, or we write a phrase. Sometimes we search for more information, the names of the dead, to know about their lives and families.

Was there a gun?

So much of how we read the situation seems to hinge on that question.

In 1835 Poe wrote to Thomas White about the necessity of using the conventions of sensational tales to sell magazines. He comments that such stories have a common nature: "In the ludicrous heightened into the grotesque: the fearful coloured into the horrible: the witty exaggerated into the burlesque: the singular wrought out into the strange and mystical."[23] Such a description perfectly fits the genre of horror, which existed before Poe, but which he both satirized and popularized in the American literary marketplace.

The horror movie *Get Out* brings the clichés of the genre Poe mastered to bear on racial politics and America. Director Jordan Peele calls it a "social thriller"—featuring a twenty-six-year-old black protagonist, it makes visible the racial paranoia and the everyday fear in black experience.

But *Get Out* does so much more—it explores the way white culture both objectifies and idealizes blackness, while seemingly rejecting the humanity of black people as individuals. In other words, the film lays bare the appropriative logic of primitivism—the historical exploitation of black culture as a way to reinvigorate a lifeless white one first popularized in early twentieth-century art and literature, and inherited by liberal white culture. The film takes this trope and literalizes it, so that the black body, emptied of active black consciousness, becomes the object through which white consciousness can live on, and experience black embodiment. All the subliminal references to slavery (a bingo game that is actually an auction, a black body cuffed at wrists and ankles, cotton that must be picked from the chair) suggest that enslavement is still the governing logic of race relations, though borne out of a desire for blackness, rather than a rejection.

"They treat us like family."

Peele has reversed the premise of Poe's famous tale "Ligeia," in which the protagonist's blond wife, Rowena, dies after three drops of a blood-like liquid are poured into her cup by some mystical spirit. Rowena's body is reinvigorated by the spirit of the dark-haired Ligeia, the former wife of the protagonist, who was of unknown ethnicity (with her "Hebrew nose") and mysterious parentage. Though the reliability of the tale is upended by the narrator's opium haze, "Ligeia" ends with her ripping off her death shroud to reveal a white body taken over by a darker one.[24]

In *Get Out*, Chris, the young photographer protagonist (played by Daniel Kaluuya), claws his way out of the abduction plot by killing the nefarious mad scientist relatives of his white girlfriend in self-defense with anything but a gun. Instead, he narrowly saves his life by wielding a deer head trophy, a bocci ball, and a car, but ultimately is thwarted from escaping by Rose's white grandfather trapped in the body of a black groundskeeper. With the house (and evidence) in flames, and the ground littered with dead bodies (as well as the injured body of Chris's girlfriend, who he almost strangles but leaves alive), police arrive on the scene, sirens blaring.

This is the true climax of the movie, and the moment when the film's particular genius shines forth. When police enter the scene while a hero is mid-escape, it's usually the moment when the audience knows that the hero's life is finally safe, when the evil characters are contained by the law. This time, though, as the police pull up, I feel utter dread. They won't believe the far-fetched truth, or that he is innocent amidst the scene of blood and gore, and Chris, because he is black, will go to jail for murder. This is when the horror of systemic racism, and its connection to the police, becomes clear.

Jordan Peele discusses this implied ending (though not the actual one) on the podcast show *Another Round* with Heben Nigatu and Tracy Clayton.[25] Peele reveals that he wrote a number of possible endings to the film, including one where police do arrest and lock up Chris, presenting no way to "get out" of a racist culture. He conceived of and wrote the movie during Obama's presidency as a way to right the misconception of a "post-race" era. After the murders of Trayvon Martin and Michael Brown, though, Peele decided a different ending was necessary, one that does show a way out, an escape, a possibility.

He filmed Chris's friend Rod showing up, not in a police car, but what turns out to be a TSA vehicle with sirens. Rod, the conspiracy theorist, who jokes that all white people are crazy, is the only one who believes Chris. He is the only one with a clear grasp on reality. He collects his injured, traumatized, bloody friend, and drives him away from the horrific scene.

Peele's ending, a stunning reversal of expectations, suggests that the institutions here to protect people, most notably the police, are incapable of actually perceiving the truth of any situation where race is concerned. The only thing that allows us to escape whatever is out to get us is our friends, who listen to us and believe us, no matter how far-fetched the truth may be. We make sense of what we don't know when we linger in conversation. It's when he can no longer converse with his friend, when he can no longer get through, that Rod knows Chris is in trouble.

One of my favorite poets, Erica Hunt, in the late 1990s wrote a poem called "Risk Signature," which circles around the ways in which we converse with ourselves in our minds about the kinds of dangers we are perpetually up against (who constitutes the "we" is up for discussion), how a "she" "erects / scaffolding for her critiques / then isolates her objects with a deft / twitch of the knife."[26]

One is always in conversation with the affective toll of our thoughts, and we use mental knives to pare back and simplify, to think. This is one tentative reading of the line, which, as in all of Hunt's poetry, asks us to consider the multiplicity and tentative nature of the sense we make of her language—of what happens to us when we are not rooted in understanding.

> The entries list the blood counts,
> pound in the head as warnings to the wary, little
> deaths configured into road kill
> specimens collected, dried snake
> smashed turtle, white bird skull.
>
> What about danger?
>
> Danger is engaged
> as much as possible.
> Organization entails foresight.
> She tries to see things coming.[27]

The poem ends with the suggestion that this mental calculus is a kind of natural history of the daily assault of living in an oppressive culture. She gives us an image of collecting the dead things, of mapping them, studying them. This process can teach us, if we take note of the details, how to deal with danger, which must be "engaged / as much as possible." To organize here is both a physical and mental act: not only bodies protesting in the street, but the mental work of remembering and naming the dead, not as rap sheets, but as evidence of a culture that runs over, in blatant disregard, various forms of life.

Whether we watch the videos or not, we are witnesses to their deaths.

If there is something to learn from gun violence, we might learn more by lingering than trying to understand.

To look deeply into eyes of Carolyn Bryant Donham rather than looking once again at the violence done to black bodies.

My ways of looking have made my gaze what it is: compromised, discontinuous, credible, floating peripherally, a guarantee against itself.

It must be possible to find new ways to write about the trauma of gun violence in order to honor the lives of the dead, and feel for the necessary fictions that we can sometimes touch, lingering there beside ourselves.[28]

HOMAGE TO BAYARD TAYLOR

Benjamin Friedlander

In this slightly abridged version of the essay, two sections dealing with Bayard Taylor's complex relationship to Walt Whitman have been left out, along with some ancillary notes on method. A few other adjustments have been made to accommodate house style.

I

Bayard Taylor's "Love and Solitude" (1852) is a poem I have often returned to since first reading it at least a decade ago. More than that, surely, but ten years is when I began working on a poem in homage, eventually set aside. The poem—mine—was descending into ickiness (for want of a better word), reproducing qualities of Taylor's nineteenth-century verse I had hoped my twenty-first-century idiom might redeem. In fact, my efforts only succeeded in losing the intensity that did redeem his poem. Why I had thought to attempt an homage in the first place—the basis for my attraction—is now lost to me, but I suppose it had something to do with the poem's strangeness, though my grasp of that strangeness was dim at best. Attempting now to reconstruct that original response, I believe I was attracted by the poem's emotional extravagance, but also put off by it, misrecognizing my own mixed feelings as a quality of the text. What I deemed strange and wanted to work through was a projection of myself, which I was able to value when credited to Taylor, and which I began to devalue when my own role in its production could not be ignored, as occurred in my abandoned homage. Taylor too had mixed feelings, not quite the same as mine, and these too produce the effect of strangeness. In Taylor's case, he was pulled in one direction by a whole-hearted commitment to delineating a situation that, pulled in the other direction, he had no heart to name. Maximum expression of effects; minimum disclosure of cause. The manner of expression is decidedly antebellum, fitting well within a horizon of sentimentality. Taylor's relationship to disclosure puts the poem within a different horizon, not only because of his obliqueness and abstraction, but also because his thematic treatment of disclosure describes a nearly Freudian notion of repression. The poem, in other words, belongs to an earlier time in terms of art, yet reaches toward our time in sense of personhood, with an irresolution of fit between these aspects that gives it a strangeness in either time: awful or magnificent, depending on where you stand, or which aspect you attend to. The oscillation I experienced between these two qualities—between the poem's awfulness and magnificence—was a symptom of my own fixed place in time. Taylor's time was out of joint, his poem's temporality queer.

To read Bayard Taylor's unjustly forgotten, apparently suppressed poem with anything like comprehension requires the suspension of what ordinarily facilitates comprehension: experience and judgment. These involve more than mere fact and interpretation: resting on certain assumptions, looking toward certain aids to orientation (earth and star, urge and law, datum and concept), experience and judgment are also forms of location. Cut off from experience, comprehension becomes groundless; without judgment, the urge to comprehend loses direction. Experience, then, is the matter of our lives, particular. Judgment, general, is the realization of why experience does matter. Comprehension is the two together, fused so fully that their subsequent distinction seems a purely formal gesture: body and identity, relation and society—the former giving shape to the latter, the latter giving meaning to the former. This fusion of experience and judgment, particular and general, yields the context without which acts—or texts—become incomprehensible. And how natural it is that we should bring that context to bear on the acts of others. Problems arise, however, when we apply our context to such others, like Taylor, whose assumptions and orientations are <u>un</u>certain. Encountering them, we need to think free of context, suspend our fusion of particular and general, let experience acquaint itself with new meaning, judgment with new matter.

II

This sense of the poem's strangeness—its estrangements—is much clearer than the one I acted on in my abandoned homage. At that time, I inclined toward a different clarity, having read the section on Taylor in Robert K. Martin's *The Homosexual Tradition in American Poetry*. According to Martin, Taylor, "certainly conscious of his own sexual nature," suffered "the consequences . . . of the discrepancy between an apparent public heterosexuality and a private homosexuality (expressed publicly in indirect ways)." A principal figure among the genteel writers, Taylor hints at a possibility sadly unrealized in his work overall—and in the genteel tradition overall: a melding of "frank sexuality and direct confrontation of the social and political issues of sexuality" with "a real strength and purity of language." The work that Martin does approve of takes two general forms: a homoeroticism "diverted" from frank expression, and, less commonly, a frankness only partly realized as art.[1] The former is exemplified by the brief narrative poem "Hylas" (1852), about which Martin writes:

> [I]t is deeply related to Taylor's understanding of himself
> as homosexual. His choice of the Hylas myth as a poetic
> subject is part of an attempt at self-definition and also part
> of an attempt to situate himself in a poetic tradition which
> will justify his own emotional life. The failure of the poem
> comes from Taylor's inability fully to avow his real subject:
> the love of Hercules for Hylas and his own for young men. . . .
> His language is luxuriant but finally vague; unable to depict
> directly the body of love, it wanders off into repeated similes.[2]

The latter is exemplified by Taylor's "lush, melodramatic, and sentimental" novel *Joseph and His Friend* (1870), "not merely a political argument in favor of rights for homosexuals" but "also a depiction, although in highly romantic terms, of the realization of love between two men." Martin admires the "considerable courage" it took to write the novel, but he clearly wishes that Taylor had brought that same courage to bear in his poetry, the concealments of which are rued.[3] On this point Martin is equivocal, if not contradictory. Writing of the genteel poets in general, he notes sympathetically, "It seems likely that the emotional price for . . . concealment was high, although the tensions created by the need for a constant disguise may also have been the source of a certain artistic strength."[4] Almost immediately, however, a more damning conclusion follows: "[T]he authors . . . did not in fact produce great art. . . . The strategies adopted . . . contribute to a weakening of focus and a fatal indirection." Artistic strength or fatal indirection, the reticence of Taylor's poetry is also a lure, leading later readers such as Martin to name directly and discuss frankly what the work itself kept unnamed. This, indeed, is what I too did when I first read "Love and Solitude." Though Taylor delineates his emotional state with exquisite care, leaving unde-lineated the particulars giving rise to it, I made the particulars my focus, presumptuous in my belief that I knew them. Inverting Taylor's own interest in the poem, I placed greater emphasis on "cause" than "effects," naming that cause—as Martin did—"homosexuality."[5]

An important portion of the poem poses some difficulty for this interpretation; not insurmountably, but I wish I had given it some thought, as I might have seen sooner a crucial feature of "Love and Solitude," one that distinguishes it from poems such as "Hylas." Since one followed the other when the two were first collected, it makes sense to read them together: "Love and Solitude," the structure of an experience; "Hylas," its content. But what is this content? In the Greek version of the story, told by Theocritus in Idyll XIII, there is a framing narrative, with Herakles first joining then abandoning Jason's *Argo*. In between, there is the story of Hylas, who bathes in a stream and falls into the clutches of the Naiads, who rape and drown him.[6] The drowning is used to explain why the demigod went missing: Herakles, who "loved . . . the beauteous Hylas,"[7] goes off to find the boy, who left camp to fetch water and never returned; the *Argo* departs while Herakles is searching. In Taylor's version, Herakles barely partici-pates, appearing only at the close, though mentioned briefly near the start, and Jason's ship is likewise mentioned briefly at the two ends. In between—all but 21 of the 159 lines—we attend to Hylas at the stream: his decision to bathe, his disrobing, his rape by the Naiads, his death.

Taylor's intensity of focus is explained, I think, in a passage where he uses the word "line" to trace the boy's naked form. Becoming ekphrastic instead of dramatic, he puts us in a Victorian parlor, perusing an album of erotic art:

> The thick, brown locks, tossed backward from his forehead,
> Fell soft about his temples; manhood's blossom
> Not yet had sprouted on his chin, but freshly
> Curved the fair cheek, and full the red lip's parting,
> Like a loose bow, that just has launched its arrow;
> . . . .
> Dewy and sleek his dimpled shoulder rounded
> To the white arms and white breast between them.

Downward, the supple lines had less of softness:
His back was like a god's; his loins were moulded
As if some pulse of power began to waken;
The springy fulness of his thighs, outswerving,
Sloped to his knee, and, lightly dropping downward,
Drew the curved lines that breathe, in rest, of motion.[8]

One cannot tell from this passage if Taylor is discreetly but directly invoking the boy's erection, or indiscreetly suggesting it while describing something else; the effect is of a delirium, a sensual overload—a quality that Byrne R. S. Fone captures well, comparing Taylor favorably to Whitman:

> [I]t is certainly an intensely erotic description, indeed daringly so. . . . At that intimated point where "downward the supple lines had less of softness," Whitman's frank "masculine muscle" is also answeringly ready to waken. Here is the "hard stuff of nature indeed," Whitman's "well-hung" rough. Taylor's gaze is fixed upon Hylas's loins and thighs just as Whitman's gaze is fixed in equal fascination upon the tight fitting trousers of his firemen in "I Sing the Body Electric." Taylor is fascinated—almost to the point of incomprehensibility—not only by the decreasing softness but also by the rising "pulse of power" that awakens to "springy fulness" and soon becomes "outswerving," dropping, quite amazingly, to his knee.[9]

One can almost hear a gasp in that last comment—it reaches *where*?

Fone's juxtaposition of Taylor and Whitman has some historical justification, as Taylor in 1866 initiated a fleeting correspondence, commending *Leaves of Grass* for "two things . . . I find nowhere else in literature, though I find them in my own nature": "the awe and wonder and reverence and beauty of Life, as expressed in the human body, with the physical attraction and delight of mere contact which it inspires, and that tender and noble love of man for man which once certainly existed, but now al-most seems to have gone out of the experience of the race."[10] Turning back to "Love and Solitude" from "Hylas," then, and in light of Taylor's later letter to Whitman, one might suppose that the object of affection in "Love and Solitude" is male, that the love under "ban" is homoerotically charged; but here I must mention the difficulty cited above: in the eighth section of the poem, indulging in his fantasy of an island haven, a place where he and his love might live "Each within each involved, like Light and Air, / In endless marriage" (8:4–5), Taylor strongly suggests that this metaphorical marriage will find its literal fulfillment in offspring:

> Year after year the island shall become
> A fairer and serener home,
> And happy children, beautiful as Dawn,
> The future parents of a race
> Whose purer eyes shall face to face
> Look on the Angels, fill our place,
> And be the Presence and the Soul, when we have gone. (8:20–26)

One could argue, of course, as Martin does in similar contexts, that the passage is pure dissimulation; one could also argue that Taylor is fantasizing "a race" born solely of fathers. He seems to support that second reading in his bitter dismissal of this fulfillment as *mere* fantasy:

> Forgive the dream. Love owns no human birth
> And may not find fulfilment here
> On this degenerate Earth. (9:1–3)

No certain conclusion about the gender of his beloved is possible. Attending to the problem, however, did help me see that the act of concealment is what Taylor wants us to understand, not the thing concealed. When all is said and done, the poem leaves us with a model of experience applicable to all manner of affection: it is not the object of love that matters, but its proscription. In this respect, reading "Love and Solitude" and "Hylas" together suggests that in the former the crucial problem is not the gender of Taylor's object, but the nature of his desire for it: a desire at once intense and corporeal, transgressing convention, even unlawful.

"Love and Solitude" is an anguished tribute to a potent, transgressive desire unsustainable in society, hence requiring both secrecy and escape. The poem tells no story about this desire, and reveals no information about its object, enacting the very secrecy it evokes with

such extravagance. The account is structural, relentlessly focused on the subjective dimensions of an objective condition: we get a model of personhood, not a person's biography; we learn a great deal about effects, nearly nothing of cause. The poem shares and withholds in the same gesture, communicating what it can of an experience it will not divulge. Yet this very refusal communicates crucial information: Taylor's occluded account of his experience, in its maintenance of secrecy, makes possible an understanding of maintenance itself. Following Taylor's extended architectural metaphor in the second section, we might say that his poem is hospitable where open, requires a key where closed. Yet even from the locked portion certain inklings are let loose. Thus Taylor: "The heart has . . . / . . . secret halls, . . . / Dark crypts, beheld of none," where "darker powers, that flee the sun," are "heard at intervals / When all is still, and through the trembling walls / Some guilty whisper calls" (2:13–19). The nature of these "darker powers" is never brought to light, and Taylor will not share with us the content of their "whisper." Instead, he gives expression to the affects generated by it, to the turmoil experienced in maintaining dark powers in his heart.

III

Two types of law are cited in "Love and Solitude," both in the third section. The first, though embodied in government decree, evoked with an image of shackles, is, in origin and impact, a perversion of religion:

> Men from their weakness and their sin create
> The iron bonds of State,
> Soldered with wrongs of olden date,—
> The heartless frame, the chance-directed law
> Which grows to them a grand, avenging Fate,
> And fills their darkness with its awe.
> States have no soul. (3:6–12)

The second is a counter-law, scarcely equal in power and administered by "Love," who "hath his own world"—a sovereignty unrecognized in "the world of men" (3:1–2). Trapped in society, Taylor remains obedient to Love, "Not hopeless . . . , but hoping much in vain" (3:14).[11] There is thus an undertone of pessimism in Taylor's ironic claim of being *bound* to his lover; the two may have escaped, but not necessarily to freedom:

> [A]liens we, who breathe a separate air
> In regions far away!
> Thou art my law, I thine: the links we wear,
> If not of Freedom, dearer still,
> And binding both in one harmonious will. (3:17–21)

Harmonious and whole together, though unable to be together where state and church hold sway, Taylor and his Thou are driven apart, and inward, away from "the common ground, / Where gloom is born of gloom, and pain / From pain unfoldeth ever" (3:26–28). As a consequence, what the poem largely presents is an account of the inner life, much of it given in the form of fantasy, a dream of futures yet to be attained. Influenced by Martin, I understood this dreaming as an effect, the cause of which I presumed to think I could name, not out of any great insight, but simply because of my historical vantage. I had terms and concepts unavailable to Taylor. I assumed, of course, that what Taylor lacked the ability to name nonetheless existed, and did so in a form I would recognize; that history, mediating between us, rendered Taylor more legible, not less.[12] I understood that my reading was anachronistic, but not that my anachronism might limit understanding. I thought, with false superiority, that *my* world, swallowing *his*, was the larger; that *my* way of seeing gave *his* life dimension. Like an art critic judging the painting's back, forgetting that it is a back, I forgot why the poem even mattered. Even if my interpretation was correct, I was wrong. The effect was what Taylor had given to art; the cause he kept for himself. The effect he was willing to share; the cause he could not. *That* was the point, the essential solitude: driven inward, Taylor yearned for an impossible explicitness.

Was my supplying of explicitness the right response? I no longer think so. I had become, so to speak, a parent turning on the light, revealing the monster as a shadow on the curtain. My explicitness was meant to soothe, dispelling what the poem trembled to present. In doing so, however, I also drained the poem of its strange power, emptied the effect of its effect. Once more, however, I am being smug. In any ordinary genealogy, Taylor would be the parent, not the child; we the progeny, not he. Guessing at Taylor's secrets—at what he withheld from us—I neglected to consider what was nonetheless passed down. That inheritance is more than just a record of concealment, for despite Taylor's opacity regarding gender, and his vagueness about certain other details, he does disclose his feelings. Those, presumably, are what he wanted to bequeath to his island's "happy children," the "future parents of a race" he could not quite permit himself to expect. In preparing this legacy, moreover, he falls neatly into that condition Christopher Nealon calls *foundling*, a relationship to history that

> entails imagining, on one hand, an exile from sanctioned
> experience, most often rendered as the experience of
> participation in family life and the life of communities and,
> on the other, a reunion with some "people" or sodality who
> redeem this exile and surpass the painful limitations of the
> original "home."[13]

The queer writers who concern Nealon belong to a later period than "Love and Solitude," and they worked from a notion of sexuality already distant from Taylor's. They were trying to think beyond a discourse of gender inversion, which "Love and Solitude" precedes. Yet like those later writers, Taylor's stake in history is a fleeting one, sustained by emotion.

---

*The secrecy and escape of "Love and Solitude" are means of protection that Taylor explores both formally and thematically, using abstraction to maintain his privacy while giving free rein to fantasy in order to concoct a life where privacy would not be a concern. The poem, then, is not merely anguished; enacted also is the freedom it yearns for, with Taylor seeking out in two flights of fancy two plausible havens: "a glorious Valley, hidden / In the safe bosom of the hills that part / The river-veins of some old Continent's heart" (5:6–8), and "Some Island, on the purple plain / Of Polynesian main, / Where never yet the adventurer's prore / Lay rocking near its coral shore" (6:5–8). That Taylor might have decamped to such a safe zone is not far-fetched: he was already the author of two travel narratives (*Views Afoot; or, Europe Seen with Knapsack and Staff *[1846]* and *Eldorado; or Adventures in the Path of Empire *[1850]); soon after the poem was published, he became a member of Commodore Perry's Japan expedition. It was, indeed, as an adventurer that Taylor—like Melville, whose* Typee *(1846) is perhaps invoked in the poem's island—was best known. Like Melville too, Taylor bore witness to erotic attachments between men, most notably in his novel* Joseph and His Friend *(1870), described by Martin a century later as "a political argument in favor of rights for homosexuals,"[14] and by Taylor himself as depicting "the impulse of . . . manly love, rarer, alas! but as tender and true as the love of woman."[15] For many recent scholars, the epistemological and terminological disjunction between the precise, anachronistic term "homosexuals" and Taylor's imprecise, resonant "manly love" is a productive one, drawing attention to "the permeable borders separating queerness and normativity."[16] There, erotic attachments prove rich but indeterminate in meaning, manifesting in "affects, styles, and cathexes" rather than sex as such.[17] This methodological consideration is especially useful for thinking about Taylor, whose biography is rich with border crossings of all sorts. In his travels, of course, Taylor crossed literal borders, but figurative ones were* *also transgressed, abroad and at home, in feeling as well as act. As he put it in "Love and Solitude," speaking for himself and his beloved:*

> *For us the world contains no ban;*
> *In the profoundest measure given to Man,*
> *We love, we love! (1:3–5)*

IV

That Taylor is concerned in this poem with histories and legacies is only incidentally suggested in a few brief passages, turns of phrase that one might easily overlook, or take as merely figurative ("imperfect destinies" [1:7], "heir to all delight" [1:15]). In some places, this concern is expressed optimistically:

> Through blindness and through passion came the clear,
> Calm voice of Love, thenceforth to be
> The revelation of diviner truth
> Than ever touched our sinless youth,—
> A power to bid us face Eternity! (4:4–8)

Elsewhere, with pessimism:

> Forgive the dream: here never yet was given
> More than the promise and the hope of Heaven.
> The dearest joy is dashed with fear,
> Our darkest sorrow may be then most near. (9:4–7)

Primarily, however, the optimism and pessimism are blended, with Taylor projecting hypothetical legacies he scarcely dares imagine possible. The most powerful of these projections, already cited, has its point of origin on an island—an "isle," as he eventually puts it (10:12), meaning an *I will*:

> There, when the sun stands high
> Upon the burning summit of the sky,
> All shadows wither: Light alone
> Is in the world: and, pregnant grown
> With teeming life, the trembling island-earth
> And panting sea forebode sweet pains of birth
> Which never come. (6:16–23)

The projection here begins optimistically and ends in pessimism, but even the pessimism places Taylor *in* rather than outside history, and in precisely the manner Nealon proposes: through a "strong emotion" that allows Taylor to "'feel historical' despite a daily problem of feeling pathological."[18] In this case, the strong emotion is foreboding, a relationship to the future perpetuated by anxiety. The birth projected in this passage is allegorical, a pregnancy of light; in a subsequent passage, the birth is literal. Each time, a future teeming with possibility is imagined, then retracted. The emotional labor of conceiving, so to speak, "A fairer and serener home" miscarries (8:21). The solace of belonging to a new race, if only in retrospect, gives way to mourning, arguably an even stronger emotion. This mourning marks Taylor as a foundling; had he been able to sustain the solace, he might have become—virtually at least—"a member of the tribe," Nealon's next stage of queer identity.[19] Or perhaps not; Taylor's opacity and vagueness make it impossible to ascertain if the island people he imagined attain the anthropological richness of an ethnicity, which is what Nealon means by *tribe*. Certainly, however, he imagined those people as living the next stage in queer history, projecting himself among them when most hopeful, as here, declaring:

> We
> Will leave this splendid misery,
> This hollow joy, whose laugh but hides a groan,
> And teach our lives to write a perfect story. (4:11–14)

Taylor's dimeter "We love, we love!" (1:5) might be read (or, admittedly, overread) as no repetition, but a joint declaration, a giving voice to his twofold desire, the simultaneous pull he evinces toward "normativity" and "queerness." The former is well represented by his two marriages, the first to a childhood sweetheart who died young, the second to the niece of a German who befriended Taylor in Egypt. Taylor's passionate friendship with this German, by no means the only such friendship he maintained, is a meaningful instance of his pull away from normativity. Evoked in Taylor's dimeter line or not, these different directions are given some dimension in the havens he concocts in "Love and Solitude." One is figured in feminine terms—the womanly bosom of the hills protecting his valley. The other haven is masculine—the phallic "prore" (prow) of the ship off his untouched island. It would be a mistake, however, to see this duplicity as equivocation. The entanglement of marriage and friendship is a major theme of Joseph and His Friend. *As "Philip Held," the friend of the title, tells Taylor's "Joseph": "A man's perfect friendship is rarer than a woman's love, and most hearts are content with one or the other: not so with yours and mine!"[20] The novel is in many ways a thought experiment, a working out of what not choosing between one and the other, of what not being content with just one, might mean.*

V

Rereading Taylor by way of Nealon helped me to put aside my presumptions of knowledge, substituting for Martin's "homosexual tradition" a more modest term of description, one that was still retrospective, but no longer ahistorical. Through the "foundling," my relationship to the past—and of the past to me—became an object of study in its own right, distinguishable from the art object and artist; and the art object and artist in turn became distinguishable from my relationship to them. Where "homosexual" asserts a continuity between epochs, a stability in modes of erotic life, Nealon's term assumes alterity, the apprehension of which stirs thought and feeling. Not to overstate my shift in thinking; I was familiar already with Foucault's *History of Sexuality* and had some knowledge of "the uneven transition"—see Christopher Looby—"from the Foucauldian regime of acts to the ensuing regime of identities."[21] I assumed, however, an essential continuity in behaviors; that consciousness and culture might change—change utterly—but not what bodies do. I had failed to grasp that consciousness and culture were sexuality's province; that the body is not sovereign there, but subject. I suspect I was not alone in this misapprehension, since, in recent years, a number of scholars have arisen to correct it. For these new scholars, the slow coalescing of *homosexual* and *heterosexual* as terms and concepts, indeed ways of life (a process that had scarcely begun at the time of Taylor's death), was also a slow erasure of all that got replaced. What remain are impressions and smudges, stray letters only partially legible. Making out that old meaning thus begins in part by ignoring as well as considering the meaning written on top, as the new will only sometimes be a revision of the old, only sometimes an aid to understanding. Where the new meaning sets aside the old, guesses about the latter based on the former will go astray. A starting point, consequentially, is recognition of sexuality as an issue for epistemology as well as ontology, philology as well as hermeneutics. As put by Christopher Castiglia and Christopher Looby, "'sexuality' is neither transhistorical nor innate, easily discoverable . . . nor conventionally comprehensible."[22] Compressed in their neat definition are two methodological coordinates: the first pair of terms—"transhistorical" and "innate"—locates the familiar issue of essentialism; the second pair—"discoverable" and "comprehensible"—locates a new issue, putting "sexuality" itself in question. The resulting scholarship, taking constructivism for granted, asks, with regard to previous epochs, "Can we even know what it is that was constructed?"

For some time, constructivism has been concerned with the transformation of acts into orientations, of orientations into identities, but this emphasis on transformation has often meant that only acts meaningful in retrospect are considered; erotic life as we understand it now mediates our perception, exaggerating the significance of some things while minimizing that of others. Undoubtedly, this has also influenced our estimation of past authors; reading their work in light of the present, we often give in to what Michaël André Bernstein called "backshadowing," "a kind of retroactive foreshadowing in which . . . knowledge of the outcome of a series of events . . . is used to judge the participants in those events *as though they too should have known what was to come*."[23] Those judged unknowing are left to oblivion, or the library annex; their books no longer handled, only dredged for information; authorship irrelevant, as suits their virtual afterlife, out of copyright. Lost in such dredging necessarily is the information authorship itself provides, by which I mean those things we can learn from lives spent fashioning art and the art that fashioned lives.

Care for that lost fashioning is the distinguishing feature of Peter Coviello's work, though the authors to whom he attends are still remembered. His project is "restorative"; what he rescues from obscurity, however, is not a text consigned to the past, but a past consigned to the text.[24] No single past emerges from this study; each lost possibility seems as unique as the author preserving it—Thoreau's "exquisite carnal ravishment by sound,"[25] Jewett's "assemblages of erotic life," wherein the object is "a scene of sociability,"[26] not simply a person or persons—yet aspects of each resonate with certain moments in Taylor's work I had found mysterious or simply overlooked. For me, Coviello's readings thus served as a gentle reminder of how much presumption remained in my setting aside of presumption—my trading in of certainty for its opposite, which again left the text poorly read, now because unreadable. Could I learn to read? Perhaps not; but I could learn to see better what I yet failed to grasp, taking Taylor's world-building efforts more seriously, as "ambitions for and yearnings after a discursively uncaptivated sexuality,"[27] not mistaking my own failures of understanding for his repression, his dissimulation. I do not want to exaggerate the difficulties; there are aspects of Taylor's erotic life I could at least recognize as such: "relations that are friendly, but not chaste; carnal, but not matrimonial; filial, but not organized by the ties of family."[28] What I could not make out was the experience of living those relations: how they felt, what they meant, where they fitted, who shared in their knowledge, why they resisted fuller articulation. What to make, for instance, of Taylor's life-altering encounter with the German aristocrat August Bufleb? There is more than enough documentation of its emotional intensity to suggest an erotic aspect; the issue is not *if* eroticism was involved, but *how*. How, above all, was this eroticism managed, both between the two men and by the men in relation to others? Documentation notwithstanding, the story exemplifies the problem of understanding as Coviello conceives it, signaling to us as if from a different present's past—"a scene of broken off futures, of possibilities skewed toward inarticulacy by time's unfolding."[29]

When the two men met in 1851—on board a steamer en route to Egypt—Taylor was a recent widower and Bufleb was twenty years Taylor's senior, well-ensconced in marriage; yet the intensity of their connection was not at odds with the other affects and relationships that organized their lives. The centrality of Taylor's losses to his bonding with Bufleb is attested to in a letter sent by Taylor to his mother soon after Bufleb's return to Germany:

> For two days before our parting he could scarcely eat or
> sleep, and when the time drew near he was so pale and
> agitated that I almost feared to leave him. I have rarely been
> so moved as when I saw a strong, proud man exhibit such
> an attachment for me. He told me he could scarcely account
> for it. . . . I told him all my history, and showed him the
> portrait I have with me [of Taylor's deceased wife, Mary
> Agnew]. He went out of the cabin after looking at it, and
> when he returned I saw that he had been weeping. . . .
> Almost the last thing he asked of me was to look at it once
> more before leaving.[30]

That Bufleb's marriage posed no conflict is also attested to; a few months after the parting in Egypt, Taylor wrote to George Boker the following:

> I think I spoke to you . . . of my German fellow-traveler, to
> whose sympathy and noble nature I owe the best part of my
> enjoyment of the Nile. I find here two letters from him—
> letters so full of devotion to me and care for my safety that I
> have been strangely affected by them. His wife also writes to
> me the most sweet and beautiful of letters, thanking me for
> my friendship toward her husband. It is a new phase of
> human affection, which I have never known before. As I
> said, he is a man of fifty, proud and self-willed, and
> accustomed all his life to wealth and authority. But he clung
> to me with a love like that of a woman. He had no secrets

for me; all his past life, good and bad, was revealed to me.
I looked into the recesses of his nature which he had never
before exposed to the eye of another. He entered into my
sorrow as if it had been his own, and wept, as a mother
might have done, at the recital of my history. . . . He says
that Nature has no longer an intelligible language to him,
since we parted.[31]

In 1855, Bufleb purchased a house and prepared it for Taylor, urging a visit ("In spite
of our long separation and remoteness from each other, your heart I know could never
tell you of any change in my feelings and thoughts"[32]), and during his subsequent stay
Taylor met and became engaged to Bufleb's niece, Marie Hansen, entwining the men's
friendship in another, more conventional relationship.

What to make of this entwinement? The world-building involved in the ongoing
Taylor-Bufleb relationship—and there is more of the story I could tell—is immensely
suggestive, but what it suggests in our time is not necessarily what it did in Taylor's, a
condition of knowledge that makes me clumsy when I would grasp with precision, as
if my very interest in the past knocked it away, as if reading were a magnifying glass
that burned what it enlarged. Situating Taylor in a gay male lineage, as Martin does,
comparing his life choices with those of Whitman, does little justice to the facts as we
know them, but I have no alternative understanding that might do better; with regard
to Taylor's friendship with Bufleb, I remain caught in the same anticipation invoked by
his biographer Russell H. Conwell, who wrote in 1879, the year after Taylor's death, "It
will be like a romance, when told in all its detail, as it might be now, and will be when
the present generation passes away."[33]

"What are the codes of legibility," asks Coviello, "that allow us even to recognize
something . . . as sex, or sexually invested? What have those codes of legibility to do
with what gets to count, not only as sex or sexuality or sexual identity, but as History as
well?"[34] Taylor's friendship with Bufleb was counted as history already in the nineteenth century, but its legibility as something "sexually invested" was put on hold, left
to a future that in the interval broke off.

---

*Whether the issue be the concordance of two lovers or of two kinds of love, the iambic
repetition "We love, we love!" does more than give expression to a private feeling. A performative utterance, the line makes real what it describes by making the private public. It*

constitutes a vow—and Taylor refers to vows explicitly in section nine. Acknowledging the full effect of this performance—this "sacrament of language" in which the speaker is "himself at stake in his speech"[35]—Taylor immediately follows with a comment that bears directly on the work his poem undertakes:

> O, in that sound, completion lies
> For all imperfect destinies. (1:6–7)

In the context of the poem as a whole, "imperfect destinies" must be the unsustainability in society of the concordance both enacted and celebrated by the vow. Referring to his vow as "that sound," however, Taylor also indicates that the utterance's language is not merely descriptive or referential, but involves an aural dimension, an aspect of speech most fully developed in poetry. By "sound," of course, he also means that the words must be spoken aloud to be effective; but in speaking them—in giving them both breath and a hearable form—he is certainly conscious of their rhythmic power. Hence the lines he gives next:

> It is a pulse of joy, that rings
> The marriage-peal of Nature, brings
> The lonely heart, the humblest and the least,
> To share her royal feast. (1:8–11)

Taylor's word choice, "pulse," emphasizes the link between rhythm and body. In this way, his poem, affirming in its content the union of lovers in a vow, affirms formally the fact that those lovers are embodied; their joy is felt physically, in the flesh.

VIII

Commentators who have paid attention to Taylor's queerness have for good reason been drawn by Taylor's interest in the homoerotic,[36] the "manly love" of man for man; their inattention to "Love and Solitude" is surely due to the absence of that interest, though the poem certainly acquires more meaning when read in light of it. In keeping with the poem's subject—the repression of love by society—the particularities of the speaker's erotic life are smoothed away. Putting it anachronistically, the poem is not concerned with homo*sexuality*, but homo*phobia*. Anachronism, of course, will not do; apart from the risk of mistranslation, the poor fit that occurs between present-day names and past actions, there is the problem of reconciling our distinctions with Taylor's. Though his often-cited, polemical preface to *Joseph and His Friend* does seem to split erotic life along lines of gender, equating "man's love for man" with "man's love for woman," the split was something he wanted to repeal. Heterosexuality as we conceive it was as unknown to Taylor as homosexuality; the bend toward convention that concerned him was not "love for woman," but marriage, a social institution answering to nature, which he sought to reconcile with a nature no social institution accommodated.[37] The irreconcilability and antagonism Martin saw between Taylor's "public heterosexuality" and "private homosexuality" was experienced by Taylor himself as a problem of wholeness, not choice. Married twice, he was clearly drawn toward that convention; he was also drawn toward experiences that transgressed it. Relinquishing one tendency for another was not a solution to his problem, but another version of it.

This, in any case, is my thesis: Taylor, lacking our categories of sexuality, was not in need of them; what he needed were new categories of sociality. His fissure ran through "life," not the "erotic." Marriage made possible for him a public integration of one form of affection, but this very integration relegated others to secrecy. The metaphors of marriage in "Love and Solitude," arising from that secrecy, do not strike me as ironic, but as an expression of hope for alternative modes of integration. This is not to say he idealized marriage; *Joseph and His Friend*, as the plot plays out, is clearly an indictment. Still, the "nature" accommodated by marriage was not at odds for him with the inclination that led Taylor to admire *Leaves of Grass*.

When Taylor praised Whitman for recording those things "found nowhere else in literature, though I find them in my own nature," his preposition, "in," suggests a nature with capacity, able to encompass *many* inclinations. The architectural model of personhood in "Love and Solitude"—nearly Freudian in its play of light and dark, "airy tower" (2.12) and "awful crypts" (2.24)—renders vivid the disciplining of his nature by society. Pitched against that disciplining are the various modes of sensual experience to which Taylor yielded nonetheless, through which a model of being prior to personhood is also set forth. In "Metempsychosis of a Pine," published alongside "Love and Solitude" and "Hylas" in 1852, he comes to comprehend this prior being, assisted by "strange sympathies," and an inner "wisdom . . . / Whereof nor creed nor canon holds the key."[38] Once upon a time, Taylor tells us, "somewhere in the world," he enjoyed a more "Rooted" existence as "a towering Pine"; the alterity of this prior existence—in which he persisted "for centuries"—is expressed with erotic intensity:

> Through all my fibres thrilled the tender sigh,
>   The sweet unrest of Spring.
>
> She, with warm fingers laced in mine, did melt
>   In fragrant balsam my reluctant blood;
> And with a smart of keen delight I felt
>   The sap in every bud,
>
> And tingled through my rough old bark, and fast
>   Pushed out the younger green, that smoothed my tones,
> When last year's needles to the wind I cast
>   And shed my scaly cones.
>   . . . .
> I felt the mountain-walls below me shake,
>   Vibrant with sound, and through my branches poured
> The glorious gust: my song thereto did make
>   Magnificent accord.

"Upwrenched" from this natural state, the pine becomes a mere object of human use, "All sense departed," "A mast upon the seas."

Though ultimately a story of loss, the recounting of this prior life is also stirring; nowhere else in Taylor's work is the potency of his yearning evoked so grandly, or offered up so explicitly as the source of his poetry:

Yet still that life awakens, brings again
　　Its airy anthems, resonant and long,
Till Earth and Sky, transfigured, fill my brain
　　With rhythmic sweeps of song.

Thence am I made a poet: thence are sprung
　　Those motions of the soul, that sometimes reach
Beyond all grasp of Art,—for which the tongue
　　Is ignorant of speech.

And if some wild, full-gathered harmony
　　Roll its unbroken music through my line,
Believe there murmurs, faintly though it be,
　　The Spirit of the Pine.

To these early quatrains I would link, from the other side of Taylor's career, the preface to his 1870 translation of *Faust*. There we find, rendered in language more recognizably erotic, the earlier defense of poetry, more mature in form, but arising from the same sources as the "pining" without language of Taylor's youth:

> Poetry is not simply a fashion of expression: it is the form
> of expression absolutely required by a certain class of ideas.
> Poetry, indeed, may be distinguished from Prose by the
> single circumstance, that it is the utterance of whatever in
> man cannot be perfectly uttered in any other than a
> rhythmical form: it is useless to say that the naked meaning
> is independent of the form: on the contrary, the form
> contributes essentially to the fullness of the meaning. In
> Poetry which endures through its own inherent vitality,
> there is no forced union of these two elements. They are as
> intimately blended, and with the same mysterious beauty,
> as the sexes in the ancient Hermaphroditus. To attempt to
> represent Poetry in Prose, is very much like attempting to
> translate music into speech.[39]

To fashion life as one does a poem is only possible if the outward form—the social form—contributes essentially to the inner vitality, assisting in its fullness of expression.

Though first printed in 1852, "Love and Solitude" was reprinted with slight but significant abridgements in 1856 and 1865, then dropped altogether from Taylor's posthumous Poetical Works *(1880), though the editor's preface declared an intention "to make the following collection of Taylor's poems as complete as possible, and to omit from it nothing in a poetical form . . . to which he once gave his serious attention."[40] The editor went on to produce a long, angry sentence that made the omission all the more perplexing—for this very sentence might well have served as a comment on the text:*

> *It is consoling to know that throughout [Taylor's] laborious life, which brought his sensitive, poetical nature into daily contact with stupidity, ignorance, grossness, and with the consequential vulgarity of conceited dolts, he had something to cheer and to comfort him in those solitary hours through which less imaginative men brood over the wrongs and the disgusting histories of their world, and harden themselves against the future in a crust of cynical misanthropy.[41]*

This is an outburst, and Taylor's poem was a cry, but the twenty-eight years between the two was no easy interval, and this perhaps explains the difference in tone between them. "Love and Solitude" signified differently in 1852, 1856, 1865, and 1880, marking off a trajectory that ended, apparently, in deletion from the record. Simply put, secrecy and escape had proven ineffective, at least for the poem's would-be editor. The carefully protected meaning of 1852 had become by 1880 both unprotected and, as a consequence, altered in meaning. As if the seal had broken on a jar of preserves, turning the sweetness of Taylor's "sensitive, poetical nature" into the rot of his editor's anger, the poem had become inedible. An Oedipal age was dawning, with homosexuality identified, pathologized. Taylor's prophetic evocation of the unconscious might have enjoyed success then, but what his unconscious contained—and expressed—could not. His depiction of repression was repressed.

IX

There are no books of Bayard Taylor's poetry in print and none has appeared recently enough to remain in copyright. As near as I can tell, the last edition was the 1902 version of *The Poetical Works of Bayard Taylor*,[42] which differs in important ways from the 1880 volume of the same name. That 1902 version, reprinted in 1907, contains a preface by the editor (Taylor's second wife, Marie Hansen-Taylor), and reorganizes the contents, trimming a few poems along the way. The superseded text, which appeared only two years after Taylor's death in 1878, had also trimmed a few poems from the previous edition, which Taylor himself prepared. That differently titled volume, *The Poems of Bayard Taylor* (1865), was the last to include "Love and Solitude" (interestingly, the 1865 text was also reprinted in 1907, now with an introduction by Albert H. Smyth, whose 1896 biography was the last of three to appear in the nineteenth century). Taylor also made a compilation in 1856, *Poems of Home and Travel*, a companion to *Poems of the Orient*, which appeared the year before; the 1856 volume drew from two earlier books, supplementing these with poems of more recent vintage. On two occasions, then, Taylor reprinted earlier poems, often incorporating revisions, some significant. In the case of "Hylas," the revisions were minor: the 1856 printing made twenty-four alterations to the 1852 text, twenty-three of which involved spacing, punctuation, or spelling, and a twenty-fourth that cut three lines of description; the 1865 printing made three more changes of punctuation and cut two more lines, again of minimal significance. With "Love and Solitude," the revisions were more extensive: the 1856 printing made thirteen adjustments of punctuation and wording to the first nine sections of the 1852 text and cut the tenth section entirely; the 1865 printing made six additional adjustments and cut the ninth section. The poem was then dropped from the posthumous editions, perhaps on Taylor's own instructions; "Hylas" was retained. The effect produced by the dropped sections is interesting to consider. In its original printing, "Love and Solitude" concludes with "a dream divine / Of larger freedom":

> Death
> Is here, and Pain, and sobbing breath;
> But souls so blent may reach some radiant spot
> Where these are not:
> *One* isle is ours . . .
> There we are free in truth, there only free,
> There only happy, lifted far above

Strange laws of men, not made for such as we,
For whom all founts of Nature overflow:
And Love hath bid us know,
All things are justified to those who love. (10.4–5, 10.8–12, 10.16–21)

In 1856, the penultimate section became the ultimate, altering the poem's conclusion from hope to resignation; "love" no longer had the last word:

Even with the will our passion lends
We cannot break the chain;
Against our vows, we must remain
With common men, and compass common ends . . .
We cannot shift the burden and the woe
Which all alike must know,
Which Love's Elected through the countless years
Have known, and, knowing, died: God Wills it so. (9:8–11, 9:14–17)

Then, in 1865, a year before his letters to Whitman commending *Leaves of Grass*, five years before *Joseph and His Friend*, Taylor cut what was originally the antepenultimate section, altering the ending yet again; this third ending edged away from the resignation of the second, reaching again toward hope, but not with the defiance expressed in the first ending. Instead, Taylor looked toward the future, foundling-fashion, bequeathing his hopes to a race yet to come. Taylor's original text rejected that future, giving in to resignation, then setting resignation aside by trusting in love, asserting its right to flout the law in the present. In making his edits, Taylor was clearly less concerned with matters of craft—with how his experience was told—than judgment; his deletions were a management of the reader's comprehension.

Taylor's own relation to "Love and Solitude" is no less telling than the editor's. His two reprintings show continual tinkering with the text, and two important deletions that altered the poem's ending. This suggests a volatility touched off by the poem, and an effort by Taylor to manage the effect. A similar attempt to manage volatility can also be seen in his response to Whitman, whose celebration of the body and love between men Taylor privately praised but publicly mocked. These various disavowals, however, are not a turning away from what "Love and Solitude" reveals, but a part of its delineation. Whatever

*the experience worked through in the poem, repression is a constituent feature of its struc-
ture. That very feature, moreover, is what Whitman found interesting in the work of
Taylor we know he read. Sometime in the 1850s, in pencil, in response to Taylor's third
collection,* Poems of the Orient *(1854), Whitman recorded the following comment:
"Bayard Taylor's Poems . . . are polished, oriental, sentimental, and have as attributes
what may be called their psychology—You cannot see very plainly at times what they
mean although the poet indirectly has a meaning."*[43] *One might have expected the homoeroticism in Taylor's poetry to earn remark, but this is not what Whitman responded to;
nor was it any literary quality of the work. The formal finish of Taylor's verse, its exoticism
and extravagant feeling, were all well and good, but the work's "psychology" was better:
not the visible, but its hidden "attributes"; not meaning, but its management.*

X

In retrospect, my abandoned homage to "Love and Solitude" was an exercise in managing *in*comprehension: though I would not have put it this way at the time, I was trying to translate Taylor into Hart Crane's language, or at least into a language that like Crane's made havoc of sense, not sense of havoc. In deference to Taylor's narrative through-line, I was working with larger units of utterance than Crane did. His repurposed words stretch the very guts of grammar, tightening strings to be plucked or bowed; my clumsier repurposing was slack, unmusical, losing both the tautness of Crane's havoc and Taylor's mellifluous ardor. Wanting no exact correspondence between my poem and Taylor's, only a point of correlation to organize the difference, I began each line with the same letter as the corresponding line of "Love and Solitude." The end result was an acrostic that spelled out nothing but my debt to the earlier text. Thus, where Taylor has these eleven lines:

> Earth knew no deeper life since Earth began,
> And scarce the Heaven above:
> For us the world contains no ban;
> In the profoundest measure given to Man,
> We love, we love!
> O, in that sound, completion lies
> For all imperfect destinies.
> It is a pulse of joy, that rings
> The marriage-peal of Nature, brings
> The lonely heart, the humblest and the least
> To share her royal feast . . . (1.1–11)

I have these:

> Elegant figures demanding a better showing,
> A better angle. After the mirror closed their eyes,
> Feeling returned to their extremities. They woke,
> Ignorant of their place in our inner sanctum.
> We dream of them. And thus they become our reflection,
> Our trace, the surface of comprehension.

Faces with a tale to tell, their lips are dull. Like tips of a frag-
Ile crayon,
They will not submit
To being sharpened.

Textually, my ties to Taylor's poem were nominal. Apart from the acrostic, I took some
cues from his word choices and images, but I did so arbitrarily, intermittently. His
"pyramid of light" (7.48) suggested my "transparent cylinder of cold air," but I trans-
posed it to an earlier section; his "balmy breath . . . breathed upon the land" (2.1) I kept
in the same section, though on a different line, in an altered form: "No balmy breath is
strong enough to thaw his speech." But then, midway through section three, I stopped;
in the typescript, my labored havoc gives way to mere erasure:

Torn like a smile, might admit xxx
All embracing sunlight, all em-
Bracing sunlight
I
T
I
Ahhhhhh
Why follow the law?
B
O
T
W

—and so on.

Returning to Taylor, this time as a scholar, I found myself faltering yet again. The
history I wanted to work through, the poems I wanted to quote and interpret, all
proved too much for my prose to hold, for my thought to round in a single text. I
wanted to carve out some meaning from Taylor's oblivion, telling it as a story to give it
wholeness, in tribute to the meaning I found there; but wholeness eluded me, as it did
Taylor.

Reconsidering my plans, I went back to the start, remembering the homage I had
wanted to compose ten years before. Why not a new one? In prose this time, constrain-
ing myself in form instead of meaning, matching my text to Taylor's again, but by

number this time instead of letter, a way of saying, perhaps, "The poem *does* count." To this end, I aimed for a text in ten sections, the same number as the poem in its first printing; and for each section I sought to compose the same number of sentences as the equivalent section of the poem had lines—quotations and footnotes excluded.

An early version of this essay attended narrowly to questions of method, and I thought to retain that text as a shadow underneath, giving the top over to stories—my own, in relation to the poem; the poem's, in relation to Taylor; Taylor's, in relation to Whitman—as if to demonstrate the irreconcilability of method and story, rigorous intention and the messiness of life. True to life, however, the distinction broke down, though the shadow continued to follow, ten italicized sentences at a time; neither irreconcilable nor complementary, the two parts of my essay shared their object—Bayard Taylor—in obedience to a form they might better transcend. But *might* is a future the essay could not—cannot—reach. It offers a hand backward instead, in friendship.

When I read poetry, it is with eyes shaped by modernism, but through the corrective lens of my own experience; in this regard, my encounters with the past are irrevocably mediated by the very intervals of change I read to overcome: straining to focus, I adjust to a blur. What I need, to quote Emily Dickinson, is another way to see. Scholarship is the closest I come to this other way, most of which involves a certain patience, a certain willingness to question my response—that is, to consider it an affect rather than a judgment, yielding more insight about me than the work, my own epoch than its. There are, of course, texts in which my poetic and scholarly interests coincide, poems legible, but in different ways, from each side of the modernist divide. Sometimes, this coincidence only amplifies the differences between perspectives, with the poem becoming a site of conflict. Other times, the coincidence counteracts divergence; I fasten on a poem whose different legibilities lead to unexpected syntheses. When this occurs—as it did with Taylor—the break I feel between the two sides of my intellectual life mends itself in dialogue. As in many a dialogue, this internal one includes a lot of talking at the same time; and when I listen in—when I reread what I have written—it can be quite hard to tell whose voice I am hearing. Am I a scholar or a poet in my embrace of Taylor's work, which, despite all obvious weaknesses, still stirs my imagination? Am I a poet or a scholar in my holding it at arm's length, the better to consider what stirs me?

REVISING *THE WASTE LAND*

BLACK ANTIPASTORAL
& THE END OF THE WORLD

Joshua Bennett

> In what I am calling the weather, anti-blackness
> is pervasive as climate. The weather necessitates
> changeability and improvisation; it is the atmospheric
> condition of time and place; it produces new ecologies.
>
> —CHRISTINA SHARPE, *IN THE WAKE*[1]

> You can pull the trigger or you can build an ark
>
> —JANELLE MONÁE, "DANCE OR DIE"[2]

> and
> as I watch your arm/your
> brown arm
> just before it moves
>
> I know
>
> all things are dear
> that disappear
>
> *all things are dear*
> *that disappear*
>
> —JUNE JORDAN, "ON A NEW YEAR'S EVE"[3]

I

According to an obituary published in the *Middletown (NY) Times Herald-Record* immediately following her death on August 4, 2016, Kea Tawana was "born on a [. . .] reservation [and] ran away from home at the age of 12."[4] But by Tawana's own account of things—and thus the narrative recorded in any number of national newspaper profiles and journal articles concerned with her trajectory—the artist was born in Japan in 1935, moved to the United States with her father and two brothers when she was twelve years old (her mother and sister, Tawana claimed, were killed by an air raid during World War II), and eventually settled in Newark, New Jersey. It was there—in a city known for its exceptional artists and contentious political history[5]—that she would complete her masterwork five decades later. It was there that Kea Tawana would assemble her *Ark*.

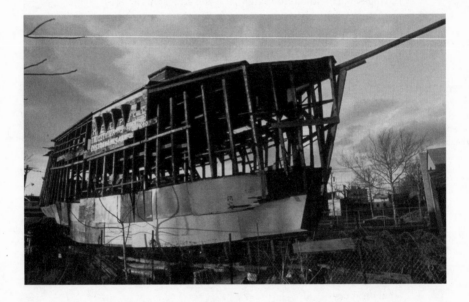

II

The *Ark* was a wonder to behold in person. It stood over three stories high, spanned eighty-six feet in length, and was built from the ground up with materials that Tawana gathered from various abandoned locales throughout the city. The base of the boat was built from plywood and sheet metal. The rest of its body came from planks, paneling, an assortment of seemingly random objects marked up by local aerosol artists and casual dreamers, all of it bearing the trace of homes and businesses destroyed at the tail end of the city's blood-stained race toward the twenty-first century. In his 1987 profile of Kea Tawana and her *Ark* project, Chip Brown of the *Chicago Tribune* writes:

> The ark is an elegy to the lost communities of the Central Ward. Everything but tar paper and nails has been scavenged from the ruins of her environment. She has reused the lumber of demolished homes and bars, columns of churches, pieces of orphanages and synagogues. Her 48-star flag came from an old school. The bowsprit is a refurbished clothesline pole. The clear acrylic for the portholes hails from a hockey rink. The ship is ballasted by tons of paving block from the city's old stone sidewalks....
>
> She envisioned three masts, carrying 12,000 square feet of sail, and a 650-horsepower engine. She was determined to keep the keel under 100 feet, afraid the federal government might invoke its wartime right to seize boats over 100 feet for use as minesweepers. She figured an at-sea food storage capacity of 120 days and freshwater storage of 1,400 gallons. Her sketches called for a chapel, a library, a museum, a conservatory, a greenhouse, a bakery, a laundry, a sick bay, a stained-glass studio and metal shop. She anticipated a crew of a captain, a first officer, six seamen, a cook and two cats.
>
> She also envisioned that the ark would be able to mount a credible defense with an arsenal of six quartz pulsar lasers and four 2.5-inch rocket tubes.[6]

What Brown's description makes clear is that Kea Tawana was readying herself for war. And it was war that she found, though not the sort where rocket tubes or pulsar lasers would have been of much use. Tawana's fiercest battle would come in the form of the elected representatives of the city of Newark, a constellation of local government agents tasked with the destruction of the *Ark* between 1982 and 1987. The vessel was said to have violated multiple zoning codes, in addition to being seen as a blight on the city; its rugged, piecemeal exterior was in direct contrast to the image of a streamlined, modern metropolis. The story might have ended right there, with the state-sponsored destruction of the *Ark* in the first year of its existence, if not for the generosity and courage of a local group of black parishioners: the membership of one Humanity Baptist Church.

As soon as news of the *Ark*'s imminent destruction became public, the members of Humanity stepped in and offered the vacant lot next to their church as a resting place for the ship: it would remain there several years while Tawana battled the city over the right to keep her doomsday vessel intact. Tawana initially built the *Ark*, she claimed, because there was "no safe place on land." This idea—the ineluctable danger of everyday life within white civil society—animated this specific artistic and architectural project, and also served, we might imagine, as the condition of possibility for her peculiar relation to the predominantly black membership of Humanity Baptist Church, as well as to the predominantly black citizenry of Newark, a community that reacted rather favorably to Tawana's project even as it was decried, and ultimately destroyed, by the machinations of a state agency. That the black parishioners of Humanity offered safe harbor, *sanctuary*, to Tawana's ship demands both study and deeper reckoning. Who else would step in, step up, in this moment of danger? Who else but those who knew very well just how unsafe, unjust, the land is and always has been? The radical hospitality of Humanity Baptist Church comes to us in the present as a call toward ethical relation, and radical imagination, in the face of certain doom.

What was it, exactly, that the black denizens of Newark envisioned when they gazed upon the *Ark*? What vision of the world or possible future? What did Tawana see in the city of Newark that compelled her to build there? Not only to construct the *Ark*, but to work odd jobs in the neighborhood, fixing boilers and replacing stained glass windows for folks that lived nearby? How might we situate this project historically, given the long-standing tradition of black artists crafting arks of all kinds—and here I'm thinking not only of Sun Ra's famous Arkestra, but also Marcus Garvey's Black Star Line, Romare Bearden's famous painting of Noah's Ark, as well as the speculative ark of Countee Cullen's *The Lost Zoo*[7]—in response to a global order that depends upon their subjugation for its very coherence?

Given this uncanny, still-expanding archive, I wonder how we might use the occasion of the life and legacy of Kea Tawana's *Ark* to theorize the poetic as well as the political uses of a certain strain of *black apocalypticism*: a mode of black thought which is not only centrally concerned with the world's end in a Césairean register, but grounds that concern in rigorous study of the relationship between blackness and the earth in another, double sense: that is, blackness as planetary thinking, blackness as ecological thought at the edge of the known, or knowable, universe. In Camilo Vergara's 1987 *New York Times* Opinion piece, "Why Newark's Ark Should Be Saved," he cites the observation of a six-year-old girl from Newark named Aisha, who claimed that "the ark should be a monument, like the Statue of Liberty."[8] Vergara's analysis is grounded in Aisha's insistence that the *Ark*—as opposed to any number of more traditional, US Americanist symbols—is a steady, life-affirming reminder of the promises and possibilities of black freedom struggle; indeed, that the *Ark* represents all that could ever truly belong to black people in modernity: the water, the weather, the earth that is yet to come.

III

Hence, over and against a historical vision of black life *qua* resistance, or else the history of black resistance as that which is thought most rigorously through the lens of what we might call, to riff on Sianne Ngai's notion of "ugly feelings" (though in a divergent direction) *affirmative affects,* I offer in this essay an alternative approach, one carried out primarily through an extended meditation on the role of blueness—a term I am using to signify that which operates at the nexus of melancholy and misery, despair and righteous rage—in antipastoral poetry produced by twenty-first-century black writers. This approach doubles as a call to re-think the role of ugly feelings in African American literary history, as well as the present-day centrality of literary theory that engages the role of black feeling as it appears within the western philosophical tradition broadly construed. My emphasis will be on the writings of nineteenth-century poet James Monroe Whitfield and contemporary poet Phillip B. Williams.

My aim in assembling this particular constellation of works is, first, to assert the political significance of blueness as a mode and means by which we might imagine the end of an anti-black world and the dawning of a more equitable social order. Second, to highlight the distinctly *ecological* tenor of the image systems that black writers have historically constructed in undertaking this larger destructive project. These writers call to the fore a vision of the natural world in which gratuitous violence against black people is not aberrational but algorithmic—which is to say, inextricably bound up with the normative order of things—but they also provide a critical vocabulary through which we are able to imagine other, more ethical methods of organizing human and nonhuman life. Rather than embracing a triumphalist approach wherein the conditions of modernity might be transcended through the sheer force of affirmative affect,

Whitfield and Williams instead call us to weaponize sorrow. They do not believe in the promise of the present world, and thus encourage the living to cast our lot with *the earth* in its utter opacity, and all that such unfettered, unfathomable darkness makes possible. In an attempt to extend Aimé Césaire's contention that "the only thing worth beginning is the end of the world," I want to place Whitfield and Williams's writings in a much larger context, situating them within an extensive and ever-expanding collective of writers, a cloud of witnesses, who are crafting a kind of *black geopoetics*[9]: a poetics of ground, a poetry of mud, of earth, of the black planet Public Enemy claims we are all made to fear, even and especially those of us who stand to benefit from its arrival. What sort of poetics rises to the fore when home is defined in the first instance not by filiation, or belonging, but by an ongoing antagonism? By what Colin Dayan and others have described as an existential experience marked, and marred, by not only *civic death*, but also the myriad forms of life, of *living*, that are energized within its field of reach?

Within the universes fashioned by Whitfield and Williams, the hard distinction between the grave and the living landscape is softened, blurred, made hazy by the fact that antiblackness is the air itself. Through the harsh reality that these poems refract, these poets grant us a new and more elaborate human vision, one wherein the world has already in some sense ended, or else is in the process of ending, and black living, which is distinct from and operates as an unrelenting critique of a normative discourse of Life, can flourish. In these poems, black flourishing and a kind of black critical blueness are coeval and co-constructive. What appears as blueness in Whitfield and Williams is also always and already a form of *Afrofuturism*, a willingness to take seriously the idea that any apocalypse is also, quite literally, a *revelation*, or opening— and here, again, we hear echoes of not one ark but an entire fleet, a figure returning throughout the tradition to signal the coming of a new way—one wherein black human beings can improvise a radically divergent order of things. In this vein, it is as the old saints say. *We are in the world but not of it.* We desire the end of the world because of a black love that demands such radical dreams. Because, as Henry Dumas writes, we "have to adore the mirror of the earth."[10] It is in the name of the black earth, the black shambling bear and favorite daughter of the universe,[11] that these writers militate against the position of the denizen of the world, and dare to imagine the destruction of the parasitic, geopolitical order that derogates their people at every turn. In no uncertain terms, this is a poetics of demolition. These are poems that kill. And set ablaze. And build.

IV

James Monroe Whitfield's "The Misanthropist" is an ur-text for the historical and conceptual overlap between black geopoetics and the critical blueness that animates so much contemporary writing throughout the African diaspora.[12] The title foregrounds a certain skepticism, indeed, an outright hatred, toward the figure of the Human as the poem's condition of possibility. We can assume from the outset that what we will encounter in the lines to come is not some extended celebration of Man, but rather a critical unmooring, an unmaking, of the Human as a site of transcendent moral value:

> From earliest youth my path has been
> > Cast in life's darkest, deepest shade,
> Where no bright ray did intervene,
> > Nor e'er a passing sunbeam strayed;
> But all was dark and cheerless night,
> > Without one ray of hopeful light.
> From childhood, then, through many a shock,
> > I've battled with the ills of life,
> Till, like a rude and rugged rock,
> > My heart grew callous in the strife.
> When other children passed the hours
> > In mirth, and play, and childish glee,
> Or gathering the summer flowers
> > By gentle brook, or flowery lea,
> I sought the wild and rugged glen
> > Where Nature, in her sternest mood,
> Far from the busy haunts of men,
> > Frowned in the darksome solitude.[13]

From its earliest lines, Whitfield's poem demands that its readers wrestle with their most deeply engrained frameworks and categories. Youth is presented not as a period of unfettered play, an epoch of innocence upended by adulthood's brutal encroachment, but a radically divergent experience: one marked by an unmitigated darkness which is described as devoid of hope or cheer, a somber solitude that is inextricable from the elasticity of the natural world. The speaker's self-described despair, his callousness, is bound up with the figurative darkness of the environmental spaces where he feels most recognized. The figurative darkness of his mind—and, we find later, the darkness of his skin, the racial blackness that distances and ultimately disqualifies him from the ethical bonds of a social world he observes but never enters—is reflected in the darkness of "the wild and rugged glen," the blackness that holds him in the midst of his ongoing alienation.

The speaker's invocation of other children playing in far greener, tamer meadows strikes a layered note here. For although the young people in this scene are undeniably happier than the speaker, there is a piece of critical information in his claim that he "sought the wild," rather than taking up residence there after being banished, or scorned. The glen is a choice. It is a site of study and reflection, a space in which the speaker can retreat. In a world where the meadow is available, the speaker decides in favor of the glen, the valley, the wild, in order to dwell in a space that more closely reflects a black geopoetic sensibility: a refusal of the civil in the name of the preservation of, and care for, the earth. The speaker casts his lot with the animals, and the darkness, and the trees, instead of a certain vision of the Human community, and in absolute contradistinction to *the light*, which is always already inextricable from Enlightenment practices and protocols of Western Reason. He opts instead for *endarkenment*,[14] and in the process discovers a subterranean mode of persistence truer to the precarious dance between life and death that is black human being and becoming. The speaker must leave the world in order to enter this place that is no place at all—what Claudia Rankine generatively calls a *Nowhere* that we should nonetheless inhabit alongside her[15]—and in the process must lose himself, lose his mind and encounter the earth in its intractable opacity.

The speaker joins the earth in its alterity, and rather than simply inhabiting that mode as one of irreconcilable difference, refers to it as a source of radical misanthropy. This misanthropy is not a hatred for all human life. Rather, it is bound up in his critical refusal of forms of human life that correspond to Theodor Adorno and Max Horkheimer's assertion that "what men want to learn from nature is how to use it in order to wholly dominate it and other men."[16] The speaker of "The Misanthropist" understands that such a relation is not only destructive but fundamentally *untrue*, a self-annihilating illusion that also brings violence to bear against myriad forms of human and nonhuman life. It is in his effort to remain fugitive from those ways of inhabiting the earth that the poem's most powerful moments rise to the fore:

Dark visions of the night arose;
And the stern scenes which day had viewed
In sterner aspect rose before me,
And specters of still sterner mood
Waved their menacing fingers o'er me.
When the dark storm-fiend soared abroad,
And swept to earth the waving grain,
On whirlwind through the forest rode,
And stirred to foam the heaving main,
I loved to mark the lightning's flash,
And listen to the ocean's roar,
Or hear the pealing thunder's crash,
And see the mountain torrents pour
Down precipices dark and steep,
Still bearing, in their headlong course
To meet th' embrace of ocean deep,
Mementoes of the tempest's force;
For fire and tempest, flood and storm,
Wakened deep echoes in my soul,
And made the quickening life-blood warm
With impulse that knew no control.[17]

In stark contrast to the earlier lines of the poem, we see the speaker's eyes lift here from the depths of the valley to the farthest reaches and inner workings of the clouds, to the weather as a site of recognition, and reverence. The very movement of the lightning resonates with the speaker's own desire to likewise move through the landscape with power and speed, a mobility that would run counter to the ongoing, ubiquitous confinement which marks the position of the enslaved. We might even think of it, in our contemporary context, as a nodal point in a broader constellation of black writers who would later return to lightning, and electricity more broadly, as a thematic concern. Ralph Ellison[18] immediately comes to mind on this point, but I am also interested in how we can think of this trope as a useful metonym for *black power* in a figurative sense: in electricity as a source of unlimited energy, one that the speaker harnesses to imagine life beyond the limits of the human body.

The speaker does not fear the lightning at all; rather, he delights in watching its workings, considers the lightning a reflection of what he remarks upon several times as a "sterner" climatic mood. The lightning's flash is an occasion for reflection: it represents both mortal danger and uncontainable beauty. This is what, we are led to imagine, occasions the speaker's love. Lightning as portent. Lightning as reminder that the power to make live and make die does not lie solely with the administrators of civil society's murderous whims, but also in the unknowable machinations of the ecological. As Ed Roberson reminds us: "The world's desires do not run the Earth, but the Earth *does* run the world."[19] Fire, tempest, flood, and storm all resonate here as markers of a distinctly *apocalyptic* register, as signals that the end of things is on its way and in short order; that matters cannot remain the way they are, and all will indeed be washed away, or else razed to the ground. The coming of the darkness, the prominence of the opaque, unruly waters—both stand in as signposts marking the advent of a *blackened* planet, the black earth the speaker cares for and considers his kin.

In the apocalyptic moment the speaker claims to lose control and begins to feel as if his body, his joy and his anger, are his own—a description that calls to mind Paul Dunbar's mask as a kind of everyday presentational imperative for black folks in the modern world,[20] the black quotidian as ineluctably marked by coerced passivity in the face of unthinkable violence and violation. The storm in the outside world gestures toward an altogether different sort of tempest brewing within the body of the speaker. It forms a space for an anguish and rage that the speaker is disallowed by the present order. Whitfield's speaker dreams of this apocalyptic moment, as an extension of his broader political and cosmological vision: the abolition of racial capitalism and the overturning of an anti-black world.

The poem's closing lines help ground this message in terms that explicitly evoke the language of race in ways that are absent elsewhere in the poem, and work to compelling effect:

> Let others strike the sounding string,
> And in rich strains of harmony,
> Songs of poetic beauty sing;
> But mine must still the portion be,
> However dark and drear the doom,
> To live estranged from sympathy,
> Buried in doubt, despair and gloom;
> To bare my breast to every blow,
> To know no friend, and fear no foe,
> Each generous impulse trod to dust,
> Each noble aspiration crushed,

Each feeling struck with withering blight,
With no regard for wrong or right,
No fear of hell, no hope of heaven,
Die all unwept and unforgiven,
Content to know and dare the worst
Which mankind's hate, and heaven's curse,
Can heap upon my living head,
Or cast around my memory dead;
And let them on my tombstone trace,
Here lies the Pariah of his race.[21]

One is left to wonder whether the invocation of "race" in the poem's closing line is a gesture toward the speaker's phenotypical appearance—and thus rooted in the claim that his melancholy, his unwillingness to "sing," has made him an outcast among other black writers—or if this section serves as the continuation of a thread of thinking wherein we might count this poem as a critique of the western philosophical tradition, particularly its limited conceptions of the Human. If we linger in a zone of indeterminacy between these two readings, new questions and theoretical vistas become available. Invoking the language of darkness, gloom, and a world without light, Whitfield's speaker appears to grapple with the social cost of despair, despair as that which estranges us from "sympathy" or even the care of friends. Although this reading, on its face, lines up well with Whitfeld's characterization of the speaker up to this point, I wonder what thinking against the grain of these final lines produces in the way of imagining this speaker as part of a lineage of black misanthropists and reprobate loners: the Invisible Men and Bigger Thomases throughout the African American literary tradition who likewise saw no outside to their sorrow, no possible end to their sufferings. Is there a way for us to take seriously their assertion of absolute alterity and nonetheless push back against it?

Might we offer, alongside this reading—and always in the face of overwhelming, unrelenting violence—a vision of an endless stream of Pariahs, numberless black boys and girls and men and women who are likewise barred from the protections of the universal rights of Men? The speaker of "The Misanthropist" provides great insight into just such a vision, and lays the theoretical groundwork for an understanding of apocalyptic aesthetics, and by extension any rigorous interpretation of black geopoetics, as intimately bound up with this particular problem for thought. That is, the means by which we might theorize a kind of black loneliness that nonetheless means one is never alone, always multiple, always linked to the dead and the undead alike via the dark, endless thread of The Color Line. The poem's conclusion recalls Countee Cullen's timeless quandary: "Yet do I marvel at this curious thing / to make a poet black and bid him sing!"[22] "The Misanthropist" displays in great detail what happens when the black poet answers the call to song but refuses to make it beautiful, and instead engages in the critical embrace of ugliness, mourning, unbounded and irreducible blueness. It is not a song solely for the living, but rather for all that persists. All that refuses. Remains.

V

The radical abolitionist dream of a more robust, rigorous language with which to think of the ligaments linking freedom and enslavement, confinement and mobility, beast and overseer, extends far beyond the nineteenth century. Contemporary poet Phillip B. Williams's "Mastery" is deeply concerned with such matters. The poem opens with regicide on its mind:

> The masters are yet dead. Wanting to be human,
> I tried to rewrite *The Waste Land*. The canon's reach
> casts ruinous light. The masters' pens breach
> this page where, above, my own hand spectates. Babylon
> risen, exorcism in reverse, whose nature upended now?
> If I remember my own name, then I can ego
> my way through this crowd of shadows
> that cross the bridge of my back mid bow.
>
> I slept in the Fifth House of Modernism
> beneath stars that offered no light—dust
> full of fear, my own dead skin encrusting
> room corners and my mind in a schism
> between image and luck. When I awoke,
> the empire rose in me and I was risen
> from its dead letters to the letter, chiseled
> by my own invisibility, this war between smoke
>
> and reflection, between self versus self conniving
> in the longest hall of my fear to remain there.[23]

In Williams, as in Whitfield, the juxtaposition of darkness and light occupies center stage. And although Williams seems to be working along a vector altogether asymptotic to Whitfield's existential concerns—Williams's speaker casts the question as a conflict over craft—it is nonetheless striking to observe the similarities in the ways that both writers approach the question of being-in-the-world for the black (anti-)citizen, the black child, the black writer. The masters in question here each die a death that lacks finality, or closure; even from the grave their influence delimits the choices that are available to our speaker. Note the critical inversion of the light/dark binary as it appears in these lines. Rather than offering wisdom or transcendental power, Williams's speaker describes the cultural knowledge passed down by the masters as "ruinous." Still, this light provides a path to walk by, illuminates the signposts our speaker might follow on the path toward human community. Herein lies one of the central problems of "Mastery," as well as a primary object of interest within Williams's broader oeuvre.[24] Understanding, as he does, this historical relationship between mastery of the Word and the anthropomorphic machine described by Giorgio Agamben[25] and others, Williams's speaker evocatively locates his desire for the safeguards of the human in his ability to practice mimesis, to echo the forms and broader protocols handed down by Eliot, among other canonized white writers. The specter of this influence—their ghosts lingering in his mind, upon his shoulder, beneath his tongue—threatens to tear the page asunder.

Williams's speaker strains against this influence through his invocation of other authorial traditions, other canons. One example is his use of the phrase "the bridge of my back," which calls to mind the 1981 feminist anthology edited by Cherríe Moraga and Gloria Anzaldúa, *This Bridge Called My Back*,[26] and in the process works to upset the very domination that Williams presents as an overarching problem for this figure from the outset. Movement is indeed possible, we are told, but only through recourse to the knowledges made available by ancestors, the languages and lyric sensibilities that have always thrived on the underside of the modern world system. Though the speaker goes to bow, attempts to reconcile his dark body and the Eurocentric body of work he must learn in order to survive, the shadows of the darker tradition he calls home nonetheless remain attached to him, refusing to die in the wake of the western canon's ruinous enlightenment. The speaker is at war with himself, with his sound colonial education, and names this conflict as a matter of cosmology, as part and parcel of a much larger, systemic, geological antagonism between the acknowledged Living and all those said to be dead or else animate objects without interior worlds:

"Away! Away! I wish the masters dead." To be freed
I tried to revise *The Waste Land* but blacker,
where Margaret Garner speaks to Margaret Walker
on a barge crossing the Mississippi River. I see
the aftermath of this convenience, slow
in the river mud fondling the delay.
They will make it across. They will pray.
They will drown beneath what they know,

that the living have undone so many
and the river's dark portion was the color
of a baby's dried blood, the neck wound dolorous
in its grin-shaped curve, another mangled
bridge into history.[27]

Williams makes an explicit turn toward the antipastoral here, invoking a river that refuses any symbolic association with a straightforward, historical telos—an arc or swift movement toward justice perhaps, or else the soothing music of a premodern idyll—and instead forces us to confront the histories of brutality and exchange that mark such spaces. In the speculative historical vision painted by Williams, Margaret Garner—the enslaved woman most widely known for killing her infant child rather than returning to bondage with her baby in tow, and whose story served as the source material for Toni Morrison's *Beloved*—and Margaret Walker somehow encounter each other and exchange stories of what they have seen and survived. The river itself works as a reminder of what these women have loved, lost, destroyed, and yet they continue to move along its currents, refusing to bow or break under the weight of history. Williams's speaker describes this survival as a kind of drowning, an ongoing war between the knowledge these women hold and a social order that refuses not only that knowledge but their very capacity to hold it, *to know anything worth knowing* or claim any rights it is bound to respect. Williams stages this entire encounter against the antipastoral, apocalyptic backdrop of a river the color of a black child's blood. In doing so, he calls upon the plagues in the Book of Exodus, so that the poem's setting works as a fusion of both the first plague, the transformation of various bodies of water into blood, and the last, i.e., the death of the firstborn.[28] In the end, the reader is left with no concrete sense of the words shared between these two women. In this vein, Williams echoes Morrison directly: their story is not one to pass on.[29]

Midway through the poem, the river appears again in a rather dazzling moment of prosopopoeia, one that expands and expounds upon any number of the poem's central objects of interest:

> The river unfurls its god tongue
> in Nigger Jim's voice. He speaks of rivers
> as the river, soul grown deep into a river
> carving a country like an infant's throat.
> There are many ways to freedom, with a hymn's
> lithe blade or a butcher knife. Even now the blood
> that runs through the river runs through my hand,
> black as a cock that caws for dawn hilt-to-hide till mum.
>
> Dawn does not know it cannot drown me.
> Sunrise gilds all water the same dull pageant
> and I am water after all. Sun-rinsed,
> my skin coal-hisses, a conquered city, the first flame.
> Call me Chicago, call me Lake Michigan.
> I, an unnatural mirror for enlightenment,
> spit back ash rivaling Pompeii. Relent
> to whom, for what? Night will come again.[30]

And, only a stanza later:

> This is the end of the world.
> Even an ended world needs a mythology.
> Like snow, like breath, like rust, like feet,
> night will come again and over a sobbing
> woman who has found her mother's grave
> for the first time and succumbed to elegy.
> Her cries bleed over the dirt with a strange insistency.[31]

This, then, is how the world ends. With a mythology blurring the borders between black flesh and animate objects of all kinds: animals and rivers, darkness and dirt, monsters, corpses, coal. In a dizzying series of deft, allusive gestures, Williams summons a cohort of characters from across the literary landscape, repurposing their images toward radical ends: Jim, Sethe, Garner, Twain, Melville, Hughes. Even the black rooster from Morrison's *Song of Solomon* makes an appearance.[32] Each of these figures function as a critical component of the broader black antipastoral aesthetic that Williams maintains throughout "Mastery," one in which we are bound to the bodies held within the earth, and all the unfathomable darkness therein; the darkness that refuses to be drowned by dawn, or shattered by a policeman's sirens. Williams's speaker is unkillable because he refuses a dominant vision of the Human in favor of the ground, the dust, the water of which he is made and that once, many centuries ago, served as his ancestors' condition of emergence within the Americas. Williams's mythology for the ended world begins in the dark and remains there. It ignores the call of daybreak, and chooses to linger in the spaces outside the ever-expanding reach of modernity's wartime instruments, its brutal, anti-black imagination. This work calls us into other practices of gathering, other modes of sociality and study alongside nonhuman forms of life and death. It does not ask us to dream that the end of the world is on its way. It invites us to celebrate as if it has already arrived.

HENRY OSSAWA TANNER

NIGHT OVER NIGHT

Cole Swensen

We're considering only the later works because it's only in them that night becomes built of light and lets contradiction lock into place as the principal engine of Tanner's oeuvre. It is a contradiction that he lived all his life, this active disruption of the distinction between dark and light, between black and white. Night, in which things become unfixed, unhinged, his late paintings—something flies apart in them; something flies within.

Christ walking on water, 1907, as is natural for him in his natural environment. And thus he becomes it, becoming just a slight stripe of the luminous, a vertical streak up the evening sky, as he walks toward the disciples through the lapis dusk, soft and dense.

And walking softly; this too epitomizes Tanner, a gentle man for whom painting a landscape was a mode of displacement, a form of travel, not only from one place to another
        but from self to self,
                          one hand on the handle of a door.
        One paints the handle, and then opens the door.

Le Touquet, c. 1910, on the Normandy coast, near their house in Trépied in the moon in the clouds
                    over the azure
      is such an ocean heralding form
                      two people are heading home and two trees
      that are still there, now in the sun.

Tanner became a leader of the artists' community centered in the nearby fishing village of Étaples. International in nature, it thrived from the early 1880s to 1914, but never quite recovered from the war.

Tanner, however, continued to live there, with his wife and son and best friends, Atherton and Ingeborg Curtis. When his wife died in 1925, he moved to a different house, internalizing the shroud, and continued to live there until almost the end of his life, which he spent more or less rewriting the Bible from the perspective of night:

> Sweep and glimpse
>
> > across a street
>
> the ghost of blue
>
> > with a corner of the night sky in its eye
>
> dotted with streetlights
>
> > or torches held up, allowing the sharp
>
> leap into sight
>
> > to continue moving forward,

drawing the painting along in its wake, the disciples, the foolish virgins in the middle of this life in which night is the alive lit from within.

And given that painting is all about seeing,

> > to focus on the point at which
>
> seeing breaks down,
>
> > breaks out into other senses,

puts pressure on intuition, on reflection, on invention, and every other way by which we see.

Tanner first left the US in 1891 on his way to Rome via London and Paris, but once in Paris, he simply didn't move on, but instead started classes at the Académie Julian.

Tanner: *Strange that after having been in Paris a week, I should find conditions so to my liking that I completely forgot when I left New York I had made my plans to study in Rome and was really on my way there . . .*[1]

But let's go back to the night,

and via the proposition that, for Tanner, paint-
ing offered a vehicle for overflowing circumstances and context, i.e., for flowing out of
the United States, thereby eroding the boundaries of nation, self, and personal history.
By focusing on the night which is inherently borderless—within it, things have no
edges, things live indeterminate, less themselves alone, they begin to participate in
others, they start suggesting and transforming—in evening is the transformation of
the world—

Tanner made a particular study of twilight be-
cause in it, the seen and the unseen strike a perfect balance, and in it, light has more
layers than at any other hour.

He found himself, in the summer of 1891, in the artists' colony of Pont Aven, made
known by Sérusier, Bernard, and Gauguin. 1892, again summer, and another spot in
Brittany, Concarneau. And then, 1897, to "the Holy Land," sponsored by a patron who
thought he needed to see the actual sites of his scenes.

Once there, however, he painted what was there:

A Mosque in Cairo,

The Jews' Wailing Place,

A View of Palestine stretching out past tree-lined
ravines to a peacock sky, his interest in religion seeming to evenly embrace them all.
And often through architecture—the mosque, the wall, the architecture of faith picked
out in right angles by the architecture of light.

He also continued painting the Bible: Nicodemus, 1899, who will much later bring the
spices for the embalming, now sitting on a terrace across from a young Jesus behind
whom the city is not so much a matter of buildings as it is of the density and tangibility
of evening turning air into powdered cobalt, a material that came to the center of
Tanner's research; it became a land in itself, increasingly where he lived, sieved in pale
prescience.

In the 1927 version, they are sitting on a rooftop and the night has gotten bluer. There's a small pile of it in the hand that Jesus holds out as if weighing it against what will be said.

This 1897 trip, following his initial journey to Europe, crystalized travel as an infrequent but determinate aspect of his life. Perhaps having grown up as an outsider, he was tempted to keep on going, getting more and more outside, to see how far it went and what one might find, until ultimately it manifests as total inclusivity, as every bit of territory you cross, once behind you, becomes internalized. Thus the farther you go, the larger the inside grows, until, in fact, it's all inside; it's just a matter of time.

And yet his travels also returned him to the biblical stories on which he'd been raised, however going back physically made it apparent that any return is also entering new territory. The son of a bishop in the African Methodist Episcopalian Church, Tanner was a committed believer, though at some point, he exchanged the church for the painted night to convey the unexplained in a pencil drawing of the unsaid in the margin of a small carnet—

> "this is what you missed

that now so misses you."

But practically speaking, biblical themes were also very popular and sold well at the end of the 19th century, fluidly fusing with the Symbolist spirit, as well as with that of the Nabis and various other post-impressionists. And so he continued to paint them:

The *Good Shepherd*, 1902–03, beneath the moon and two great oaks while off to the right distance accrues a ridge behind which the void begins in periwinkle blue.

And the oak comes back: *Abraham's Oak*, 1905, in smoke gray of the great age of the full moon of an endless tree (Isaiah 61:3).

(In 1852, a bolt of lightning struck off a branch and it took eight camels to haul off the wood.)

And yet still
a small white house—well in the distance—persists.
And persists in difference,
as white as its moon, a square against a circle
alight, and so thrives.

The theme of difference was ever-present for Tanner, which he addressed through a stylistic focus on indeterminacy—indeterminacy radicalizes difference by making everything suddenly different from itself, by disrupting the stability that anchors a "normal" from which things are or are not different. Instead, we see all elements in relative motion, with each creating the others and being created by them, paradoxically both making them all more distinct and erasing all apparent boundaries between them as they fuse into an intricate system. Another of the contradictions that drove him. Drove him into the shadows, and shadows make us listen

acutely and heighten

the tactile attention
that lies in a thin layer all over the skin
kinetically within

shadow-heft

the lilting time
of time lost back

and the backward time of blue.

The century turned, and Tanner developed a new palate in which usually cool colors—again from within—turned warm—greens and steels in the heat of the moon whose light is made of mica
layered amid and ricocheting within.

Tanner spent years perfecting his glazes, refining his recipes, balancing fragility and transparency, the delicate snap of anything transparent, even in the evening, through which his figures walk lightly, almost shell becoming dust beneath their way.

He laid glaze upon glaze

        until they were looking down through ice

suspended in which

        as if the trite

metaphor of time as a river

        had suddenly frozen over, there hovered

a face

        turning away

to walk back down the road

        to Bethany (oil on canvas,

1902–03, Musée d'Orsay)

        with two others

who have already turned completely

        into that earlier era

which has, in turn, turned warm again—a summer night outlined in moon.

Atherton to Tanner in a letter from the early 30s:

        I hope there was some blue or green paint among those you unpacked. It would be a pity if you had to substitute red for blue and paint sunsets or things on fire instead of moonlight.[2]

        Moonlight, Walls of Tangiers, 1913—the grey luminosity washing the sky across the face of the building.

More travels: two trips to North Africa, 1908 and 1910, soaking his purples in the sun. The North African paintings are pretty much the only ones outside in broad daylight, even drenched in it, light running down the walls and doorways and arches—

        we are looking through an Arabic arch

        and the light pouring through

makes a halo of the head of the back-lit figure walking in.

This, of course, simply records the reality of the place, but perhaps it's also a metaphor for the relative lightness that he felt upon finding himself for the first time in a society not dominated by white Europeans and their descendants, even though the issue of race had largely ceased to be a limiting factor in his life since he'd moved to France. And though not completely free of the French colonial gaze, he avoided its clichés and depicted North African cities and people in an unusual light—both frank and vibrant at the same time.

> Light as a narrative element. Light saying if
> > and what if
> and then when
> > light is a story in itself—in fact, light
> as the only story—Eakins (paraphrased): "light
> > as the principal tool"
> building buildings:
> > *Entrance to the Casbah*, 1912,
shimmering mirage of yellow rushing forth against a donkey moving slowly in the heat that warms the room in Lafayette, Indiana where the painting is currently hanging.

> *Gateway, Tangier*, 1910—again, we are led ever more inside.

And, as always with Tanner,

> we also go inside the night—
> > *Algiers, Old Buildings Near Ka-hak*, 1912,
up on a hill where a moon we can't see makes one of the vanilla buildings its mirror.

Or *Palace of Justice, Tangier*, 1912–13, which is actually a flight into Egypt; the Holy Family, having, by now, been flying for almost twenty centuries, walks peacefully through the public square, late in opal, hoping never to get there.

These works marked the end of a transition he'd been making since the early 1900s toward an atmospheric cerulean based on transparencies applied serially in sheets over a bright white ground, the white increasingly covered over, through which it increasingly shone.

He worked, too, in a strangely serial manner; because each application of glaze took a while to dry, he worked on ten or twenty paintings at a time, which must have made him feel like he was wandering the entire Bible, passing through the Annunciation, the Visitation, the Last Supper, and so on like they were rooms in a mansion of which they were also the windows.

Unlike others of his era who were experimenting with form and abstraction, Tanner focused his experiments on the materials themselves, seeing in the visceral matter of his media a vitality and necessity that wouldn't be taken up again until the Abstract Expressionists.

         His experiments addressed the gaze

  as diffused

         by certain preparations of paint

  that let the glaze gaze back,

         up to 21 layers

  of fishermen coming home

         through the night now slightly

  a green thing

         in transparent chromium viridian

  adorned with warm lantern

         requiring a hand

attached to a tired man attached to a tired woman trudging uphill behind him.

Let's stop a moment at the lantern—a recurrent character and often associated with the inhabitants of Étaples—

 Return at Night from the Market (1912)

 Étaples Fisher Folk (1923)

 Fishermen's Return (1926), stark against the dark, an errant shard of sun, held in, and held in a hand or placed on the ground within reach. For a Christian, the issue of fish, fishing, and fishermen cannot not have multiple densely impacted meanings (*The Miraculous Haul of Fishes*, 1913–14) and the fact that they often work at night and bring a light home with them, the fact that a lantern is itself a small glass house, made wholly of windows, from which a light looks out alone.

This is a particularly crisp instance of one of his guiding principles: Tanner located the light inside of things, which is easier to find at night, and brought it to the surface, where it glowed, and overflowed. This is the nature of the halo.

His 1935 recipe: best linseed soaked, raw or lightly cooked, then the glue: soak goat parchment 24 hours, simmer, but do not boil. Add oil, linseed or poppy, to mastic varnish. Dissolve lanoline in mineral essence. Add 90% alcohol; it will emulsify better. Mix it all together until it attains the consistency of butter.

NIGHTS AND LIGHTS IN NINETEENTH-CENTURY AMERICAN POETICS

Cecily Parks

A farm near Uppsala, Sweden, late July: night deepens over the grassy lawn, the hunching brambles, the river gone pale gray with glints of black. Unable to sleep, nineteen-year-old Elisabeth Christina leaves her bedroom and pads with bare feet downstairs and through the large farmhouse dining room where her family ate supper hours ago. When she opens the door at the back of the house, the wind off the river pushes her nightclothes against her stomach. Cold grass underfoot, flowers wavering in the wind. Perhaps she escapes the house that night for sensual reasons, hoping for something to happen. Something happens. In the location in the garden where she knows the orange petals of the *Tropaeolum majus* to be, several flower-sized fires sparkle and flare. Perhaps Elisabeth Christina runs inside to wake her father, Carolus Linnaeus, the botanist famous for devising the classification system we still use to name plants. Or perhaps Elisabeth Christina kneels by herself in front of the flower-flame. Not hot fire but a trick of phosphorescence, she will explain when she publishes in 1762 a paper on her discovery: the *Tropaeolum majus*, commonly known as the nasturtium, glows in the dark.[1]

Across the Atlantic decades later, as botanical and horticultural texts proliferated in nineteenth-century America, so did reports of the nasturtium's nocturnal magic. Hermon Bourne writes in the *Florist's Manual* (1833): "This curious plant is said to possess the extraordinary property of *emitting flashes of light in the dark*. It exhibits an appearance not unlike the gleam of distant lightning. . . . It is often so bright as to render the plant itself entirely visible."[2] In his nasturtium entry in *The American Flora; or, History of Plants and Wild Flowers* (1849–50), Asa B. Strong writes: "*Darkness flies at your approach*. In the darkness of mid-summer's night, it is said, that the electrical sparks may be seen emanating from the flowers of this plant."[3]

· · · · ·

As an adult, the poet Emily Dickinson began gardening in the dark—before dawn, at twilight, or even at night—when she suffered an eye condition that made it painful for her to be outside in sunlight. According to scholar Judith Farr, "Her neighbors recalled glimpsing a white figure, slightly illumined by lantern light, kneeling in the darkness above her lobelia and sweet sultans."[4] What began as a medical necessity became a preference, so that when her eyes improved, Dickinson continued to dig, prune, weed, water, and sow in the dark. "We grow accustomed to the Dark — / When Light is put away —" (Franklin 428), she writes; and later, in the same poem:

> Either the Darkness alters —
> Or something in the sight
> Adjusts itself to Midnight —
> And Life steps almost straight.[5]

Darkness suffuses the movie of Dickinson's life, *A Quiet Passion*[6], fluttering through the sitting room where Dickinson and her family occupy themselves with solitary pursuits—sewing, reading, sleepily treading into the "larger — Darknesses — Those Evenings of the Brain —" (Fr 428). In another scene, a wide-eyed Dickinson asks her father for permission, which he grants, to write poems at night. This is the kind of request a child makes of her parent after she's already begun to do the thing requested, already begun to slip out of her bed after the family is asleep and pad with bare feet to her small writing table. If, on those nights, Dickinson eschewed the table for the door at the back of the house and with "Uncertain step / For newness of the night —" (Fr 428) stepped outside with a lantern in her hand, she was still practicing a poetics. The "work of poetry is to counter the oblivion of darkness" writes Susan Stewart.[7] *Darkness flies at your approach.* In this way the nasturtium is the work of poetry; gardening by lantern light is the work of poetry; stepping out of your father's house at night in your nightclothes is the work of poetry.

Mary Ruefle: "I am convinced that the first lyric poem was written at night."[8]

• • • • •

I use the term *night poetics* to think about what happens in the night that cannot happen in the day, with a specific attention to those sensual relationships with the natural world that the night cultivates. Small spots of light, which I think of as metonyms for poetry, mediate many of these relationships to the darkness and are often borne out of it. Stewart again: "When we express our existence in language . . . we literally bring light into the inarticulate world that is the night of preconsciousness and suffering."⁹ Stewart's metaphorical night cleaves closely to the darkness of the literal night, especially the nonurban night in which and of which nineteenth-century writers wrote. While this literary attention appears most publicly in Henry David Thoreau's and Thomas Wentworth Higginson's essays, which their race, gender, and privilege permitted them to publish with relative ease, these men are two stars in a larger nineteenth-century constellation that includes Emily Dickinson and the tellers of ghost stories. These less public voices, in most cases, chose night for the same reasons they chose poetry or the ghost story—because they were places for secrecy and transgressive desire. They bound their fears and desires into small books and placed them inside a box, or whispered them around a fire.

Because the nineteenth century, which saw the advent of electricity and rapid industrialization, marked the beginning of the end of the American night, these texts and traces of texts are remnants of an unrecoverable time but also, I want to point out, an unrecoverable place. I would be overlooking the safety, comfort, health, and social welfare of many vulnerable people were I to indulge in a nostalgia that says that old nights were more beautiful, and therefore better, than our present ones. I am more interested in noting that we, as humans with secret desires, used to have a physical place to seek them that we no longer have. The night, which I am thinking of in this essay as an environment, like a wetland or prairie, is being gradually eradicated in America, as in the rest of the world, by electricity and all that it illuminates. For beneficial or destructive ends, our secrets are increasingly public, shared on the internet that never sleeps, glowing on screens long into the yellow light-polluted night.

• • • • •

I first encountered the word *o'nights* in a passage in Thoreau's journal.¹⁰ Obscure and expressionistic, the word arrested me in part because of its weird contraction, which we most commonly encounter in the word *o'clock*. I assumed that *o'nights* was a word that delineated time and translated it for myself as something like *of the nights*, letting it rest that way in my mind for years. O nights. Even without looking up the word in the dictionary I could tell that it described not just one but multiple nights, as if there were a range of experiences that the night proffered or, more likely, a range of nights to experience. In the nineteenth century and earlier, those nights could only have been encountered sensually, with cold grass underfoot, the wind from the river pushing against your nightclothes, the sweet stinging of pines in your nose, the song of the whippoorwill in your ears, and the taste of nasturtium petals in your mouth.

The word, according to *Oxford*, means *at nights*.[11] Use of the word declines throughout the nineteenth century so that now, as I write this essay, Microsoft Word leaves a red ripple under the word to let me know that it is obscure and possibly wrong, and Google's Ngram viewer shows a drastically downward sloping graph for the word's appearance in publications.[12] Not alone among environmentally minded literary critics who draw attention to the relationships between language and place, Robert Macfarlane argues that the loss of the ecological signifier forecasts the loss of attention to the signified, which is a kind of loss of the signified itself. Macfarlane discovers that the most recent edition of the *Oxford Junior Dictionary* does not include words such as *acorn, beech, bluebell, buttercup, catkin, cowslip, cygnet, dandelion, fern, hazel, heather, heron, ivy, kingfisher, lark, mistletoe, nectar, newt, otter, pasture,* and *willow*. Without the words to recognize the fern and the pasture, perhaps my children will turn away from them, leave them unseen, which is a way of allowing them to vanish. In the places of the effaced flora and fauna in the *Oxford Junior Dictionary* are the new additions of our digital era: *attachment, blog, broadband, bullet-point, celebrity, chatroom, cut-and-paste,* and *voice-mail*.[13] It is not hard to imagine the twenty-first-century child waking up in the night and padding with bare feet to her computer, forgoing the darkness outside to search the bright internet with her fingertips.

Dickinson, in a letter: "How do you sleep *o nights*—and is your appetite waning?"[14]

• • • • •

In her late poem "Those — dying then" (Fr 1581), Dickinson describes losing faith in the certainty of a place with God after death and concludes that a capricious natural source of light offers a serviceable substitute: "Better an ignis fatuus / Than no illume at all —[.]"[15] *Ignis fatuus* (foolish fire) is the Latin name for the will-o'-the-wisp, the greenish light that eighteenth- and nineteenth-century travelers reportedly glimpsed flickering in wetlands and followed at their peril. It is said that over the course of her life Dickinson increasingly chose gardening over churchgoing and, before her death, requested that her coffin be carried through the flower garden she tended at night, an indication that her particular *ignis fatuus* may have resided there. When Dickinson (earnestly, I believe) offers the *ignis fatuus* as an alternative to Christian belief, she communicates not only the extent of her religious crisis, but also the fact that in that religious crisis, she might locate a religious experience outdoors, at night. Dickinson's belief in the natural world echoes Thoreau's declaration: "Unto a life which I call natural I would gladly follow even a will-o'-the-wisp through bogs and sloughs unimaginable."[16]

Thoreau's encounter with a will-o'-the-wisp occurs on an expedition in the Maine woods one night while his fellow travelers are asleep. He slips out of his blankets with the intention of stoking a low campfire and spies on a piece of firewood an "elliptical ring of light."[17] An investigation with his knife reveals a ring of sap under the bark, "all aglow along the log," whittled chips of which "lit up the inside of my hand, revealing the lines and wrinkles, and appearing exactly like coals of fire raised to a white heat."[18] The encounter prompts Thoreau to marvel: "I little thought that there was such light shining in the darkness of the wilderness for me. . . . It made a believer of me more than before."[19] A believer in what? Not in science, which he disparages in the same passage, and not in Christianity, which he disparages all the time. The will-o'-the-wisp, as he learns from his Penobscot guide Joseph Polis to call the phenomenon, makes him a believer in the poetry that the natural world offers at night. ("I shall be a benefactor . . . if I can show men that there is some beauty awake while they are asleep,—if I add to the domains of poetry," he hopes in another essay, titled "Night and the Moonlight."[20]) Thoreau kept the chips, splintered relics, and the following night tried to make them glow again. They did not.

• • • •

It wasn't until the middle of the nineteenth century that the word *jack-o'-lantern* came to signify a hollowed-out pumpkin with a candle inside it. So while later renditions of Washington Irving's ghost story "The Legend of Sleepy Hollow" feature a headless horseman who carries a jack-o'-lantern under his arm as he gallops through the woods at night, it surprised me to find that the original published text (1820) does not.[21] I was also surprised to learn that until the middle of the nineteenth century, the word *jack-o'-lantern* was still used interchangeably with *ignus fatuus* and *will-o'-the-wisp* to describe an organic and possibly misleading nighttime glow. Perhaps Irving had the glow in mind when he describes newly arrived schoolteacher Ichabod Crane walking at night through the "spell-bound region" of Sleepy Hollow, when

> every sound of nature, at that witching hour, fluttered his excited imagination,—the moan of the whip-poor-will from the hillside, the boding cry of the tree toad, that harbinger of storm, the dreary hooting of the screech owl, or the sudden rustling in the thicket of birds frightened from their roost. The fireflies, too, which sparkled most vividly in the darkest places, now and then startled him, as one of uncommon brightness would stream across his path.[22]

In this sensuous forest, the too-bright firefly, like the will-o'-the-wisp, would have Crane step off the path and into the woods. Crane follows not and, placing his faith outside of nature, sings psalms that his neighbors can hear as he walks home.

The headless horseman pursues Crane one night and, with a hurled head, knocks him off his horse. A shattered pumpkin, a harbinger of the Halloween jack-o'-lantern in later renditions of the story, marks the last place the schoolteacher is seen. While the story hints that a local bully may have masqueraded as the headless horseman to frighten Crane, it fails to explain the headless horseman's previous exploits, those hauntings that the old timers share around nighttime fires. What about the original headless horseman, the one who "like a midnight blast" roams Sleepy Hollow o'nights and, at dawn, races back to the churchyard to reinter his decapitated body? For the headless horseman must be real, is how my friends and I, when we were nine or ten, understood it. How else would a bully know to dress up like him? This was in Sleepy Hollow, New York, the setting for Irving's story, the real suburban town where I really grew up in the 1980s. Why wouldn't the headless horseman be real too? On Halloween, the one time of year when I was allowed to leave my house un-chaperoned at night, I listened for galloping hooves and looked through the trees for the flickering light of a jack-o'-lantern held high and believed my friends when they said they glimpsed it.

• • • • •

Thomas Wentworth Higginson: "I detested [my head] more than ever. I thought with envy . . . of the headless horseman of Sleepy Hollow, of Saint Somebody with his head tucked under his arm." Essayist, editor, and epistolary favorite of Emily Dickinson, whose poems he published, Higginson desires headlessness on the night that he swims across a brackish river in South Carolina to spy on Confederate forces during the Civil War. Higginson, colonel of the first Union regiment of freedmen, recounts this absurd desire in "A Night in the Water," an essay he first published in the *Atlantic Monthly* in 1864, and then in his book *Army Life in a Black Regiment*.[23] Perhaps he imagines carrying his head underwater for safety. How would that submerged head reckon the watery glimmers "where the stars ended [and] the great Southern fireflies began[,]" gliding within "a halo of phosphorescent sparkles from the soft salt water"? Would it find beauty in further bewilderment, underwater in the darker dark?

Higginson, in a letter to Dickinson after the war: "I have the greatest desire to see you, always feeling that perhaps if I could once take you by the hand I might be something to you; but till then you only enshroud yourself in this fiery mist & I cannot reach you, but only rejoice in the rare sparkles of light."[24]

• • • • •

Were they afraid of the dark, and did that fear make them search for any small, even unreliable, beacon? When the moon rose, was it a comfort because it offered light, or was it a sorrow because it reminded them how dark the world was? By they and them I mean anyone who went outdoors at night to seek and sometimes find something there. By sorrow I mean the sorrow that Mary Ruefle locates in the "contrast between the moon and the night sky," which she interprets as "more conducive to sorrow, which always separates or isolates itself,"[25] and which yields "the isolated sensuality of so much lyric poetry."[26] On one hand, this sorrow can be kind of romantic, driving the daughter out of bed and out the back door at night, or driving the bachelor to build a small cabin for himself in the woods, or driving the night-writing poet to cry out:

> Wild nights — Wild nights!
> Were I with thee
> Wild nights should be
> Our luxury![27]

• • • • •

The poem happens at night, when they are alone. The poem happens when she kneels in front of a glowing flower. The poem happens when her fingers reach into the garden dirt, digging not unlike a ghost at daybreak to get back inside a grave, because she is no longer afraid of death. The poem happens at night, when he holds pieces of glowing wood in his hand, and the poem is the glowing wood, the glowing flower, the phosphorescent wavelets, and the weird globe of light over the swamp.

Are they real, the will-o'-the-wisp and the glowing wood? Does the nasturtium sparkle in the dark? One of the charges leveled against nature writing is that mystery is the result of forced ignorance.[28] Consider Thoreau, who, writing about the will-o'-the-wisp, rejects the idea of applying scientific investigation to nocturnal experience: "A scientific explanation, as it is called, would have been altogether out of place there. That is for pale daylight. Science with its retorts would have put me to sleep; it was the opportunity to be ignorant that I improved. It suggested to me that there was something to be seen if one had eyes."[29]

In point of fact, scientists argued about the source of the will-o'-the-wisp throughout the eighteenth and nineteenth centuries. The light, as Dickinson imagined it and Thoreau encountered it, is vaguely understood to be the result of the gases released by decomposing organic matter, though just as Thoreau could not make his wood chips glow the night after he found them, contemporary scientists have to this day been unable to replicate a will-o'-the-wisp in a laboratory. Sightings of these flickers are no longer reported, and they remain what one scholar calls "one of the longest unexplained historical natural mysteries."[30] Because we have clear-cut and drained the woods and wetlands that were the habitat of these lights at an increasingly rapid pace since the middle of the nineteenth century, it is not a stretch to conclude that the will-o'-the-wisp may have disappeared because its habitat disappeared. A corollary: with fewer dark nights to lose ourselves in and fewer places where our smartphones do not have reception, we have fewer opportunities to look for beacons in the natural world. This not-looking can feel like sorrow.

Scientific study enables us to quantify the effects of clear-cutting and wetland drainage, of industrialization, electrification, and war. Poetry enables us to feel and mourn them. There are no longer reports of glowing nasturtiums because the nasturtium does not, in fact, glow in the dark. A German scientist in 1914 proved that "the phenomenon is optical, a result of the way our eyes perceive the flowers' colors in the twilight."[31] Even so, it is not wrong to believe in the sensuous. Late at night during slumber parties when I was a child, my friends repeated "Light as a feather, stiff as a board" as I lay down in an imitation of death and they, after placing their fingertips under my body, lifted me off the ground. The chanting made me weightless: I floated. Though I couldn't have articulated it then, knowing that I was alive in the world meant knowing I would die, knowledge I first obtained in the night. Now that I am older I can say that is an incomplete and flawed knowledge, as pleasurable as it is sorrowful, as benighted as you would expect it to be. I rely on it nonetheless because I gained it sensually, like the girl who saw the nasturtium glow at twilight and believed, and why should she not, her eyes.

THE EARTH IS FULL OF MEN

Brian Teare

"The poet is the sayer, the namer, and represents beauty," Ralph Waldo Emerson writes in "The Poet." "He is a sovereign and stands at the center."[1] These potent declaratives assert Emerson's belief in a poet whose truck with divinity allows *him*—for there can be no doubt about his sex—an elevated status. "For the world is not painted, or adorned, but is from the beginning beautiful; and God has not made some beautiful things, but Beauty is the creator of the universe." Emerson continues, "Therefore the poet is not any permissive potentate, but is emperor in his own right." Why? Because the poet represents Beauty, and Beauty is synonymous with God, therefore the poet represents God. Emerson's tautological rhetoric ushers his poet onto the kind of throne accorded to those who speak on behalf of the divine, and crowns his poet the one who both resides in "the condition of true naming" and resigns "himself to the divine *aura* which breathes through forms."[2] And as heretical as Emerson's theology was at the time—in his "Divinity School Address" he downsized Christ to a "mere" historical figure in order to allow the individual access to unmediated knowledge of God, a gesture that earned him his early infamy as a radical—his vision of the poet is more likely to strike us today as "problematic" than as something to aspire to the way Walt Whitman did. In the age of Trump, it's hard to take—and hard to take seriously—all that supremely monarchic figurative language that was, for Emerson the idealist, just barely figurative. What poet would readily admit to coveting such sovereignty? Who today would claim to speak for God? Who among us would openly aspire to head an empire?

These questions are questions about the power of poetry itself, and to pose them now, early in the twenty-first century, only raises more questions: What sort of power does poetry retain in the digital age? And does the poet remain "the sayer, the namer"? If so, do all poets have access to this power? Or only "true" poets? "Naming is basic and audacious," Kumeyaay poet Tommy Pico claims in his 2017 book *Nature Poem*, but instead of being part of his power as a sovereign, naming for Pico is "a claim . . . an attempt to maneuver from a sticky kind of ancestral sadness, bein a/NDN person in occupied America."[3] Pico's poem grows powerful from its ability to resist the kinds of sovereignty granted to Emerson's poet—a sovereignty granted to white men and implicitly reliant on the violence of settler culture—and "the magic often works // until I think *why is it so damn hard to spell maneuver* and *why does it / always look wrong.*" Pico's misgivings about his mastery over language stand as a reminder to him as an NDN poet that "my great grandparents had almost no contact / with white ppl like the shutter of a poem is the only place where I can / illusion myself some authority." And yet in its emphasis on naming and on gaining a kind of authority over experience, Pico's vision of the NDN poet interestingly echoes aspects of Emerson's sovereign poet, whose genius "repairs the decays of things."[4] But rather than asserting sovereignty over others, Pico's poetry works to "illusion *myself* some authority," the very kind of self-sovereignty that settler culture has long promised but never actually granted to indigenous peoples in the United States.

In fact, poetry itself—at least as it's often practiced by settlers—strikes Pico as just another colonial tool. "why shd I give a fuck abt / 'poetry'?" he asks elsewhere in *Nature Poem*, "It's a container // for words like *whilst* and *hither* and *tamp*. It conducts something of / *permanent* and *universal* interest."[5] Not only is the diction of quote unquote Poetry borrowed from another culture and out of date, Pico argues, the genre itself is defined by an ahistorical timelessness whose pretense to universality is just another code for whiteness, another way of controlling who has access to cultural authority and power. "I wd stroll into the china shop of grammar and shout *LET'S TRASH / THIS DUMP,*" Pico boasts in response to poetic language that reifies settler culture. Figurative language and metaphor in particular strike him as insidious aspects of the canonical poetry of settler colonialism: "metaphor [is] the traditional function of indigenous ppl in the grand / canon of lit," especially when it aids in conveying "the extinction of such-and-such tribe / in so-and-so's novel in verse, a metaphor in the narrative of a dying / relationship."[6] Given that poetry's generic tropes have traditionally been used to erase the actual presence of indigenous peoples and discredit intellectual and creative powers unique to their tribal cultures, Pico's strategy is to appropriate poetry's tropes while undercutting the genre's sometimes bankrupt humanist ideology. Calling out the pretense of universality that has often silenced or marginalized indigenous poets, Pico insists: "I'm telling YOU all about ME // in order to prove OUR intelligence, OUR right to live."[7]

Pico's insistence seems particularly necessary and timely, given that President Donald Trump and his cabinet have chosen to wage a culture war over the premise of white supremacy and the continued promise of white sovereignty. But Trump's presidency is only the latest iteration of a settler colonialism whose continued occupation depends upon the curtailed self-sovereignty and structural disenfranchisement of indigenous peoples. Pico insists on telling about himself, on making himself visible as a self-named NDN, precisely because indigenous peoples have "inherited this idea to disappear . . . descended from a clever self adept at evading an occupying force."[8] Rather than sitting at the center of things as sovereign or emperor, Pico's poet is an escapee, a survivor of others' sovereignty, a witness to the violence of empire. "Science says trauma cd be passed down," Pico reports, "molecular scar tissue, DNA / cavorting w/war and escape routes and yr dad's bad dad." And though each indigenous person inherits the trauma of settler colonialism along with whatever individual twist their family history lends it, each tribe and each generation in each tribe also has its own specific history of violence and violation. In other words, the destruction of indigenous peoples by settler colonialism is both the historical context and the ongoing contemporary reality that shape indigenous subjectivity, a doubled violence mirrored by Pico's doubled position as Kumeyaay NDN and assimilated urban queer.

• • • • •

Throughout *Nature Poem*, Pico consistently refers to himself as part of the Kumeyaay tribe, and though he grew up surrounded by family on the reservation, he is quick to suggest his difference from his parents, who still practice traditional Kumeyaay culture and talk to the plants they harvest for the family: "*I am nothing like that . . . I went to Sarah Lawrence College / I make quinoa n shit.*"[9] The tribe to which Pico belongs and from which he also attempts to distance himself is local to far southern California as well as Baja Mexico, and thus was subjected to multiple waves of colonial pressure as first Spanish, then Mexican, and then US settlers muscled onto tribal lands. Particularly dangerous for indigenous peoples, Pico suggests, was Manifest Destiny's state-sponsored expansion of capitalism to the West:

> In the mid 1800s, California wd pay $5 for the head
> of an NDN and 25¢ per scalp—man, woman, or child.
> The state was reimbursed by the feds.

The destruction of indigenous life was profitable for individual settlers and integral to the larger economic project of the USA. The genocidal pact between settler colonialism, the feds, and capitalism intensified with each passing year of the ensuing centuries, and, as the Dakota Access Pipeline has shown, continues to be a crucial feature of contemporary neoliberal economics. "My dad texts me two cousins dead this week, one 26 the other / 30,"[10] Pico writes. In the national context of the high mortality rate and greatly reduced lifespans of indigenous peoples, "the fabric of our lives #death."[11] Pico's poetry argues that this centuries-long campaign against indigenous survival and self-sovereignty proves inescapable even for an assimilated "weirdo NDN faggot" living in Brooklyn.[12] "Who is the 'I' but its inheritances," asks Pico, gesturing toward the fact that indigenous subjectivity is formed as much by family and tribe as by the colonial context that grants the white poet his imperial sovereignty.[13] "Let's play a game," he challenges us:

> Let's say Southern California's water is oil
> Let's say Halliburton is the San Diego Flume Company
> and I am descended from a long line of wildfires
> I mean tribal leaders
>
> The Cuyamaca Flume transported mountain runoff and river
> water into the heart of San Diego. Construction began illegally,
> in secret, in the 1880s. The creek bed dried. The plants died.
> The very best citizens of San Diego called it "deluded sentimentality"
> to give Indians any land or water. As if these are *things*, to be owned
> or sold off.
>
> I am missing many cousins, have you seen them?
>
> The sadness is systematic. Suspicion is the lesson that sticks.

Pico's game is one in which we entertain an analogy between nineteenth-century water and twentieth-century oil. The analogy is one in which settlers of both centuries profit from appropriating "natural resources" such as water, land, and fossil fuels. "Water was a battlefield," Pico writes, "and within just twenty years, from 1850 to 1870, the indigenous population / fell by 60%." Pico points out that the ideological frameworks of property and capitalism erase not just the cosmology and value systems of indigenous peoples, but also the indigenous peoples themselves, who need land on which to live and water to drink. Inherent in this game is the implicit colonial analogy between indigenous peoples and Nature itself, an analogy that has been central to settler ideology because it allows settlers to see indigenous peoples not as people at all but rather as a kind of natural resource to be mined, managed, and thrown away. "It's hard to unhook the heavy marble Nature from around yr neck," Pico writes, "when history is stolen like water."[14]

• • • • •

Let us now return for a while to the nineteenth century, to an American literature in which metaphor elides indigenous peoples with Nature, and thus to a literature that—sometimes more and sometimes less—steals history out from under the very people it erases under the name of Nature. Both William Cullen Bryant's poem "The Prairies" and Margaret Fuller's *Summer on the Lakes, in 1843* were penned after Andrew Jackson's Indian Removal Act of 1830 laid federal groundwork for permanent legal challenges to indigenous sovereignty and self-determination, and both offer literary renderings of landscapes that were then part of the Northwest Territory of Illinois. In 1832, poet, journalist, and *Evening Post* editor William Cullen Bryant toured the territory in the company of his younger brother John, who had settled there as a homesteader after their brothers Peter and Cyrus had successfully done so. This visit provided Bryant with the first glimpse of the biome that would inspire one of his best poems. As he writes in a letter to his friend Richard Henry Dana on October 8 of that year:

> These prairies, of a soft fertile garden soil, and a smooth, undulating surface, on which you may put a horse to full speed, covered with a high, thinly growing grass, full of weeds and gaudy flowers, and destitute of bushes or trees, perpetually brought to my mind the idea of their having once been cultivated.[15]

Bryant—who used his editorial post to promote Jackson's controversial legislation—sees the landscape as a garden, but one that has been left uncultivated, "full of weeds and gaudy flowers" instead of crops. Further, it is "destitute of bushes or trees" that would signify the presence of a settlement. It is ironic that "These prairies . . . perpetually brought to my mind the idea of their having *once been* cultivated," given that the Removal Act was only two years old, that southern and central Illinois had seen the increasing retreat of tribal peoples throughout the early nineteenth century, and that one thousand members of three Illinois tribes—the Sauk, the Fox, and the Kickapoo—were, throughout Bryant's visit to the territory, engaged in the Black Hawk War on lands north of where the Bryant family had settled.

Given the historical context from which it emerges, "The Prairies" is ripe for a rereading through the lens of settler colonialism, a lens that enables us to reimagine Bryant the poet and the canon itself as *active* agents of this ideology, with Bryant's settler sublime a frontier iteration of the kind of sovereignty Emerson would soon grant his poet. Not only was Bryant's family homesteading on the very prairies from which the poem takes its name, but Bryant himself in late 1832, after he'd returned east, bought land not far from the town of Jacksonville, Illinois, where his brothers had settled. But even before he literally invested in the frontier, he had a personal stake in the Black Hawk War, which had resulted in raids on settlers and panic among homesteaders. News of recent raids reached Bryant while he was en route to meet his brother John, and he was forced, as he confides to his wife Frances on June 4, "to relinquish my projected route to Chicago which is said to be unsafe in consequence of the neighborhood of savages."[16] In contrast to such letters from his travels, and echoing Pico's accusation that indigenous "history is stolen like water," Bryant's literary descriptions of Illinois present a landscape he's *made* to seem long abandoned and uncultivated. Where indigenous presence is imagined, it is only as an absence, as a past possibility that already seems ancient to Bryant's settler mind; such absence all but guarantees Bryant's sovereign poet an uncontested claim on all he sees.

"These are the gardens of the Desert," the poem begins, in an echo of Bryant's letter to Dana, "these / The unshorn fields, boundless and beautiful, / For which the speech of England has no name— / The Prairies." Bryant spends the first stanza of the poem's supple blank verse in rapturous praise of the vistas that surround his speaker, and produces some truly beautiful description of the movement of wind through the grasses. In awe of the deist sublime he finds there, he proclaims, "Man hath no power in all this glorious work." And though he means that the prairies were made not by humans but by "the hand that built the firmament," his imagination is everywhere informed by the settler's predisposition to imagine the prairies as shaped more by God than by centuries of inhabitation by indigenous people. The poem's second stanza introduces the possibility of such a presence, but, as in his letter to Dana, it is largely as absence, as a civilization long past, that indigenous peoples figure into his imagination:

> Are they here—
> The dead of other days?—and did the dust
> Of these fair solitudes once stir with life
> And burn with passion? Let the mighty mounds
> That overlook the rivers, or that rise
> In the dim forest crowded with old oaks,
> Answer. A race, that long has passed away,
> Built them . . .[17]

Bryant on the prairies in 1832 can't be troubled by the presence of these mound-builders who have "long . . . passed away" in what he imagines is a cycle of rising and falling
cultures fueled "by the quickening breath of God," which "Fills them, or is withdrawn."
It is true that the Upper Mississippi region is even now home to the mounds of former
ceremonial centers built by vanished indigenous tribes; and it is also true that, as the
poem goes on to narrate, other tribes succeeded the mound-builders and sometimes
waged war on each other. In June of 1832 the Black Hawk War was not yet over, and
Bryant could not know that this successful military operation would permanently
open up the entire territory of Illinois to settlement after the defeat of Black Hawk and
his warriors and the relocation of most of the remaining tribes to eastern Iowa. But
these were events unfolding during Bryant's time in Illinois, which makes his description of the mound-builders' "disappearance" particularly revealing: "the mound-builders
vanished from the earth. / The *solitude of centuries* untold / Has settled where they
dwelt" (my emphasis).[18]

As historian of science Laura Dassow Walls tells us in *Seeing New Worlds*, in 1832
a new "idealistic" science argued that cultures "naturally" succeed one another in
cycles of growth, supremacy, and subsequent decay. Victor Cousin's *Introduction to the
History of Philosophy* promotes the notion, Walls notes, that "War, for instance, is
useful because it causes both the 'defeat of the people that has served its time,' and the
victory of 'the people which is to serve its time in turn, and which is called to empire.'"[19]
Bryant's reading of indigenous history borrows heavily from the idealistic and deistic
Romanticism that also characterizes Cousin's intellectual project, not only in the way
he renders violence between tribes and the death of indigenous cultures in the wake of
settler colonialism as equivalent, but particularly in his sense that the cultural changes
brought by settlers are nothing more than natural change writ large:

> Thus change the forms of being. Thus arise
> Races of living things, glorious in strength,
> And perish, as the quickening breath of God
> Fills them, or is withdrawn. The red man, too,
> Has left the blooming wilds he ranged so long . . .

Such phrasing—"The red man, too, / has left"—erases both how recent this departure
was and who occasioned it; the settlers whose increasing presence had put enormous
pressure upon the tribes of Illinois do enter the poem, but only later, and only as a
daydream. The logic of "The Prairies" implicitly justifies the genocide of indigenous

peoples not only as natural but also as ordained by God's own design. As Walls reminds us, Cousin himself argues "the vanquished is always in the wrong."[20] Echoing Cousin's too-convenient certitude, Bryant's poem closes first with an auditory dream of settler culture overtaking the prairies, a future equally reproductive and Christian: "From the ground / Comes up the laugh of children, the soft voice / Of maidens, and the sweet and solemn hymn / Of Sabbath worshippers." It's only after listening to this dreamt settlement of the prairies that the speaker can declare, famously, "All at once / A fresher wind sweeps by, and breaks my dream, / And I am in the wilderness alone." Effective and affecting as it is, Bryant's poem lays bare a remorseless ideology, a settler imaginary that sees settlement as the inevitable result of a "natural" order: "Thus change the forms of being. Thus arise / Races of living things, glorious in strength, / And perish." Just as importantly, despite actively knowing that the North American landscape is shaped by its inhabitation by indigenous peoples, Bryant's sovereign poet ultimately imagines the prairies as "a wilderness" in which he is alone.

• • • • •

Pico's *Nature Poem* reminds us that the collapse of indigenous peoples into the category of Nature has long served the ideological and financial interests of settler colonialism, and, in doing so, has expedited genocide. Drawing on this long history, Pico's *Nature Poem* attempts to refute the very category it nonetheless embodies, using the phrase "I can't write a nature poem" as a refrain throughout the book. The reasons Pico can't write a nature poem are most often ideological—"bc it's fodder for the noble savage / narrative"[21]—"bc English is some Stockholm shit, / makes me complicit in my tribe's erasure"[22]—"bc that conversation happens in the Hall of / South American Peoples in the American Museum of Natural History."[23] But the existence of *Nature Poem* as a published book suggests that Pico has in some fashion succeeded in writing the poem that the book insists he cannot write. Indeed, *Nature Poem* can be read as Pico's attempt to decolonize the concept of Nature by making it signify on his own terms, an attempt "to illusion himself some authority" that also allows Pico to assert a certain degree of self-sovereignty over himself and his poetry as an NDN subject both created by and subjected to settler culture.

Fittingly, the book tells the story of Pico's ambivalent relationship with the concept of Nature by setting up Nature not as a colonial-made figure for the indigenous but rather as an NDN-made figure for the settler, a gesture of savvy re-appropriation. Pico's relationship with this figure begins with the aforementioned characteristic disavowal—"I can't write a nature poem / bc it's fodder for the noble savage / narrative"[24]—a disavowal that Pico immediately complicates by following it up with a story about getting cruised and propositioned by a straight guy at a pizza parlor. "He puts his hands on the ribs of my chair, asks do I want to go into the / bathroom with him," Pico reports before summing up his response: "Let's say I literally hate all men bc literally men are animals— / This is a kind of nature I would write a poem about." And though Pico claims to hate the animality of men in a way that calls to mind the dismissive vernacular truism that "men are pigs," what seems to actually irk him is the way some men—white men in particular—are acculturated to their own sexuality, their libidinal impulses bound up in "naturalized" narratives of gendered and racialized privilege. So it's fitting that Pico's relationship with Nature begins intercut with the stories of dates, hookups, and interactions with white boys who project onto Pico their own unexamined colonial ideologies:

> This white guy asks do I feel more connected to nature
> bc I'm NDN
> asks did I live *like in a regular house*
> growing up on the rez.[25]

Pico's experiences teach him that the erotic dynamic between a white man and an indigenous man is always already an expression of settler colonialism, a dynamic so naturalized, such a routine part of our national ideology, that a white man will tend to exploit it unselfconsciously *as though* it were utterly unfamiliar to him. But it remains a dynamic all too familiar to Pico. "When I express frustration, he says *what?*" Pico reports, "He says *I'm just asking* as if being earnest somehow absolves him from being fucked up // It does not."

> He says *I can't win with you*
> because he already did
> because he always will
> because he could write a nature
> poem or anything he wants, he doesn't understand
>
> why I can't write a fucking nature
> poem.

> Later when he is fucking
> me I bite him on the cheek draw
> blood I reify savage lust.

Throughout the writing of *Nature Poem*, Pico returns again and again to such instances of resisting settler colonialism: he resists writing "a nature poem," resists collapsing indigenous peoples into the category of "the natural," and resists the category of Nature itself. He resists being fucked—and fucked over—by drawing blood, a gesture he mockingly claims reifies "savage lust." Over the course of the book, we come to understand that, for this assimilated urban "weirdo NDN faggot," the concept of Nature *is* settler colonialism, *is* an earnest, clueless white gay boy. Which is why Pico turns his rhetoric of critique and resistance into a narrative by eventually allowing Nature to appear as the allegorical figure it always already is. "*My primary device is personification,* says Nature" to Pico's speaker early on in the book, and thereafter Pico dutifully personifies Nature as a sinister suitor or disastrous hookup:

> Nature keeps wanting to hang out . . .

> Every date feels like the final date bc we always find
> small ways of being extremely rude to each other, like
> mosquito bites or deforestation

> like I think I'm in an abusive relationship w/nature.[26]

Part of the reason the relationship is abusive has to do with the ideology inherent in "natural" philosophies like that of Victor Cousin, which simultaneously supports "the noble savage / narrative" *and* "my tribe's erasure," a nobility made all the more piquant for settlers *by* the tribe's erasure, a disappearance with which the settler has the luxury of forgetting their own complicity. "Absence," Pico fumes, "as if Kumeyaay just didn't show up, as if it slept in, as if there / weren't a government intent on extermination."[27] Because of the alleged "natural" order in which indigenous peoples inevitably succumb to the "superior" culture of settler colonialism, Pico describes himself throughout the book as an inheritor of both historical and ideological traumas, as not responding "well to predation,"[28] as eternally on the defensive, and as unable to "tell the difference btwn the / faces / of attention and danger."[29] Given the high stakes of being seen by an unwitting avatar of the colonial project, given the potentially disastrous consequences of being the object of a settler's desires, it's no wonder, as Pico writes earlier in the book, "Suspicion is the lesson that sticks."[30]

• • • • •

Let us return again to the nineteenth century, this time to a text that displays a wide, unsettling range of relations to settler colonialism—from complicity to critique—and to indigenous peoples themselves—from received racial stereotypes to first-hand sympathetic portrayals. Margaret Fuller's *Summer on the Lakes, in 1843* (*SOL*) records a journey to the Northwest territories not unlike the one William Cullen Bryant undertook in 1832. But where Bryant went south to Baltimore and then west across country to St. Louis by coach before heading north up the Mississippi, Missouri, and Illinois rivers by steamboat, Fuller took the northern route, traveling by train through Albany and Buffalo to Niagara Falls, after which she returned to Buffalo, where she boarded a steamboat that traveled west across the Great Lakes to Chicago. And unlike Bryant's trip, Fuller's travels took place after the Black Hawk War resulted in the formal, forced removal of the remaining indigenous tribes from the territory and the opening of all of Illinois to settlers. And also unlike Bryant, who traveled to visit his settler relatives during an armed conflict with displaced tribes, Fuller traveled as a journalist and tourist in search of an encounter with "the romance of democratic America."[31] For Fuller, this romance included the fate of indigenous peoples, and she actively engaged in research, both reading about the tribes of the region *and* seeking out encounters with the remaining tribes in the Upper Midwest. This is not to say that *SOL* is not deeply inflected by settler colonial ideology, but it *is* to say that, especially toward the end of her journey, Fuller attempts to undercut her own investments in that ideology.

As Charles Capper, Fuller's most insightful biographer, points out, Fuller's letters and journals show that she struggled "with the rival claims of the real, the Romantic, and the picturesque" throughout her trip, and *SOL* dutifully reflects the conflict between Fuller's idealistic investment in European Romanticism, her at times unselfconscious acceptance of the basic tenets of Manifest Destiny, and her eventual recognition of the genocide imposed upon indigenous peoples by settler colonialism.[32] In fact, one could argue that *SOL* begins with an unproblematized Romanticism and ends more squarely in the real without ever fully giving up on the picturesque. But after a journey largely devoid of actual indigenous peoples, Fuller begins to recognize the costs of westward expansion toward the end of her time in the Midwest, a recognition sparked by firsthand encounters with members of the Chippewa and Ottawa tribes who gathered at Mackinaw Island for "their annual payments from the American government."[33] In fact, it is only in "Mackinaw," the book's penultimate sixth chapter, that she truly allows herself to complicate and sometimes undercut her bookish research and idealistic philosophy with real-life encounters with actual people, encounters that, though often marked by unexamined white supremacy, highlight her clear recognition of the injustice and racism that drive settler colonialism:

> Our people and our government have sinned alike against
> the first-born of the soil, and if they are the fated agents of a
> new era, they have done nothing—have invoked no god to
> keep them sinless while they do the hest of fate.
>
> Worst of all, when they invoke the holy power to mask
> their iniquity. . . .
>
> Yes! slave-drivers and Indian traders are called
> Christians, and the Indian is to be deemed less like the Son
> of Mary than they! Wonderful is the deceit of man's heart![34]

Here, without ideological equivocation, Fuller decries the hypocrisy of Manifest Destiny, which often disguised its economic rapaciousness with the rhetoric of Christian charity—saving souls while divesting bodies of life and land. In doing so, she might seem to be throwing off the settler sovereignty granted to her by her race and education. But even in the midst of her own encounters with indigenous peoples, Fuller largely relies on books written by settler men to frame those encounters, so that just as often as not, she parrots settler truisms such as "Nature seems, like all else, to declare that this race is fated to perish."[35] It is only when she relies on her own intellect and experience that Fuller can access unequivocal rhetoric and a clear-eyed appraisal of the real. It is important for us to remember that Fuller could pen such passages, given that much of the rest of *SOL* falls back on a mixture of ready-made Romantic ideologies that showcase "the rival claims" at work in her interpretations of her experience of indigenous peoples and, in the book's third chapter, the "picturesque" prairie landscape west of Chicago, in north central Illinois.

Most important to this essay is the fact that, early in *SOL*, the Romantic wins out over the real, and it is in this victory that Fuller's text both most resembles Bryant's *and* most radically departs from it. After a first chapter of ironic cosmopolitanism recounting a skeptical visit to Niagara Falls, and a second chapter of genteel travel from Buffalo to Chicago by steamboat and from Chicago by covered wagon through the Illinois prairies, Fuller's third chapter sends her to the Rock River, a spot that proves to be the apotheosis of her search for a peculiarly American romance. But Fuller's romance with Rock River—and particularly with the view from the bluffs at Eagle's Nest—is predicated on an erasure of indigenous presence nearly as complete as that of Bryant's "The Prairies." Just a few paragraphs before ascending the bluffs, Fuller describes the site of a former indigenous settlement:

> The aspect of this country was to me enchanting,
> beyond any I have ever seen, from its fullness of
> expression, its bold and impassioned sweetness . . .
> How happy the Indians must have been here! It is not
> long since they were driven away, and the ground,
> above and below, is full of their traces.
> *"The earth is full of men."*
> You have only to turn up the sod to find
> arrowheads and Indian pottery.[36]

Unlike Bryant, Fuller acknowledges how recently the tribes were forced from the land. But Fuller's romance can only be successful and sustained by confronting the fate of indigenous peoples indirectly, through their traces, artifacts that easily support, even decorate the pastoral quality she ascribes to what she called in a letter to Samuel G. Ward "the Rock River Edens."[37] Indeed, through arrowheads, ceramics, and the site a tribe once chose for their village, Fuller can most easily extrapolate values similar to those of a settler culture itself derived from Europe. "They may blacken Indian life as they will, talk of its dirt, its brutality," she writes in an earnest defense of indigenous peoples, but

> I will ever believe that the men who chose that
> dwelling-place were able to feel emotions of noble
> happiness as they returned to it. . . . The whole
> scene suggested to me a Greek splendor, a Greek
> sweetness, and I can believe that an Indian brave,
> accustomed to ramble in such paths . . . might be
> mistaken for Apollo. . . .[38]

Even though she knows, as a letter to her brother Richard demonstrates, that "it is only five years since the poor Indians have been dispossessed of this region of sumptuous loveliness, such as can hardly be paralleled in this world,"[39] Fuller's public record of her first encounter with the Illinois prairies suggests it first put her in mind of the ancient "Greek splendor" that a Romantic like Shelley saw as "proof of the perfectibility of the human race."[40] Fuller's American deployment of this idealistic trope—which arose in British Romanticism before the Greek Revolution of 1821—both deploys the "noble savage" stereotype by casting "an Indian brave" as the god Apollo *and* sets the scene for Fuller's visionary experience on Eagle's Nest, a bluff high above the Rock River.

Fuller was by no means the first white person to publish an idealized rhapsody in praise of the natural beauty of what was then described as the frontier—Bryant got to the Illinois prairies a full decade before her. But she was, perhaps, the first and only one to allegorize her experience of a rapturous frontier sublime as a pederastic relationship. After she ascends to Eagle's Nest, Fuller finds herself overwhelmed by the emphatically American vista she sees before her:

> I visited one glorious morning; it was that of the fourth of
> July, and certainly I think I had never felt so happy that I
> was born in America. Wo to all country folks that never saw
> this spot, never swept an enraptured gaze over the prospect
> that stretched beneath. I do believe Rome and Florence are
> suburbs compared to this capital of nature's art.[41]

As her biographer Capper has pointed out, it is here on Eagle's Nest that Fuller achieves fullest communion with the spirit of American romance she had been seeking on her journey, and her prose "transmutes the event into a Transcendental patriotic conversion experience."[42] But Fuller does not stop the transmutation there. *SOL* employs a generic strategy borrowed from the vernacular practice of the commonplace book: Fuller interleaves her own poetry (much of it occasional verse) throughout the narrative as a kind of counterpoint to and commentary on the action, much in the way Thoreau will later do in *A Week on the Concord and Merrimack Rivers*. So there at Eagle's Nest, Fuller "thought of, or rather saw, what the Greek expresses under the form of Jove's darling, Ganymede," and in response to this vision "the following stanzas took form," stanzas in which Ganymede waits for Jove to send an eagle down to carry him up to Olympus and give meaning to his position of eternal servitude.[43]

How startling, how strange Fuller's vision is! Where Bryant's putatively heterosexual settler daydreams of children and maidens who will inevitably overtake the prairies, Fuller's settler lobbies on behalf of Ganymede and asks Jove's eagle to "answer the stripling's hope, confirm his love, / receive the service in which he delights, / and bear him often to the serene heights."[44] Drawing on the work of Danish sculptor Bertel Thorvaldsen, who made five different sculptures of Ganymede, including one of the youth offering an eagle a drink from his famous cup, Fuller's "Ganymede to His Eagle" transplants the Greek myth to American soil where it flowers as a homosexual Romance. Simultaneously skirting and flirting with the pederastic "service" with which Ganymede is traditionally associated, Fuller posits a surprising analogy between herself as poet-witness to an American frontier sublime and Ganymede as a boy waiting to be transported to Jove's erotic attentions. In this analogy, and in the lines of verse resulting from it, Fuller encodes a peculiarly nineteenth-century idealism concerning metaphysics, nature, poetry, nation, and even, by implication, sex: that they are "by nature" aspirational, or inspire aspiration. Each is a great force driven, or driving us, upward by desire, by design. But Fuller's analogy also rests on an erotic power imbalance between boy and god, and in doing so admits to a kind of pleasure, a kind of subjection, and a kind of pleasure in subjection, that Emerson's poet never could.

Fuller's poet is no sovereign, no emperor; rather she is like a cupbearer whose ecstasy depends on fulfilling her duty to a higher power. In contemporary gay parlance, Fuller's poet is a total bottom. Fuller is more honest than Emerson about the ideology that "raises" the poet up in communion with the divine because she recognizes that such elevation comes—as it did for Ganymede, whose servitude to Jove and the other gods was eventually repaid with immortality—at the price of a kind of rapturous subjection. It's notable that Fuller's vision of Ganymede, "willing servant to sweet love's command," comes to her on *Independence* Day, and serves to mark not only the highest elevation she attains on her trip to Illinois, but also the apotheosis of her delight in being American. It is there, at Eagle's Nest,

> Where hands that were so prompt in serving thee,
> Shall be allowed the highest ministry,
> And Rapture live with bright Fidelity.[45]

It's also notable that the root of *rapture* is *rapere*, Latin for rape or seizure: the eagle is a raptor. In many versions of the myth, the dynamic between god and boy is characterized less as love and more as rape, and in all versions the erotic hinges upon power imbalance: the man's desire to seize the boy's beauty. And so in the landscape of Illinois in 1843, "bright Fidelity" to the idea of America lives in love with violence. Fuller has after all just passed through an abandoned "Indian village, with its regularly arranged mounds," and is now standing on a high bluff where "certainly I think I had never felt so happy that I was born in America." It is here, out of this sentiment, in the visible absence of indigenous peoples, that she sees Ganymede waiting for Jove to claim him—and if we're encouraged to see Fuller the poet in Ganymede, "a willing servant to sweet love's command," then who is her Jove?[46] Who is "the thought which ruled the world"?[47] Is it the idea of America itself? Is it Manifest Destiny? It's not for nothing that, like Bryant, Fuller invested in land in Illinois after her Midwestern sojourn—her younger brother Arthur settled on that "two-acre plot" and started a school there later in 1843.[48]

• • • • •

Pico's *Nature Poem* surveys what remains for twenty-first-century indigenous peoples in the wake of such nineteenth-century aspirations—particularly since the categories of metaphysics, nature, poetry, and sexuality have since been thoroughly critiqued, deconstructed, and shown to be ideologically fraught. Indeed, it seems notable that the epithet "American Renaissance" has recently been co-opted by a white supremacist organization, the New Century Foundation, as the name of their monthly online magazine. As awful a gesture as this appropriation is, it nonetheless raises essential questions about the settler agenda sometimes hidden in the idealistic, aspirational thrust of Transcendentalism and the work of mid-nineteenth-century writers like Bryant and Fuller. As Joshua David Bellin reminds us in his entry on "Native American Rights" for the *Oxford Handbook of Transcendentalism*: "On the whole, the Transcendentalists' attempts to 'speak for the Indian' were far from praiseworthy," even in the case of Fuller, whose ultimate outrage on the behalf of indigenous peoples never approached anything like the activism elicited by abolitionism.[49]

So at first it might seem ironic that Pico, like Fuller, codes the relation between the speaking subject of lyric poetry and the settler agenda as a homoerotic bond between partners of unequal power. Like Fuller's Ganymede, Pico is subjected to predation, and like Fuller's startling analogy between nationalist poet and cupbearer, this predation is predicated implicitly on settler colonialism. But unlike Fuller, Pico is not transported upward by the rapture of this dynamic, and unlike the putative isolato of Bryant's poem, he does not daydream of the inevitable reproductive future of settler culture. Instead, in regards to a text from Nature, who wants to hang out again after a first date, Pico responds: "I'm both charmed and suspicious, which is probably redundant."[50] But as the book progresses and Pico and Nature become more intimate, his charmed ambivalence becomes more heightened and even more contextualized by the long history of predation and violence of which the nineteenth-century frontier sublime is only one part:

> Nature kisses me outside the movie theater
>
> I can't tell if it was a romantic comedy or a scary movie bc
> of politics
>
> When Nature palms my neck I can't tell if it's a romantic
> comedy or a scary movie bc the clarity of desire terrifies me . . .
> comfort only leads to predation, and anything marvelous
> becomes holy in the Google translate of humanity
>
> I prefer to keep it very doggy style
>
> bc holy roars untouchable, tempers flare
> and ppl die, violently, all over the world throughout time.[51]

"[T]he clarity of desire" terrifies Pico because he knows that truly desiring Nature would lead to disaster. Pico *has* to remain skeptical and critical of Nature because it has acted as a cover or blind behind which settler colonialism has acted with a "clarity of desire" whose end result has been genocide: Nature as raptor, as rapist. This genocidal ideology has traditionally been decorated by the metaphysical language of settler religions—the "holy"—which has served a) to disguise the violence of their cosmologies by reifying the sacred as "untouchable," and b) to justify the cultural and physical violence with which they enforce indigenous conversion and their own supremacy. In the face of the high seriousness and high stakes of such an agenda, Pico's version of skepticism is most often an ambivalence delivered as flip queer irreverence, a "doggy style" that serves to deflate both his own anxiety and the inflated language of settler metaphysics that characterizes both Bryant's and Fuller's Illinois experiences.

Ultimately, *Nature Poem* rejects the settler sublime that is Nature, arriving instead at a tentative acceptance of a relationship with the natural world Pico associates with his parents and their tribal practices. But given the long colonial history of conflating indigenous peoples with Nature, Pico's is a thoroughly ambivalent acceptance. After insisting he will "never write a nature poem w/feather imagery or booze or that /

describes a slow pocket of dew in a SoCal Feb AM,"[52] after arguing that "You can't be an NDN person in today's world // and write a nature poem,"[53] after claiming to "hate nature—hate its *guts*," Pico asks at book's end: "What if I really do feel connected to the land?"[54] Because his entire sense of self has been predicated on questioning the authenticity and ideological implications of such a feeling, his first response to this question is to reject it: "I get so disappointed by stupid NDNs writing their dumb nature / poems like grow up faggots." But by this point in the book, Pico's "very doggy style" approach fails to account for his own vulnerability and seriousness, and he's ready to call himself out on the self-hatred implicit in his total dismissiveness of these allegedly "stupid NDNs": "I look this thought full in the face and want to throw myself into traffic."[55]

Coming at the end of a book titled after the very subgenre of poetry it rejects, such a moment of self-reckoning is perhaps not surprising. "The first stars were born of a gravity, my ancestors," Pico admits, "our sky is really the only thing same for me as it was for them, / which is a pretty stellar inheritance."[56] That he can at last admit to such an inheritance—even while making the etymological pun on *stella*—is moving both because of the way Pico subjects himself to the same decolonizing scrutiny he brings to settler colonialism, and also because he refuses to let (white) readers feel that he has either fully embraced "the nature poem," or fully submitted to the ideology such an embrace would entail. "Admit it," he taunts readers soon after his meditation on his ancestral stars, "This is the poem you wanted all along."[57] Even as he critiques his resistance to a tradition of relating to nature that his own ancestry and family embodies, he asks readers to police any satisfaction they may have derived from a moment in which Pico seems to acquiesce to the equation between indigenous peoples and "the land."

Employing the power of a campy ambivalence, of being of two minds, Pico remains in control and refuses to subjugate himself to a higher power of any kind, even of the ancestral sort. He's neither the sovereign poet Emerson imagines channeling the divine, nor a vanished tribesman whose absence Bryant argues "naturally" made way for settlers, nor the submissive cupbearer whose fidelity Fuller envisions as embodying a particularly American ecstasy. It's not that Pico doesn't see poetry as a lofty and important enterprise. "Poems were my scripture and the poets, my gods," Pico confesses before adding, "but even gods I mean especially gods are subject to the artifice / of humanity."[58] Pico's contemporary queer NDN understanding of artifice allows him to characterize the poem as the "absence of an answer, yet suggestion of meaning," a meaning suggested in part by history and cultural context, yes, but not granted by capitulation to settler culture. Nature does not offer "all her creatures to him as a picture-language" the way it does to Emerson's poet;[59] nor does "The solitude of centuries untold" settle where Pico's family still dwells, as it would in Bryant's version of indigenous history; nor does Pico's poetry offer "The meaning foretold by the boy the man cannot disclose" the way Fuller's Ganymede-poet promises to.[60] Instead, Pico abjures the affective privileges of sovereignty and rapture given to poets complicit with the violence done by settler colonialism, concluding that "It's hard to be anything // but a pessimist // when you feel the Earth rotting away on so many home pages."[61] Ever very doggy style in its approach to making meaning, *Nature Poem* ultimately refuses any easily characterized NDN relationship to the natural while remaining steadfast in its critiques of the settler sublime. "The air is clear," the book ends cheekily, "and all over Instagram—the peeps are posting pics of / the sunset."

MAKING BLACK CAKE
IN COMBUSTIBLE SPACES

M. NourbeSe Philip

It don't come, never arrive, had not—for the first time since she leaving, had left home, is the first, for the first time in forty years (the) Mother not standing, had not stood over the aluminium bucket with her heavy belly, whipping up the yellow eggs them and the green, green lime-skin. "People buying cake in New York," she says, (the) Mother had said, "not making them."[1]

These are the opening words of a short story of mine, "Burn Sugar," written more than two decades ago. I was, at that time, in the early stages of my lifelong experimentation with language and, particularly in this case, with the Caribbean demotic,[2] trying to find the written form of this "language . . . nurtured and cherished on the streets of Port of Spain . . . in the mouths of the calypsonians . . . the cuss buds, the limers, the hos (whores), the jackabats, and the market women . . . custodians and lovers of this strange, wonderful, you tink it easy, jiveass, kickass massa day done . . . ole mass, pretty mass, pansweet language."[3]

As I reread it, I'm aware of a certain discomfort with the language, some of that because I feel more adept all these years later at how to work with the Caribbean demotic; some of it perhaps still lingering in the shame-tinged margins of it not being "proper" english.

Every year it arrive, arriving, use to, in time for Christmas or sometimes—a few times well—not till January; once it even come, coming as late as March. Wherever she be, is, happens, happening to be, Jamaica, London, Toronto, it coming wrap and tie up in two or three layers of brown paper, and tape up in a Peak Freans biscuit tin—from last Christmas—black black from the oven and address on both sides—"Just to make sure it getting there," she hearing, hears (the) Mother saying—in (the) Mother funny printing (she could never write cursive, she used to say). Air mail or sea mail, she figuring out (the) Mother finances—whether she having money or not.

The car speeds along the snow-banked highway; it's filled—two parents, two grown children, one thirteen-year-old grandchild, one small dog, and all the usual stuff and more that one packs for a few days out of town over the Christmas season. It's December 23, 2017, and we have to make one stop to pick up some seasonal Caribbean food, including a traditional Black Cake, one of the culinary axes around which Christmas celebrations in the Caribbean circle. I have never bought Black Cake before, so I'm breaking with tradition. It's not black enough, I think when I first see the cake, and this concerns me, but I pay for it and we are back on the road headed to our destination on Georgian Bay.

About an hour into the trip the radio begins a podcast about the poet Emily Dickinson and her recipe for Black Cake.[4]

When she cut, cutting the string, she use to, would tear off the Scotch tape—impatient she rips, ripping, would rip off the brown paper, and prizing off the lid she pauses, pausing . . . sitting back on her haunches and laughing her head off—the lid don't, doesn't, never, not matching the tin, but it there all the same—black and moist. The cake—Black Cake.

It's a disjunctive moment—the image of Emily Dickinson making Black Cake. Is it the same Black Cake that now sits in the back of the car? A traditional Christmas delicacy that is woven into my memory of home, childhood, my mother, loss, exile, and the (im)possibility of women like my mother making poetry, or any art for that matter, at a time when manual work extended from sunrise to sun-down.

The podcast does establish a Caribbean connection, referring to the many spices in the recipe such as nutmeg and cinnamon that come from the area. "This is a cake that calls for nineteen eggs!" writes Emilie Hardman.[5] My mother's calls for twenty-four! And 2 lbs. of butter like Dickinson's. "All assembled it's 19 lbs 4 oz," Hardman continues. I have never weighed my mother's. "And that's before you put the brandy in!" We used rum in which the dried fruit would have been soaking weeks, if not months, ahead. "The black cake first appears in the 1840s in cookbooks," according to Hardman, and is "Caribbean in its origin—the cinnamon, the mace, the nutmeg, it's very tied up with the sugar trade and molasses." My mother used burn sugar, not molasses.

The weeks them pass, passing, used to—she eating the cake sometimes alone by herself; sometimes sharing, she shares a slice with a friend. Then again—sometimes when she alone, is alone, she cries, does cry as she eating—each black mouthful bringing up all kind of memory—then choking, she chokes—the lump of food and memory blocking, sticks, sticking up in her throat—big and hard like a rock stone.

From the comfort of a snug, warm cottage I gaze directly out at the white, snowy landscape of the lake, which is actually one of the many small, beautiful coves of

Georgian Bay, all part of Lake Huron. The water is calm though unfrozen and the beauty of the bay before me is in stark contrast to the history of shipwrecks the lake is known for. The surrounding area, traditional home to the Petun, Iroquois, and Ojibway First Nations, is also home to what was once the northernmost terminal of the Underground Railroad, Sydenham, now known as Owen Sound. Over the next few days the winds will whip the water like my mother whipped the eggs for Black Cake that she, Emily Dickinson, and I are all connected to in the creation and consumption of Blackness rooted in certain brute, historical facts.

She not knowing, doesn't know—when she beginning to notice it she don't know, but once she noticing, it always there when she opening the tin—faint but undeniable; musty and old, it rise, rising up, an odour of moldiness and something else from the open tin, that making her nose twitch. Is like it casting a pall over her pleasure, shadowing her delight; it spoiling and clouding the rich, fruity, Black Cake smell, and every time she taking a bite, it there—in her mouth—hanging about, it hangs about her every mouthful. (The) Mother's advice is to pour some make-sure-is-good-Trinidad rum on it. Nothing helping—the smell just there, lingering.

Knowing, she know that something on its annual journey to wherever she happen to be, something inside the cake change, changing within the cake, and whether is the change that causing the funny smell, or the journey to her that causing the change that causing the funny smell . . . she not knowing . . . It not tasting like this back home is what the first bite telling her—back, back home where she hanging round, anxiously hanging about the kitchen, getting in (the) Mother's way—underfoot—waiting for the baking to start.

In her commentary, mentioned above, Emilie Hardman refers to the sugar trade, not the slave trade, or slavery for that matter, although the latter was the foundation, the *sine qua non*, of the former. The sugar trade, as Hardman euphemistically refers to it, would bring sugar, molasses, and spices to northern states like Massachusetts; slavery and its brutal legacies would bring Dickinson in contact with African Americans in Amherst. According to author Aífe Murray, they, along with the Irish immigrants who eventually displaced them in the Dickinson household, as well as indigenous people uprooted from their homelands, comprised the serving classes in Amherst;[6] indeed, this was the pool of people from whom the servants in the Dickinson household would have come. Some would also have been itinerant, selling goods or wares at the Dickinson Homestead. Murray's thesis, based on extensive archival research and some speculation, is that the maids, labourers, and trades people from these diverse backgrounds residing at, or passing through, the Dickinson Homestead would have had an impact on Dickinson's life and work. The impact, she argues, can be seen both in the quantity of work Dickinson was able to produce—when she had good and steady help, her output increased—as well as in her poetic diction. The vernacular speech patterns of these individuals, some of whom, like the Irish maid Margaret Maher, worked cheek by jowl with Dickinson in her home and particularly in the kitchen, would, Murray insists, have influenced the poet in many ways, not least of all her unique poetic diction and style. "Emily's writing suggests influence by her servants' Hiberno-English and African American Vernacular English [the term linguists use for Black English]; . . . even adopt[ing] some of their linguistic and social strategies . . ."[7]

Murray refers to Dickinson's kitchen as a "combustible space" where "maid's and mistress's lives and languages rubbed off on each other."[8] In this "combustible space" we have Dickinson and her servants making Black Cake, a delicacy which is itself the result of what I call the "combustible space" that is the Americas and the Caribbean. I am suggesting here that there was something else at work beyond the simple, and perhaps simplistic, exchange that the metaphor of "rubb[ing] off on each other" implies. Murray asserts that it was "conversation . . . especially with servants whose language backgrounds were different from the poet's, [that] informed her ear and helped explain her unusual language gestures."[9] Along with the aural presence of the Other, whose oral linguistic practices complicate and diversify the "combustible space" that is not only the kitchen of the Dickinson Homestead, but all of the Americas and the Caribbean, there is the Othered nature of the recipe's ingredients—the spices and the sugar that stand in for another theatre of terror, albeit invisible: the Caribbean. These ingredients, Caribbean ingredients, sugar, nutmeg, and mace, represent an early infusion of other Afrosporic currents and discourses into the United States, discourses which, while still then unheard, linger on the tongue sweetening the stench of that which should never have been, or allowed to be. We could argue that Black Cake is a kind of blackness that Dickinson's privileged life allowed her to consume, even as she aurally consumed and absorbed the "African American Vernacular English" among others.

"Wash the butter!" (The) Mother wanting to get her out of the way, and is like she feeling the feel of the earthenware bowl—cool, round, beige in colour—(the) Mother pushing at her. Wash the butter, wash the butter, sit and wash the butter at the kitchen table cover with a new piece of oilcloth for Christmas; wash the butter and the sun coming through the breeze blocks, jumping all over the place dappling spots on her hand—it and the butter running competition for yellow. Wash the butter! Round and round . . . pushing the lumps of butter round with a wooden spoon.

Every year she asking the same question—"Is why you have to do this?" and every year (the) Mother telling her is to get the salt out of the butter, and every year she washing the butter. The water not looking any different, not tasting any different—if she could only see the salt leaving the butter . . . (the) Mother catching her like this every year, and every year she washing the butter for hours, hours on end until is time to make the burn sugar.

The bought Black Cake is, predictably, disappointing. Tasty yes, but its sweetness, unchallenged, remains unscathed like "the myth in the white dress . . . then you think about her in the kitchen. The physicality of that cake—of making that cake that you share with people. It's a social cake! This is a woman who is doing something that we think so counter to Emily and her remove from the world."[10]

Now! She stopping—(the) Mother not telling her this but she knowing and (the) Mother knowing—it is understood between them. The coal-pot waiting with its red coals—(the) Mother never letting her light it—and the iron pot waiting on the coal pot, and (the) Mother waiting for the right time. She pushing her hand into the sugar bag—suddenly—one handful, two handful—and the white sugar rising up gentle gentle in the middle of the pot, two handful of white sugar rising gently . . . (the) Mother never letting her do it herself, but to the last grain of sugar, the very last grain, she knowing how much sugar going into the pot. She standing close close to (the) Mother, watching the white sugar and she knowing exactly when it changing—after she count to a hundred, she deciding one year; another year she knowing for sure it not changing while she holding her breath;

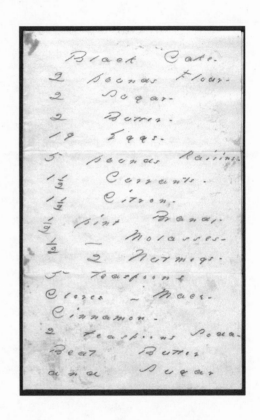

and last year she closing her eyes and knowing that when she opening them, the sugar changing. It never working. Every time she losing, disappointing herself—the sugar never changing when she expecting it to, not once in all the years she watching, observing (the) Mother's rituals. Too quick, too slow, too late—it always catching her—by surprise! First, the sugar turning sticky and brown at the edges, then a darker brown—by surprise!—

smoke stinging, stings her eyes, tears run running down her face, the smell sharp and
strong of burning sugar—by surprise!—she not budging, standing still, watching, watches
what happening in the pot—by surprise!—the white sugar completely gone, leaving
behind a thick, black, sticky mass like molasses—by surprise! If the pot staying on long
enough, she wondering if she seeing the sugar changing back, right back to cane juice,
runny and opaque . . . catching her by surprise.

(The) Mother grabbing a kitchen towel, grabbing the pot and putting it in the sink—
all one gesture, clean and complete—and it sitting there hissing and sizzling. (The) Mother
opening the tap and steam for so rising up and brip brap—just so it all over—smoke gone,
steam gone, smoke and steam gone leaving behind this thick thick, black liquid.

She looking down at the liquid—calling it her magic liquid; is like it having a life of it
own—its own life—and the cake needing it to make it taste different. She glancing over at
(the) Mother—maybe like she needing (the) Mother to taste different. She wonder, won-
dering if (the) Mother needing her like she needing (the) Mother—which of them essential
to the other—which of them the burn sugar? Sticking a finger in the pot, she touching the
burn sugar, turning, she turns her finger this way and that, looking at it in the sunlight,
turning it this way and that, making sure, she makes sure she not dropping any of the burn
sugar on the floor; closing her eyes, she closes them, and touching she touches her tongue
with her finger . . . gently, and tasting she tastes the taste of the burn sugar. She screwing
up her face then smiling it tasting like it should—strong, black and bitter and it making
the cake taste like no other cake . . .

Every year I turn my hand to making blackness. And bitterness. First, you pour a
heaping mound of white granulated sugar into a pot (preferably done outdoors since
the process will set off fire alarms); heat the sugar until it becomes caramelized, then
past that to the point at which it becomes black in colour, by which point the sugar,
now liquid, will be bubbling in the pot. Wait for it to become sufficiently black; add
water enough to make a syrup, the thicker and more bitter, the better.

That process of rendering the white sugar black always appears magical to me, akin
to what I imagine alchemy to have been like, except this appears a reversal, albeit
partial, of the alchemical process, which begins with the *nigredo*, the black stage,
which, in turn, becomes the *albedo*, the white stage. The following stages, the yellow
and red, finally yield the goal of the transformation—the prized philosopher's stone.[11]
I am curious to know where the practice of using burn sugar among the descendants
of the enslaved, like my mother, comes from and have yet to find the source. It is a
puzzle because the molasses that Dickinson's recipe calls for would have been readily
available in the sugar economies of the Caribbean, yet the key ingredient of Black Cake

as I knew (and know) it, the ingredient that gives it its unique taste, dare I say, as prized as the philosopher's stone, is burn sugar, not molasses. It is, however, a tradition that, like many others, is being impacted by the easy availability of commercial browning products. Making burn sugar—making blackness from whiteness—remains a challenging and difficult process for me. In all respects.

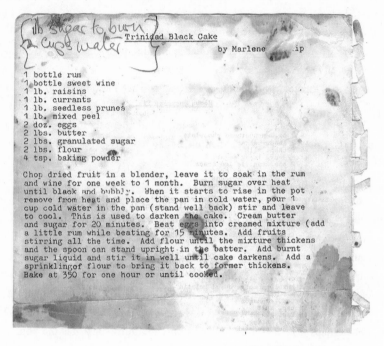

(The) Mother's Recipe—

The imagination, Gaston Bachelard writes, "is . . . the faculty of deforming the images offered by perception, of freeing ourselves from the immediate images; it is especially the faculty of changing images."[12] Alchemical work, through deformative processes such as burning or putrefying is intended to deform nature with the goal of creating the philosopher's stone. In a similar way, preparing burn sugar deforms the white sugar, itself the product of earlier deformative processes—the deformation of the African into the non-existence of a negative blackness, through the terrifying, exhaustive, and exploitative practices of transforming and deforming the sugar cane plant into sugar—white sugar. The outcome and legacy of the transatlantic trade in

Africans is a layering and mirroring of deformations between the enslaved, the land they worked, and the crops which they produced. Are these deformative processes reversible? the young narrator in "Burn Sugar" wonders, as she gazes at the rendering of white into black, yet another deformation, through the application of heat—in "combustible spaces." If enough heat were applied long enough, would the blackness of the burn sugar transform into the original cane juice, thin and somewhat opaque, that is expressed from the cane stalk? Can we move past the oppositional binary of black and white to a place that resists clarity and transparency and offers a refuge, a place of maroonage, perhaps, with echoes of Edouard Glissant's insistence on the right to, and possibly even the necessity for, opacity?[13]

The result of the first deformation, which occurs when black bodies in "combustible spaces" are forced to deform the sugar cane plant, is twofold—material and non-material. Sugar and whiteness, the latter being simultaneously the product of deformation that is sum of the practices of empire, colonialism, slavery, and racism, as well as the instrument of continued deformation.

The result of the second deformation process is the black bitterness of the burn sugar, which reminds us of all that is forgotten, unremembered, or seldom spoken; it rescues the sweetness of the cake from being unscathed, lending it a certain memory of a bitter, deformed history that lingers, an aftertaste on the tongues of those descendants of that original deformation, as much as the taste of the sugared spices of the Caribbean lingered on the tongues of the inhabitants of the Dickinson Homestead, also deformed, though unaware, by the same history of empire, colonialism, and racism. It is a bitter history we consume as we consume the rich Blackness that is Black Cake, but perhaps, like the philosopher's stone, the burn sugar has the potential of generating transformative possibilities within and for us.

To return to Dickinson's Black Cake and Murray's analysis of the generative role the kitchen and her various servants and helpers played in her work: Can we perhaps interpret the role of these familiar unfamiliars with their distinctive vernaculars, people who as servants and labourers would have been marginal in nineteenth-century life in the United States, people whose histories contained and spilled trauma—the Irish famine, the Indigenous genocide, and the transatlantic trade in the Africas—as catalysing a certain deformative process in Dickinson's linguistic imaginings, much like the burn sugar (which she didn't use in her Black Cake) does? Could we, perhaps, say that her tongue acquired a taste for that linguistic bitterness, coming out of a deformed history of colonialism, racism, and classism that would have been present in her household, which, in turn, resulted in a poetry that refused to be unscathed?

... *(The) Mother nodding her head and at last she knowing that now is the time— time for the burn sugar. She picking up the jar, holding it very carefully, and when (the) Mother nodding again she beginning to pour—she pouring, (the) Mother stirring. The batter staying true to itself in how it willing to change—at first it turning from yellow to beige to brown—just like me, she thinking, then it turning a dark brown like her sister, then an even darker brown—almost black—the colour of her brother, and all the time (the) Mother stirring. She emptying the jar of burn sugar—her magic liquid—and the batter colouring up now like her old grandmother—a seasoned black that sometimes whitish flecks of butter, egg and sugar still betraying, and (the) Mother's arm not stopping beating and the batter turning in and on and over itself . . .*

"THE TINGE AWAKES"

READING WHITMAN AND OTHERS IN TROUBLE

Leila Wilson

It was a day I was teaching Walt Whitman, and I temporarily lost my vision. I felt my-self warm and my vision speckled. At first, I thought myself moved. It was a day Whitman looked from his ferry and watched as the gulls' "glistening yellow lit up parts of their bodies," saw their "slow-wheeling circles."[1] His "eyes dazzled by the shimmer-ing track of beams," he looked "at the fine centrifugal spokes of light" surrounding his reflection in the water.[2] My vision warbled, and I felt for the desk. During these blurs, I saw peripherally, marginally, around floating, vibrating lumps of light. What started as specks, as sparkles, became orbs I hoped to rub away, but they spread open in clus-ters over the page. If I moved my head to the side and looked down at my book, like a cow might look down at a fly from the corner of its eye, I could see words quavering. I pressed the desk's plane so my palms could have a place, could extend to my arms to hold this sudden planet of wind. I stopped seeing for swathes of seconds as students spoke and waited. I craned and circled and tilted my head until I could find a handle of language, until I could make out an annotation or a lever of underline. I asked a stu-dent to read. I made a joke about a ghost. Soon I called a break and felt for the wall to the door.

Oliver Sacks, who suffered from migraines and experienced accompanying visual hallucinations throughout his life, wrote several studies characterizing such optical auras, called scintillating scotoma. In describing one manifestation, he explains that the "whole visual field—or half of it—may be taken over by a violent complex turbulence, sweeping the perceived forms of objects into a sort of topological turmoil; straight edges of objects may be swept into curves, bits of a scene magnified or distorted as if stretched on a rubber sheet."[3] I developed exit strategies from rooms, breathing exer-cises on trains, pit stops to and fro; I found perches to ride out the twenty minutes of psychedelic disturbances until the surfaces around me again cohered to their reason-able forms. I chalked it up to sinus infections. Bright lights. Stress. Dehydration. Lack of sleep. I thought it possible, too, I might be touched. For about two years ocular migraines would interrupt classes, trips to the grocery store, stories to my toddler, but mostly no one knew.

• • • • •

From where did this resistance come? To admit struggle? To confess pain? What was this hesitancy, even, to say *my*, *I*, and *me*?

> The impalpable sustenance of me from all things at
>   all hours of the day,
> The simple, compact, well-join'd scheme, myself
>   disintegrated, every one disintegrated yet part of
>   the scheme,
> The similitudes of the past and those of the future,
> The glories strung like beads on my smallest sights
>   and hearings . . .[4]

Eventually the headaches that followed were too much to hold. When the doctors checked me for stroke, looked in my ears, slipped me a Z-Pak, and told me I wobbled, I guess I knew more. Later, one Saturday morning, I was back at the walk-in clinic vomiting. When the doctor entered the room, she kept the lights off. I didn't know what to answer when she asked me to rate my pain—I was numberless to gauge. "O suns—O grass of graves—O perpetual transfers and promotions, / If you do not say any thing how can I say any thing?"[5] I didn't know that I had a blood clot that could have clogged.

For a year I took NSAIDs and blood thinners. I had INRs, CBCs, and MRIs. I was told I was fine, that they may never know the cause. Months later, my platelet numbers spiked. And then my red blood cells. And then another climb. Finally, a genetic test revealed the source—I had mutated. One of my protein switches got stuck, jamming the gates and sluices of my marrow, tricking it into thickening my blood. Somehow as I had moved through the world, as my channel moved within me, I was shifted by a greater lake. In hopes of keeping my numbers in order, I would now take a toxic concoction for the remainder of my days.

"Have you guess'd you yourself would not continue? / Have you dreaded these earth-beetles? / Have you fear'd the future would be nothing to you?"[6] Caught between a longing to accept what this illness might mean and a longing to retain some hope for a future free of it, I just wanted to be with my kin. I wanted to linger longer. I lost patience with selfish people, rich people, righteous people, healthy people. I was now entering the Necropastoral, "a strange meeting place for the poet and death, or for the dead to meet the dead, or for the seemingly singular-bodied human to be revealed as part of an inhuman multiple body."[7] Never unaware of the toxicity within my surroundings and always conscious that my choices would have little effect on the mutations that have already taken hold of my body and my planet, I felt done for.

> O how can it be that the ground itself does not sicken?
> How can you be alive you growths of spring?
> How can you furnish health you blood of herbs, roots,
>   orchards, grain?
> Are they not continually putting distemper'd corpses
>   within you?
> Is not every continent work'd over and over with
>   sour dead?[8]

I still cradled some desire for connection beyond myself, for a hook into a future existence in which I might effect some change. Was this fantasy? Willful trickery? Dull denial? This human desire for continuity wasn't rooted in belief or aspiration. It was rooted in observation. Decomposition. Body. "My tongue, every atom of my blood, form'd from this soil, this air . . ."[9] I saw dirt, I saw land, as holding histories of each other. I saw dirt remaining for a future that I wanted to still, to stretch toward.

In other words, I didn't know what to do with my longing. How to write? How to speak? Toward whom or to what end? What use could my criticality be as I wondered whether my medicine would work, whether it would tamp back my bone marrow's misfiring? What could I find through language, through mutation's scrutiny, that I could openly thread out toward those beyond me? What sieve could writing be?

Questions that existed after diagnosis continue to exist: Is my illness making me dumb? Making me sappy? Making silt of thought? Donna Haraway offers a way to exist within such struggle. She offers *sympoiesis*—a "making-with"—as a praxis of "worlding-with" others in ways "complex, dynamic, responsive, situated, historical."[10] She urges us, regardless of our split inheritances and entrenched nodes of knowing, to form relations outside of family, beyond expected bonds, in acts that "cultivate the capacity to respond to worldly urgencies with each other."[11] The need here, the "urgency," is learning how to live within damage. "Staying with the trouble requires making oddkin;

that is, we require each other in unexpected collaborations and combinations, in hot compost piles. We become—with each other or not at all."[12] We turn to each other in the act of decomposition, and our materials are intermingled: through the process of sharing our stories, creating the modes of their telling, and inventing the language with which to tell them. Because, as Haraway asserts, it "matters what stories we tell to tell other stories with" and "what concepts we think to think other concepts with," we lift our gaze from our entrenched modes of making, and we decompose.[13]

• • • • •

Whitman asks me to question and reinvigorate what I believe. He compels me to wonder, to wander toward divergent possibilities, different notions of futurity. "Do I contradict myself? / Very well then I contradict myself, / (I am large, I contain multitudes.)"[14] His ways of resisting death are varied and his conclusions transform over the years: Write lasting poems! Embrace and enact democratic ideals! Take a walk! Get it on! However, I see throughout his oeuvre a lasting belief in the capacity of compost, as the practice of writing, living, and dying together. Whitman knows how muck stimulates. He admits death's envelopment. Whether or however I feel urged to pray, he consistently leads me, along with my contemporaries who are looking also toward an end, to get my house in order, to die better. Is he my prophet-bard? Not exactly, but he does get me to hoe humus with others in the midst of making. As I disintegrate, Whitman expands my kin.

The poets I look to, those I "world-with" and word-with, are skeptical and agnostic, yet they are wholly open to possibility: Carl Phillips, Saskia Hamilton, Claudia Rankine, and Christina Davis. Taught by modernists, schooled in Language poetics, and wary of neo-sincerity, their work reflects my suspicion of confession. Their poems often resist a clear narrative trajectory and refuse poetic epiphany, resisting closure and foregrounding doubt. By embracing flux and transition, by accentuating schism and slippage, they show that we exist in fragments yet still desire the sphere of the unified poem. They, too, work to resist the pitfalls of sentimentality, yet they know that without sentiment, there is no sacrifice. Without the pleasures of lyrical experimentation, of prosody's possibilities, the body of the poem has no form from which to mutate. Ultimately, these poems show vibrant meandering. Their vibrissae stretch. Their scintillas spread. They show that when we get out of the way of ourselves, we're less squelched by self-consciousness and our poems can lead the way.

In "Democratic Vistas," Whitman asks America's future poets to write "great poems of death" that "link and tally the rational physical being of man, with the ensembles of time and space."[15] He laments a declining "faith . . . scared away by science [that] must be restored . . . with new sway, deeper, wider, higher than ever."[16] This must be done by a future poet "who, while remaining fully poet, will absorb whatever science indicates, with spiritualism, and out of them, and out of his own genius, will compose the great poem of death."[17] We poets may try, but we're held back by forceful inheritances and positions that make it difficult to take Whitman's request seriously. We're rooted in practices of poetry—modes favoring doubt over declaration, pragmatism against belief, the living above the dead—that make such mandates seem maudlin at best. Many of us have come to resist the possibility—or at least resist the relevance of the possibility—of "the ensembles of time and space."[18] Tired of mere resignation yet suspicious of open belief, we are caught. We're restricted by criticality and left alone to admit our inventions of afterlife. As Donna Haraway writes, we find ourselves

> always situated, someplace and not noplace, entangled
> and worldly. Alone, in our separate kinds of expertise and
> experience, we know both too much and too little, and so
> we succumb to despair or to hope, and neither is a sensible
> attitude. Neither despair nor hope is tuned to the senses, to
> mindful matter, to material semiotics, to mortal earthlings
> in thick copresence.[19]

I want to read poets who are inviting death into their poems, who are "staying with the trouble." I, who had been consigned to waiting rooms and companion seats while helping my parents get through dozens of tests, consultations, procedures, operations, and infusions, now only want the company of poets who admit fear and who want to make something of it. These poets are thinking about finitude, not just in the way of tricking fate by writing lasting poems; not just by effecting change through social, pedagogical, or political acts; but by exploring the possibilities of unlocking land—be it horizon, crop, or city block—to form a different kind of death, to decompose for and with each other.

• • • • •

Carl Phillips's "After the Afterlife," a sonnet in a loosely pentameter form, takes as its subject the poet's effort to envision what the afterlife might look like or contain. The landscape, the afterscape, is as torqued as the syntax in many of his lines. There's no vista extending into a crystalized form. Though his sentences gesture toward clarity, their subjects slip into unstable pronoun-antecedent relationships, and gerund fragments adjoin. The speaker imagines finding "bones, for sure," and "feathers almost the white / of an eagle's undershaftings in its first year" strewn on afterlife's ground, surrounded by "any wind, that stirs."[20] What could serve as a kind of thesis for the poem—"Punishment in death / as it is in trembling"—resists closure without an operative verb and ends up establishing the artifice of afterlife. Phillips aligns death with tremor, with collapsed edges, with failed intentions: "having meant to be kind, yet / failing anyway." Death itself "can do no good." Death, in itself, offers me nothing I can extend or to which I might fasten a future.

Where I should really focus is "after the afterlife," because there lies another "afterlife." This post-afterlife afterlife hazily exists as a "stand of / cottonwood trees getting ready all over again, / because it's spring, to release their seeds." In the force of their plentitude, they remind me of Whitman's "Unseen Buds," one of the last poems he wrote before his death. They push toward potential, "urging slowly, surely forward, / forming endless . . ."[21] The performance of Phillips's blowsy seed-poofs "only look like cotton; they're not cotton, at all."[22] The cotton-like spores, maybe even clouds now, shift "across these waters." Left in a state of suspension, I am detached and variable, unable to make meaning of a line of breakages following one after the other through and into the next afterlife. The stand of cottonwood trees takes a practiced, deep breath "all over again" and releases into another time whatever fabrication it has mustered. I don't experience transcendence here, but I'm exposed to what's coming, however dissatisfying the presumed answers.

• • • • •

Whitman aspired to create a kind of democratizing poetry. His unflinching observations of his world reveal his allegiance to the living. His lists of seeming minutiae, categorizations, anecdotes, and exclamations all envelop the physical force of being-in-the-now. As Ken Chen asserts, "Whitman cared more about our world than another purer one waiting for us beyond."[23] He smeared round his recognitions to show that the living, the actual, the present, must be acknowledged, that they could be even more here in their being named. And yet, I still wonder: Are these chock-full, finely fashioned acknowledgments of life preparations for a more complete experience of death? What kind of future, what potentiality, does Whitman open for us?

• • • • •

Haraway's notion of the Chthulucene again helps me understand the potential of being fully in this world. While Whitman sometimes embraces a notion of futurity that preserves our discrete souls and other times envisions it as a shared experience of post-human boundlessness, he consistently flirts with the idea of an Edenic afterlife. The poets I turn to don't look away from their current bodies, their current damage, their current physical existence through our harmed planet. They're planting themselves in it—thickly in the midst of their experience and "staying with the trouble in real and particular places and times"—so that they may most fully live and die.[24] We are all consistently in the midst of our flawed becoming, and the land ends up containing and expressing damaged, potent presences.

The speaker in Christina Davis's "Concord" wants to commune with others and collapse time.[25] "It avails not, time nor place—distance avails not," Whitman wrote.[26] Yet the margins around death in Davis's poem aren't so permeable. The speaker of this poem understands intimately the pain caused by another's death, yet as she considers her own death, she is suspended rather than transformed. Davis opens the poem with measurements, "(from here to there) // (from me to you) // (from birth to death)," and she realizes that each of these is "not far."[27] Distance can be compressed; it neither limits nor prevents closeness. Proximity is measured by familiarity, by informality: "We could be there / this evening with our bared feet // and our first names." In becoming ourselves, without adornment, we become intimate. In Concord—in communion, concurrence, concordance—togetherness collapses time and invites us to pray. But the urges behind this prayer are not revealed.

> What at birth was proposed to us
> What at walking was perceived
> over the man-high grasses, what keeps
>
> never coming,
>
> let steps be
>
> found again.

We see horizon, distance, an awareness of human scale, and ultimately our smallness. We know death is here, but it remains apart, enigmatic, or in hiding. There's no spark or transformation, just a decision to keep moving, a desire to keep walking through and over this scape. Walking is what first exposes death to us, and it is what we must keep doing as we face our movement toward it. Walking through landscape becomes the process of accepting death.

• • • • •

For years I turned to expanses at the ends of walks. I dropped to my knees on whatever softened earth opened up. With any number of gestures, a clutch or stretch or prostration or clasp, I sought to appeal to some air. The prayers I pitched beyond reach were always for another. When things changed with my health, I didn't want to walk to the edges of places anymore. I could not project my absence.

• • • • •

In New Jersey, about an hour-and-fifteen-minute drive from Whitman's home in Camden, lies the subject of Richard McGuire's graphic novel *Here*, a book-long lyric exploring the location of what would become and what has since ceased to be his family's living room in his home town of Perth Amboy.[28] Each drawing occurs within the same location, seen from the same viewpoint, over eons of time. Every frame is dated with the year that corresponds to its captured moment, ranging from 3,000,500,000 BCE to a post-human era of 22,175 CE. The events therein are interrelated, enmeshed, overlapped, and sometimes recurrent, reflecting changes in epoch, outline, and element—in flora, family, and fashion. Each image is made even more reflexive and dynamic by McGuire's superimposed frames, reminiscent of small pop-up windows, that present splices of time taken out of their original contexts and placed within his full-spread drawings.

These windows become highly charged sub-moments, portals of lyrical associations that invite us to peer and merge. In one small frame, we see a fifteenth-century arrow mid-flight superimposed over the undifferentiated bog that McGuire imagines existed over three billion years ago. In another two-page spread dated 1938, a child's hands play cat's cradle in 1990 next to what appears to be two enslaved people in 1777 carrying away a body in a bloodied sheet. Within the span of a larger frame, dated 1995, a father is haunted by a dream in which he cannot save his children from drowning: "As soon as I save one / the next one is drowning." What traces of experience are rising to the surface in these portals? What is revealed in their correspondences? The father's home cannot tamp down the stories that originated and still remain there—and that have yet to manifest—as they continue to accumulate and integrate, pushing out.

In an earlier group of images, we see a darkened two-page spread of the living room in 1955 that holds just a tint of maroon light on its ceiling. In one portal, dated

1986, a couple of nervous, flirting teenagers accompany an archeologist on an investigative site visit. She says, "I like your T-shirt." He looks down at it, mumbling, to see what he's wearing: "Future transitional fossil." In the portal on the facing page, we see two figures in 2050 playing a game with floating screens. One player pokes his head through its vertical plane, and he's transformed into his child-self from the neck up: "Oh wow!" On the next two-page spread, we learn that the Perth Amboy home lies on the ground of a Native American settlement, perhaps over, as the archaeologist reveals, "tools," "remains that could shed light on diet," or "burial sites." In the slippages of time in *Here*, between and among experiences, McGuire resists asking his readers to gauge, classify, or rank their sympathies. He reveals the cross-fertilization of encounters within a designated space. And yet in every juxtaposition, we feel McGuire uncovering layered narratives from suppressed histories. As in Whitman, each section of this place—each portal opening into another time—is filled with a kind of sentience, and it is up to us, his readers, to recognize, draw out, and call back to such interrelations.

• • • • •

For many months, the ocular migraines I experienced presented themselves in fortification patterns—geometric conglomerations that bloomed and bumped into each other as floating, scallop-edged orbs. Though unnerving, I was eventually able to make these visual displays into opportunities to see: levitating, breaking petri dishes spilling their cultures; frost-struck weed clutches thawing and rising in sun; and ripped quilts rumpling over children. Never static and always blurred, they were my trace presences, blood wreathes, and brain splices. Because contact with my medicine could make others ill, I was told not to contaminate my bare hands with it, so I developed a system of dropping the pills from their box to my mouth so I wouldn't have to wash my hands before touching my son.

• • • • •

For John Ruskin, a fixed vision of a landscape or seascape was the means through which artists could transcend their mortal existence and tap into the eternal. "There is one thing that [distant space] has . . . which no other object of sight suggests in equal degree, and this is—Infinity."[29] Whitman, who sent *Leaves of Grass* and some photographs to Ruskin in 1879, might have agreed with Ruskin's notion that a landscape can capture unboundedness, yet his poems home in on quite particular past and future inhabitants. Boring wormholes into places to open their empathetic possibilities, Whitman ecstatically takes his "impalpable sustenance" from "all things at all hours of the day" and feels himself "disintegrated yet part of the scheme, / The similitudes of the past and those of the future, / The glories strung like beads on [his] smallest sights and hearings . . ."[30] He sees roadside "paths worn in the irregular hollows" and recognizes in them their "latent . . . unseen existences."[31] Ruskin, by Whitman's own account in a letter to William O'Connor in 1882, expressed that "*Leaves of Grass* is . . . too personal, too emotional, launched from the fires of myself, my spinal passions, joys, yearnings, doubts, appetites."[32] Though generally undaunted by criticism, Whitman admits in this letter a "*worry* of Ruskin," and he anticipates a disagreement with Ruskin about his goals for poetry. He reveals a degree of defensiveness when he imagines the poetry Ruskin must appreciate: "abstract works, poems, of some fine plot or subject, stirring, beautiful, very noble." Was Whitman, too, concerned about his lack of personal restraint? Is he self-conscious about how he captures landscape, not limiting his vistas to what is "fine" and "noble," but instead engaging his "special personality" and "the greater drama going on within [himself]?"[33]

• • • • •

Saskia Hamilton's "Flatlands" opens as a pastoral, but her poem becomes complicated with a "greater drama going on within [herself]": "Horses and geese in a sodden field."[34] Yet menace spreads around their ankles, as we see the possibility of the animals being subsumed by the saturated land. It is a place circuited by tracks and canals, and from the speaker's position on a train, she can see "solitaries with luggage on a wet platform." It is a land where we have only semblances of wide expanses, where the spread of land is contained, demarcated by a country made viable by its civil engineers. Space here is hyper-organized, rigidly striated into "a bit of land / a copse, a fold, a quadrant of wood, / lines of beech, lines of poplar." Though the speaker is caught within her train compartment, her "miniature commentary magnified / in the glass" brings the landscape closer, enlarging and immobilizing it.

The "winter streaking the window" intensifies the sense of this freezing—of the viewer being protected and the world outside being brought into sharper relief. The train itself is suspended within the tension of the poet's looking. It is both "bearing" and "not bearing the weight / within." The poet comes to recognize her own burden of seeing from behind the glass, becoming separate from her experience within a landscape, separate from even herself. Though she has the empowering mechanism of perspective, this ends up isolating her within her own perceptions. "Let this not be thought / (one thought to oneself)." In looking at the land from this vantage point, does she have the urge to transcend thought and reach pure sensation, emotion, or intuition? Something more lasting because of its being just out of reach, ineffable? The speaker risks paralyzing self-consciousness in her desire to access landscape, and yet in the process she becomes a part of "non- / thoughts of passengers on the way forward / backward through the hour." The passengers are being pulled backward toward their destination, suspended between thought and non-thought, between moving forward and moving backward, in hovering over a ground that's oversaturated with consideration. Landscape provokes her yearning to move beyond the limitations of thought, and though she does not transcend her boundaries of observation, she "stay[s] with the trouble in speculative fabulation."[35] Hamilton's speaker is "attached to ongoing pasts" and "bring[s] . . . forward in thick presents and still possible futures" herself and those with her on the train.[36]

• • • • •

Whitman wants readers to enter his texts with their own observational skills and reading practices; as he lays out in his 1888 essay "A Backward Glance o'er Travel'd Roads" he wants them to be open to "suggestiveness."[37] His work, he says, gives readers great agency: "The reader will always have his or her part to do, just as much as I have had mine. I seek less to state or display any theme or thought, and more to bring you, reader, into the atmosphere of the theme or thought—there to pursue your own flight." Though we can interpret this as another one of Whitman's attempts to justify inconsistencies within stated goals for his work, I see this as a pronouncement that's consistent with compost. As Jorge Luis Borges first lays out in "Walt Whitman: Man and Myth," all writers are conscious of their relationship to their readers, but Whitman's relationship is unique in that "you [the reader] also are Walt Whitman."[38] Given that "one of Whitman's habits is to think of himself as dead and to think of the reader as coming many centuries after him," Whitman is not only encouraging readers' symbiotic relationship with his texts, he's making readers grow out of him. Whitman's readers come to be merged, companionate, enjoined with him as peat—in a continued practice of making, "in thick copresence" through the poem.[39]

• • • • •

One of Claudia Rankine's untitled prose poems in *Citizen: An American Lyric* begins, "Closed to traffic."[40] Written in second person, it's an account of a viewer noticing what might seem inconsequential: a father pausing to watch his child enter a school building on an "unexpressive street fill[ed] with small bodies" at the start of a day. The scape isn't expansive; we don't have a sense of terrain or exact coordinates. But the location is charged, its histories pulled to the surface by a poet who trusts her readers to intuit what she notices. Rankine's particular use of the second person brings Whitman to mind, for they both enmesh readers in their scenes by activating them with their own noticing: "You can't tell which child is his, though you follow his gaze." The readers' beholding dramatizes and ultimately legitimizes what's being described. But Rankine is leaving a lot out, drawing us into a common experience of parenting while also making us aware of how few specifics are engaged. Despite the power within the father's observation, despite his palpable desire to protect his child and to deflect any possible pain or danger, Rankine's withholding is her primary gesture. Readers sense the "scope of [the father's] vigilance" largely because of his continued watchfulness, but we fill in the rest based on the context of some of the other work in the collection and our own experiences.

What pain, heartache, injustice, racism, or violence might the child confront? The poem is a prolonged moment of loving observation—empathic parenting—and serves as a clear frame around a blurry portal of exchange, a compost-dialogic. Nothing is clearly articulated, or even suggested, about the dynamics of the school or the larger context in which the school is situated, yet the rest of the volume pushes into the edges of the poem. We intuit threat, while simultaneously questioning our intuitions, which then places us within the scene. The father, "having let go of his child's hand," must continue to separate from the child and untether his gaze, despite wanting to remain.

While located within this sphere, we wonder how great the consequences are of letting go. What's the role of the imagination in this poem? How much is in our imagination, the father's fears, and the second-person speaker who does "not want to leave the scope of his vigilance"? Imagination here becomes more than possibility or potential; it becomes probable defense, necessary caution. Rankine, in staying with the trouble, expounds upon the vulnerability of "small bodies" going to school and watchful parents unable to protect them.

• • • • •

How do we learn from what ails us? How do we care for our kin while comingling with the dead? In coming into being as a person with a disease, I have had to admit that I am no longer a spectator but a participant in damage. In one version of my story, my relation to my body is an expression of our ravaged planet, and it has a narrative arc: 1) I am fine; 2) I am in pain, but I still must be fine; 3) I am sick, but others must not know; 4) I have a disease and am unlucky; and 5) I have a disease along with others on earth. In another version of my story, which I share in the dark, I have transformed in the waiting room: 1) I slip off my patient ID wristband and throw it in my bag; 2) the nurses who recognize me in the hematology office think I'm there again with my mother; 3) I tuck my wristband up into my sleeve, but I say hello to the nurses who now know I'm there for myself; 4) I look into the eyes of the others in the waiting room; and 5) I say hello. In another version of the story I write myself out.

• • • • •

In "The Old Whitman and Van Velsor Cemeteries" section of "Specimen Days," Whitman describes visiting his paternal family's gravesite on July 29, 1881: "My whole family history, with its succession of links, from the first settlement down to date, told here—three centuries concentrate on this sterile acre."[41] The next day he visits his maternal family's site, writing "this paragraph on the burial hill": looking at the "significant depository of the dead" and seeing "soil sterile, a mostly bare plateau-flat of half an acre." Whitman is not overtly critical of these burial grounds; he in fact finds them to have an "emotional atmosphere" with "inferr'd reminiscences." Yet I'm struck by the reserve with which he makes his observations. Where are the decomposing bodies that nourish the land? Where is the "Corpse" that he thinks is "good manure," which "does not offend [him]," but in fact helps grow the "white roses sweet-scented and growing" and "polish'd breasts of melons"?[42] In light of his buoyancies about the regenerative benefits of our dead bodies, why does Whitman find traditional burial practices "sterile"?[43] He regularly activates the dead and invites them into a dialogue with readers, yet his own kin seem tamped down and tepid. A jotted goal in one of his notebooks surfaces from the 1850s: "Write a new burial service. A book of new things."[44] Can we find in his poems his plan for new funeral rites? In Whitman's epitaph, drawn in part from the closing section of "Song of Myself," I think we see a business plan for this new "service":

> His poetry was a celebration of life,
> And his philosophy was a preparation for death.
>
> I depart as air, I shake my white locks at the runaway sun.
> I effuse my flesh in eddies and drift it in lacy jags.
>
> I bequeath myself to the dirt to grow from the grass I love.
> If you want me, you can look for me under your boot soles.[45]

• ● ● •

The ground allows for the dead. It seems to esteem the dead, in fact waits for the dead, where our bodies can rejuvenate it. What process of recomposition is available to us? Human composting, in fact, exists as a physically transformative, generative possibility, as an act of "staying with the trouble" in situ.[46] According to Katrina Spade, founder and CEO of Recompose (formerly the Urban Death Project), we have the potential to make nourishing soil from the deceased through a process called recomposition. It's a system to "gently and sustainably" dispose of the dead through composting practices that uses a ratio of carbon (from wood chips) and nitrogen (from bodies),[47] which allow bacteria and microbes to break bodies down in "hot compost piles."[48] "Each year, 2.6 million people die in the US, and most are buried in a cemetery or cremated, impacting land use and contributing to climate change. Wasteful, toxic, and polluting, these options undervalue the potential of our bodies and place an enormous strain on the environment."[49] It takes about six weeks for a human body to break down into finished compost, including bones.

What would it mean to compost this body? Would mine be eligible in the midst of my toxicity? I need Whitman here, "That when I recline on the grass I do not catch any disease, / Though probably every spear of grass rises out of what was once a catching disease."[50] I need an earth that's terrifying in its "calm and patient" ability to grow "such sweet things out of such corruptions" and "with such endless successions of diseas'd corpses." I learn that in the case of my particular medicine, it would take only seven days to leave the body. I am a candidate for compost, as we all are on earth. What filter, this home.

ACKNOWLEDGMENTS

The idea for this book began as a conversation between Kristen and Alexandra on a bench in Concord, Massachusetts, in 2014. Since then it has grown into a labor of love, a nurturing collaborative practice, and a collection of deeply intimate and revealing essays. Along the way the project has been supported and bolstered by an array of people who believed in the value of the work collected here. Thanks are due first to the twelve contributors whose extraordinary, brave work comprises this book, and who rose to the challenge of the brief with indelible grace and eloquence. It was our work with them that convinced us that this book is as much about intimate, risky, collaborative ways of knowing and working as it is about the North American nineteenth century. We are especially grateful to those poets who were part of this project from the very first panel we hosted on the subject in Moscow, Idaho, in 2015: Cecily Parks, Leila Wilson, and Dan Beachy-Quick. Their moving contributions helped us realize that there was room in the world for a book-shaped version of our project. Thanks are also due to Fred Moten who has been unfailingly supportive of this book.

We are also grateful to the people at Milkweed, including Daniel Slager who grasped and embraced the book's vision immediately, Abby Travis for managing the book's production, Annie Harvieux for answering an ongoing deluge of questions, Joey McGarvey for shepherding the book through its final stages, and Mary Austin Speaker for making the book look and feel beautiful. Finally we'd like to thank Haris Pelapaissiotis, Andre Zivanari, and Maria Mina, for hosting us at the Point Centre for Contemporary Arts in Nicosia in 2018 as part of an ongoing series of talks on collaboration, and where we were given the chance to ground our transnational conversation in an intimate, in-person dialogue with an interested audience. We are deeply grateful for the spaces in which this four-year series of conversations has unfolded and for the many voices who have contributed to it. We hope the music of these exchanges resonates with our readers.

• • • •

Grateful acknowledgement to the editors of the following publications:

"Thinking as Burial Practice" by Dan Beachy-Quick first appeared in *Wave Composition* 10, September 7, 2015.

A version of "Revising *The Waste Land*: Black Antipastoral & the End of the World" by Joshua Bennett first appeared in the *Paris Review* blog *The Daily*, January 8, 2018.

"Citation in the Wake of Melville" by Joan Naviyuk Kane first appeared as a chapbook published by Albion Books in 2018.

"Nights and Lights in Nineteenth-Century American Poetics" by Cecily Parks first appeared (as "Nineteenth-Century Nights and Nocturnal Lights") in *Conjunctions* 72 (Spring 2019).

NOTES

Introduction by Kristen Case and Alexandra Manglis: "Unsettling Proximities"

1. "I want to stay with the trouble, and the only way I know to do that is in generative joy, terror, and collective thinking." Donna J. Haraway, *Staying with the Trouble: Making Kin in the Chthulucene* (Durham, NC: Duke University Press, 2016), 31.

2. Christina Sharpe, *In the Wake: On Blackness and Being* (Durham, NC: Duke University Press, 2016), 13.

3. Haraway, *Staying with the Trouble*, 2.

4. Stefano Harney and Fred Moten, *The Undercommons: Fugitive Planning and Black Study* (Brooklyn: Minor Compositions, 2013), 64.

José Felipe Alvergue, "Feeling the Riot: Fugitivity, Lyric, and Enduring Failure"

All citations appearing in the text but not otherwise included in the notes are as follows:

Quoted on pages 26, 27, 29, 31–33: "Race, Rage. The Beating of Rodney King," *CNN Presents* transcript, April 29, 2012, http://transcripts.cnn.com/TRANSCRIPTS/1204/29/cp.01.html.

Quoted on pages 36–38: "Record of Fugitives," 1855, box 75, book 1, Sydney Howard Gay Papers, Rare Book and Manuscript Library, Columbia University.

1. Anthony Reed, *Freedom Time: The Poetics and Politics of Black Experimental Writing* (Baltimore: Johns Hopkins University Press, 2014), 104.

2. See, for instance, the case of Martin Tabert, whose death in 1928, following a "correctional" flogging, resulted in large enough public outcry to call into question the continued existence of the lease system.

3. See the work of architect Jorge Orozco Gonzalez.

4. Albery Allson Whitman, Canto IV, stanza XLVI, in *The Rape of Florida* (1884) (Miami: Mnemosyne Publishing, 1969), 93.

5. Whitman, Canto I, stanza I, *Rape of Florida*, 8.

6. Whitman, Canto IV, stanza XLIV, *Rape of Florida*, 92.

7. Stefano Harney and Fred Moten, *The Undercommons: Fugitive Planning and Black Study* (Brooklyn: Minor Compositions, 2013), 98.

8. The autochthonous labor of the "godless," or the "barbarous" : situated beneath an indigenous provider who stands with feet adjacent to beasts, brow adjacent to white heavens : a

bridge : liminal : in the distance, white colonial destiny in a ship, a monument to the global empirical truth, or Empire.

9. Whitman, Canto I, stanza XXVIII, *Rape of Florida*, 19.

10. George W. Cable, "The Convict Lease System," speech given to Prison Congress in Kentucky, and quoted in Ida B. Wells, "The Convict Lease System," in *The Reason Why the Colored American Is Not in the World's Columbian Exhibition* (Urbana: University of Illinois Press, 1999).

11. Harney and Moten, *The Undercommons*, 98.

12. See Cornel West, *Race Matters* (New York: Vintage, 1995); Calvin Warren, "Black Nihilism and the Politics of Hope," 2015, https://illwilleditions.noblogs.org/files/2015/09/Warren -Black-Nihilism-the-Politics-of-Hope-READ.pdf; Christina Sharpe, *In the Wake: On Blackness and Being* (Durham, NC: Duke University Press, 2016); Alexander G. Weheliye, *Habeas Viscus: Racializing Assemblages, Biopolitics, and Black Feminist Theories of the Human* (Durham, NC: Duke University Press, 2014).

13. Whitman, Canto I, stanza XII, *Rape of Florida*, 13.

14. See Jean-Luc Nancy, "Painting in the Grotto," in *The Muses*, trans. Peggy Kamuf (Stanford, CA: Stanford University Press, 1994), 69–81.

15. Frederick Douglass, "Introduction," in Wells, *The Reason Why*.

16. Achille Mbembe, *On the Postcolony* (Berkeley: University of California Press, 2001), 14. "By age is meant not a simple category of time but a number of relationships and a configuration of events," writes Mbembe, distinguishing *durée* as the multiple spontaneous experiences contained within the postcolony. While the postcolony is itself a heterogeneous epoch (age), *durée* refers to the "discontinuities, reversals, inertias, and swings that overlay one another, interpenetrate one another, and envelope one another" within its historical-material bounds. In his focus on power, Mbembe's *age-durée* entanglement is principally aligned with Michel Foucault, rather than Henri-Louis Bergson's post-Kantian ontical re-rendering of the will, via *durée*.

17. Chantal Mouffe, *The Democratic Paradox* (London: Verso, 2000), 67.

18. Eve Kosofsky Sedgwick, *Touching Feeling: Affect, Pedagogy, Performance* (Durham, NC: Duke University Press, 2003), 68.

19. Thomas DeFrantz and Anita Gonzalez, eds., *Black Performance Theory* (Durham, NC: Duke University Press, 2014), 9.

20. *source* (v.) obtain [by what means]; (n.) a rising, from the Latin *surgere*, "to rise up, get up, attack" [by what means] : "demand is that you speak with a kind of authority" : "You're an ensemble." See Fred Moten's "The General Antagonism" in Harney and Moten, *The Undercommons*, 100–59.

21. Lisa Marie Cacho, *Social Death: Racialized Rightlessness and the Criminalization of the Unprotected* (New York: New York University Press, 2012), 2.

22. Cacho, *Social Death*, 2.

23. See Calvin Bedient, "Against Conceptualism: Defending the Poetry of Affect," *Boston Review*, July 24, 2013, http://bostonreview.net/poetry/against-conceptualism/.

24. Harney and Moten, *The Undercommons*, 93.

25. See Katherine McKittrick, *Demonic Grounds: Black Women and the Cartographies of Struggle* (Minneapolis: University of Minnesota Press, 2006), 3.

26. Harney and Moten, *The Undercommons*, 98.

27. Whitman, Canto IV, stanza XXXII, *Rape of Florida*, 88.

28. Whitman, Canto IV, stanza IX, *Rape of Florida*, 81.

29. Tank and the Bangas, "RollerCoasters," Spotify track 3 on *Think Tank*, Independent, 2013.

30. Warren, "Black Nihilism," 5.

31. David Appelbaum, *Voice* (Albany: State University of New York Press, 1990), 119.

32. Adriana Cavarero, *For More Than One Voice: Toward a Philosophy of Vocal Expression*, trans. Paul A. Kottman (Stanford, CA: Stanford University Press, 2005), 148.

33. Warren, "Black Nihilism," 28.

34. Mouffe, *The Democratic Paradox*, 68.

35. Mouffe, *The Democratic Paradox*, 11.

36. Dred Scott v. Sandford, Benjamin C. Howard, US Supreme Court, Reports of Cases Argued and Adjudged in the Supreme Court of the United States, December Term, 1856 (Washington, DC, 1857), https://www.loc.gov/item/07008916/.

37. Whitman, Canto I, stanza I, *Rape of Florida*, 8.

38. Harney and Moten, *The Undercommons*, 61.

39. Whitman, Canto II, stanza XXXIII, *Rape of Florida*, 39.

40. J. H. Van Evrie, introduction to *The Dred Scott Decision: Opinion of Chief Justice Taney* (New York: Van Evrie, Horton, 1860), iii, https://www.loc.gov/resource/llst.022/?sp=3&st=text.

41. Whitman, Canto II, stanza XXXIV, *Rape of Florida*, 39.

42. Van Evrie, *Dred Scott Decision*, iii.

43. Whitman, Canto II, stanza XXXV, *Rape of Florida*, 39.

44. Colonial precedent cited in Taney's decision in Scott v. Sandford.

45. "Let it go forth, and let mankind attest, / That, Seminoles and exiles, old and young, / Upon the bosom of their country prest: / By valiant deeds are shrined in ev'ry patriot breast!" (Whitman, Canto III, stanza XLV, *Rape of Florida*). The essential confusion is in the recognition of who is and who is not American in the sense of "mankind," who, presumably represented, summoned in the speech of national *writ*. Is the American the *de facto* white body draped in symbols? Is the American the person taking fear inside and standing nonetheless, embracing the promise of an *afterward*? There is a cellphone video that complements an image of Corey Long holding an improvised flamethrower. The video is long enough to capture Richard Wilson Preston yelling out "die nigger" and (after mistakenly trying to do so with the safety on) shooting his gun at Mr. Long, then walking away with the rest of the Alt-Right demonstrators in Charlottesville, Virginia: Easily melding into the white crowd, with some children present, their parents, and others in bulletproof vests. Who is the patriot?

Karen Weiser, "Touching Horror: Poe, Race, and Gun Violence"

1. Adam Phillips, *Missing Out: In Praise of the Unlived Life* (New York: Picador, 2013).

2. Teresa Brennan, *The Transmission of Affect* (Cambridge: Cambridge University Press, 2004), 90–92.

3. Susan Howe, thinking of Charles Olson's statement "The stutter is the plot," responds: "It's the stutter in American literature that interests me. I hear the stutter as a sounding of uncertainty. What is silence or not quite silenced [as in *Billy Budd*]. . . . A return is necessary, a way for women to go. Because we are in the stutter. We were expelled from the Garden of the Mythology of the American Frontier. The drama's done. We are the wilderness. We have come on to the stage stuttering." Susan Howe, "*Talisman* Interview, with Edward Foster," in *The Birth-Mark: Unsettling the Wilderness in American Literary History* (Middletown, CT: Wesleyan University Press, 1993), 181.

4. Edgar Allan Poe, "Chapter 18," in *The Narrative of Arthur Gordon Pym* (New York: Harper and Brothers, 1838), https://www.eapoe.org/works/tales/pymb18.htm.

5. Audre Lorde, "The Transformation of Silence into Language and Action," in *Sister Outsider: Essays and Speeches by Audre Lorde* (Berkeley: Crossing Press, 2007), 40–44.

6. This essay was written during the election and early days of the Trump administration. Since then, as white supremacy groups have been emboldened, due to the early and influential role in the White House of the Alt-Right, the conversation on the legacy of the Confederacy and on the current state of race in the US has changed. Trump systematically has taken apart any protections for people of color and women that the Obama administration put in place, as if attempting to push the country back into a state of white supremacy (also patriarchy). The events of Charlottesville, i.e., the killing of Heather Heyer (a protester) by a white supremacist, and Trump's refusal to immediately condemn white supremacy and Nazism have clearly laid bare the racial dynamics at work and the terrifying strength of white supremacy movements, which have always been present but are now emboldened. These events highlight the need for more protest, not only against Trump and his policies, but also against continuing routine police violence against people of color.

7. Tamir Rice's death so clearly illustrates what Claudia Rankine famously writes in her book of poems *Citizen*: "Because white men can't / police their *imagination* / black men are dying" (my emphasis). In *Citizen: An American Lyric* (Minneapolis: Graywolf Press, 2014), 135.

8. This essay responds to current calls to move beyond a "hermeneutics of suspicion" as articulated by Eve Sedgwick, *Touching Feeling: Affect, Pedagogy, Performativity* (Durham, NC: Duke University Press, 2003); Bruno Latour, "Why Has Critique Run Out of Steam? From Matters of Fact to Matters of Concern," *Critical Inquiry* 30, no. 2 (Winter 2004): 225–48; and Rita Felski, *The Limits of Critique* (Chicago: University of Chicago Press, 2015).

9. Claudia Rankine, "The Condition of Black Life Is One of Mourning," *New York Times*, June 22, 2015, https://www.nytimes.com/2015/06/22/magazine/the-condition-of-black-life-is-one-of-mourning.html.

10. Rankine, "The Condition of Black Life."

11. Rankine, *Citizen*.

12. Rankine, "The Condition of Black Life."

13. Sarah Schulman, "Open Casket," *ArtsEverywhere* (blog), April 12, 2017, http://artsevery where.ca/2017/04/12/open-casket/.

14. Gwendolyn Brooks, "The Last Quatrain of the Ballad of Emmett Till," in *The Bean Eaters* (Whitefish, MT: Literary Licensing, 1960).

15. Schulman, "Open Casket." From the essay's introduction on *ArtsEverywhere* blog: "In offering the text to *ArtsEverywhere* for publication, Schulman noted that LitHub declined to publish the text after she refused to delete the concluding paragraph regarding the Palestinian Solidarity Movement."

16. Edgar Allan Poe, "The Facts in the Case of M. Valdemar," *American Review*, December 1845.

17. Seth Colter Walls, "Reviving the Ghostly Sounds of Maryanne Amarcher," *New York Times*, May 19, 2017, https://www.nytimes.com/2017/05/19/arts/music/reviving-the-ghostly-sounds -of-maryanne-amacher.html.

18. Arthur Hobson Quinn, *Edgar Allan Poe: A Critical Biography* (New York: Appleton-Century, 1941), 485.

19. Julia Kristeva, *Powers of Horror: An Essay of Abjection*, trans. Leon Roudiez (New York: Columbia University Press, 1982), 3.

20. Ludwig Wittgenstein, *Tractatus Logico-Philosophicus*, trans. D. F. Pears and B. F. McGuinness (Atlantic Highlands, NJ: Humanities Press International, 1992).

21. Toni Morrison, *Playing in the Dark: Whiteness and the Literary Imagination* (Cambridge, MA: Harvard University Press, 1992), 32.

22. Terence Whalen, *Edgar Allan Poe and the Masses: The Political Economy of Literature in Antebellum America* (Princeton, NJ: Princeton University Press, 1999).

23. Edgar Allan Poe, letter to Thomas W. White, April 30, 1835, Edgar Allan Poe Society of Baltimore website, https://www.eapoe.org/works/letters/p3504300.htm.

24. Duncan Faherty, "'Legitimate Sources' and 'Legitimate Results': Surveying the Social Terror of 'Usher' and 'Ligeia,'" in *Approaches to Teaching Poe's Prose and Poetry*, ed. Jeffrey Andrew Weinstock and Tony Magistrale (New York: MLA, 2008), 39–47.

25. Heben Nigatu and Tracy Clayton, "83: Incognegro (with Jordan Peele)," March 1, 2017, in *Another Round*, produced by WNYC, podcast, MP3 audio, 00:56:31, https://www.acast.com /anotherround/episode-83-incognegro-with-jordan-peele.

26. Erica Hunt, "Risk Signature," *Bomb Magazine*, January 1, 1997, https://bombmagazine.org /articles/three-poems-77/.

27. Hunt, "Risk Signature."

28. I want to thank Carley Moore, Anton Borst, Hoa Nguyen, Kristen Case, Matt Longabucco, Edvige Giunta, and Alexandra Manglis for giving me help and permission in this endeavor.

Benjamin Friedlander, "Homage to Bayard Taylor"

1. Robert K. Martin, *The Homosexual Tradition in American Poetry* (Austin: University of Texas Press, 1979), 91, 92, 105.

2. Martin, *The Homosexual Tradition*, 101.

3. Martin, *The Homosexual Tradition*, 103.

4. Martin, *The Homosexual Tradition*, 91.

5. For an excellent review of the issues involved in giving a name to Taylor's erotic life, see Liam Corley's recent *Bayard Taylor: Determined Dreamer of America's Rise, 1825–1878* (Lewisburg, PA: Bucknell University Press, 2014).

6. Martin calls the story of Hylas "one of the most important myths for homosexuals" (*The Homosexual Tradition*, 101), making delicious the fact that Tennyson would, when the poets met, recite the Greek text to Taylor over sherry, an anecdote shared by Taylor in a letter to Edmund Clarence Stedman. See Bayard Taylor, *Selected Letters*, ed. Paul C. Wermuth (Lewisburg, PA: Bucknell University Press, 1997), 305.

7. Theocritus, *The Greek Bucolic Poets*, trans. J. M. Edmonds (New York: Macmillan, 1912), 157.

8. Bayard Taylor, *A Book of Romances, Lyrics, and Songs* (Boston: Ticknor, Reed, and Fields, 1852), 33–34.

9. Byrne R. S. Fone, *Masculine Landscapes: Walt Whitman and the Homoerotic Text* (Carbondale: Southern Illinois University Press, 1992), 226.

10. Taylor, *Selected Letters*, 294.

11. This theme of law and counter-law is also prominent in Taylor's *Joseph and His Friend*, evident in the early cry, "Who built a wall of imaginary law around these needs, which are in themselves inexorable laws?"; and in the later exclamation, "[T]here must be a loftier faith, a juster law, for the men—and the women—who cannot shape themselves according to the common-place pattern of society,—who were born with instincts, needs, knowledge, and rights—ay, *rights!*—of their own!" See Bayard Taylor, *Joseph and His Friend: A Story of Pennsylvania* (New York: G. P. Putnam and Sons, 1870), 50, 214.

12. I will not take up here the methodological issues, now familiar, that follow from what Jonathan Ned Katz calls—discussing Whitman "retrolabeling," which he usefully distinguishes from *mis*labeling, arguing for a wary anachronism that accommodates historical understanding: "Homing in on the historically specific character of nineteenth-century men's love of men and friendship with them requires us to take their language, ideas and social arrangements seriously. But it *does not* require us to take those words, concepts, and institutions exactly as they were understood in the past." See Katz, *Love Stories: Sex between Men before Homosexuality* (Chicago: University of Chicago Press, 2001), 333–34. Louise Fradenburg and Carla Freccero, less concerned with accommodation, argue for a historiography grounded in desire, "a joy of finding counterparts in the past." See *Premodern Sexualities*, ed. Fradenburg and Freccero (New York: Routledge, 1996), viii. But certain writers are ill-served by this pursuit; as Liam Corley notes (*Bayard Taylor*, 139–40):

> It is too easy to judge those writers as repressed or ignorant of their own desires and thus retrospectively free them from constraints they had either chosen or constructed for themselves as an integral aspect of their aesthetic practice. . . . [W]e should resist the pull of melioristic narratives of same-sex relations which would explain the sexual alterity of a figure like Bayard Taylor as a deficiency in terms of self-understanding or aesthetic accomplishment.

13. See Christopher Nealon, *Foundlings: Lesbian and Gay Historical Emotion before Stonewall* (Durham, NC: Duke University Press, 2001), 1–2.

14. Martin, *The Homosexual Tradition*, 103.

15. Taylor, *Joseph and His Friend*, 217.

16. Christopher Castiglia and Christopher Looby, "Come Again? New Approaches to Sexuality in Nineteenth-Century U.S. Literature," *ESQ* 55, no. 3–4 (2009): 195–209.

17. Castiglia and Looby, "Come Again?," 196.

18. Nealon, *Foundlings*, 177.

19. Nealon, *Foundlings*, 4–7.

20. Taylor, *Joseph and His Friend*, 112.

21. Christopher Looby, "The Literariness of Sexuality: Or, How to Do the (Literary) History of (American) Sexuality," *American Literary History* 25, no. 4 (Winter 2013): 845.

22. Castiglia and Looby, "Come Again?," 196.

23. Michael André Bernstein, *Foregone Conclusions: Against Apocalyptic History* (Berkeley: University of California Press, 1994), 16.

24. Peter Coviello, *Tomorrow's Parties: Sex and the Untimely in Nineteenth-Century America* (New York: New York University Press, 2013), 11.

25. Coviello, *Tomorrow's Parties*, 44.

26. Coviello, *Tomorrow's Parties*, 84, 86.

27. Coviello, *Tomorrow's Parties*, 22.

28. Coviello, *Tomorrow's Parties*, 4.

29. Coviello, *Tomorrow's Parties*, 204.

30. Marie Hansen-Taylor and Horace Scudder, eds., *Life and Letters of Bayard Taylor, Volume 1* (Boston: Houghton Mifflin, 1885), 224.

31. Taylor, *Selected Letters*, 96–97.

32. Hansen-Taylor and Scudder, *Life and Letters*, 1:307.

33. Russell H. Conwell, *The Life, Travels, and Literary Career of Bayard Taylor* (Boston: B. B. Russell, 1879), 156.

34. Coviello, *Tomorrow's Parties*, 8.

35. Giorgio Agamben, *The Sacrament of Language: An Archaeology of the Oath*, trans. Adam Kotsko (Stanford, CA: Stanford University Press, 2011), 71.

36. Martin, *The Homosexual Tradition*; Fone, *Masculine Landscapes*; and Corley, *Bayard Taylor*.

37. Taylor, preface to *Joseph and His Friend*.

38. The quoted lines here and below come from the poem's first book printing. Taylor, *A Book of Romances*, 46–52.

39. Bayard Taylor, preface to Johann Wolfgang von Goethe, *Faust: A Tragedy* (Boston: Houghton Mifflin, 1870).

40. G. H. B. [George Henry Boker], preface to *The Poetical Works of Bayard Taylor* (Boston: Houghton, Osgood, 1880), iii.

41. G. H. B., preface to *The Poetical Works*, iii.

42. Bayard Taylor, *The Poetical Works of Bayard Taylor*, household edition (Boston: Houghton Mifflin, 1902).

43. Walt Whitman, *Notebooks and Unpublished Prose Manuscripts, Volume 5*, ed. Edward F. Grier (New York: New York University Press, 1984), 1771.

Joshua Bennett, "Revising *The Waste Land*: Black Antipastoral & The End of the World"

1. Christina Sharpe, *In the Wake: On Blackness and Being* (Durham, NC: Duke University Press, 2016), 106.

2. Janelle Monáe, Big Boi, and Saul Williams, "Dance or Die," *The ArchAndroid*, Bad Boy Records, 2010, compact disc.

3. June Jordan, "On a New Year's Eve," in *Directed by Desire: The Collected Poems of June Jordan* (Port Townsend, WA: Copper Canyon Press, 2007), 206.

4. "Kea Tawana," obituary, *Middletown (NY) Times Herald-Record*, August 25, 2016, http://www.recordonline.com/article/20160826/OBITUARIES/308269995/-1/NEWS14.

5. I am thinking not only of the Newark Rebellion of 1967, but the singular legacy of one of Newark's most famous sons, the late Amiri Baraka, whose film *The New-Ark* was released a year later, and signals in its title some of this essay's central concerns. See *The New-Ark*, directed by Amiri Baraka (Newark, NJ: Amiri Baraka, 1968), DVD.

6. Chip Brown, "Kea's Improbable Ark," *Chicago Tribune*, April 22, 1987, http://articles.chicago tribune.com/1987-04-22/features/8701300910_1_kea-tawana-red-pine-central-ward.

7. Countee Cullen, *The Lost Zoo*, illustrated by Joseph Low (Westchester, IL: Follett, 1969).

8. Camilo Vergara, "Why Newark's Ark Should Be Saved," *New York Times*, April 26, 1987, http://www.nytimes.com/1987/04/26/nyregion/new-jersey-opinion-why-newark-s-ark -should-be-saved.html?pagewanted=all.

9. "Geopoetics" is a gesture toward the writing of Kenneth White, and this is his own critical coinage. It is especially useful for my purposes given its etymological roots in the earth as opposed to the *oikos* of the ancient Greeks, the home, the very site which grounds the ecopoetic register through which we might otherwise approach these matters.

10. Henry Dumas, *Knees of a Natural Man: The Selected Poetry*, ed. Eugene Redmond (New York: Thunder's Mouth Press, 1989).

11. Camille T. Dungy, ed., *Black Nature: Four Centuries of African American Nature Poetry* (Athens: University of Georgia Press, 2009), 6.

12. See Jared Sexton, "Afro-Pessimism: The Unclear Word," *Rhizomes: Cultural Studies in Emerging Knowledge* 29 (2016), doi.org/10.20415/rhiz/029.e02.

13. James Monroe Whitfield, "The Misanthropist," in *African-American Poetry of the Nineteenth Century: An Anthology*, ed. Joan R. Sherman (Champaign: University of Illinois Press, 1992), 81. See also the Poetry Foundation website: https://www.poetryfoundation.org/poems/52478 /the-misanthropist.

14. I am borrowing this phrase from David Kishik, *The Power of Life: Agamben and the Coming Politics, Volume 2* (Stanford, CA: Stanford University Press, 2012).

15. See Claudia Rankine, *Citizen: An American Lyric* (Minneapolis: Graywolf Press, 2014).

16. Max Horkheimer and Theodor W. Adorno, *Dialectic of Enlightenment*, ed. Gunzelin Noeri, trans. Edmund Jephcott (Stanford, CA: Stanford University Press, 2002), 2.

17. Whitfield, "The Misanthropist," 81–82.

18. Ralph Ellison, *Invisible Man* (New York: Penguin, 2014).

19. Ed Roberson, "We Must Be Careful," in *Black Nature*, 3.

20. See Paul Laurence Dunbar, "We Wear the Mask," *Lyrics of Lowly Life* (New York: Dodd, Mead, 1898), 167.

21. Whitfield, "The Misanthropist," 85.

22. Countee Cullen, "Yet Do I Marvel," in *The Black Poets*, ed. Dudley Randall (New York: Bantam, 1971), 100.

23. Phillip B. Williams, "Mastery," *Paris Review* 223 (Winter 2017), https://www.theparis review.org/poetry/7093/mastery-phillip-b-williams.

24. See Phillip B. Williams, *Thief in the Interior* (Farmington, ME: Alice James Books, 2016).

25. See Giorgio Agamben, *The Open: Man and Animal* (Stanford, CA: Stanford University Press, 2004).

26. Cherríe Moraga and Gloria Anzaldúa, eds., *This Bridge Called My Back: Writings by Radical Women of Color* (Albany: State University of New York Press, 2015).

27. Williams, "Mastery."

28. Exod. 11:4–6, King James Version.

29. Toni Morrison, *Beloved* (Philadelphia: Chelsea House, 1987).

30. Williams, "Mastery."

31. Williams, "Mastery."

32. Toni Morrison, *Song of Solomon* (New York: Vintage, 2004).

Cole Swensen, "Henry Ossawa Tanner: Night Over Night"

1. Marcia M. Mathews, *Henry Ossawa Tanner: American Artist* (Chicago: University of Chicago Press, 1969), 54.

2. Mathews, *Henry Ossawa Tanner*, 236.

Cecily Parks, "Nights and Lights in Nineteenth-Century American Poetics"

1. Lisa Vargues, "Flashes in the Twilight," *Science Talk: Exploring the Science of Plants, from the Field to the Lab* (blog), New York Botanical Garden, December 30, 2013, https://www.nybg .org/blogs/science-talk/2013/12/flashes-in-the-twilight/.

2. Hermon Bourne, "Nasturtion" entry in *Flores Poetici, The Florist's Manual: Designed as an Introduction to Vegetable Physiology and Systematic Botany for Cultivators of Flowers* (Boston: Munroe and Francis, 1833), 138–39, https://babel.hathitrust.org/cgi/pt?id=nyp.33433006561 470;view=1up;seq=108.

3. Asa B. Strong, MD, *The American Flora; or, History of Plants and Wild Flowers* (New York: Green and Spencer, 1845–50), 186, quoted in Karen Kilcup, *Fallen Forests: Emotion, Embodiment,*

and Ethics in American Women's Environmental Writing, 1781–1924 (Athens: University of Georgia Press, 2013), 405.

4. Judith Farr, *The Gardens of Emily Dickinson* (Cambridge, MA: Harvard University Press, 2005), 33.

5. Emily Dickinson, "We grow accustomed to the Dark — / When Light is put away —" (Fr 428), in *The Poems of Emily Dickinson: Reading Edition*, ed. R. W. Franklin (Cambridge, MA: Belknap Press of Harvard University Press, 2005), 198.

6. *A Quiet Passion*, directed by Terence Davies (2017; Chicago: Music Box Films, 2017), DVD.

7. Susan Stewart, *Poetry and the Fate of the Senses* (Chicago: University of Chicago Press, 2002), 2.

8. Mary Ruefle, "Poetry and the Moon," in *Madness, Rack, and Honey* (Seattle: Wave Books, 2012), 12.

9. Stewart, *Poetry*, 3.

10. Henry David Thoreau, *The Journal of Henry David Thoreau, 1837–1861*, ed. Damion Searls (New York: New York Review Books Classics, 2009), 523.

11. *Oxford English Dictionary*, s.v. "o'nights," accessed December 6, 2017, http://www.oed.com .libproxy.txstate.edu/view/Entry/126965.

12. "o'nights," Google Ngram viewer, accessed December 6, 2017, https://books.google.com /ngrams/graph?content=o%27nights&year_start=1800&year_end=2000&corpus=15 &smoothing=3&share=&direct_url=t1%3B%2Co%27nights%3B%2Cc0.

13. Robert Macfarlane, *Landmarks* (New York: Penguin Books, 2015), 3.

14. Emily Dickinson, L29, in *The Letters of Emily Dickinson*, ed. Thomas H. Johnson and Theodora Ward (Cambridge, MA: Belknap Press of Harvard University Press, 1986), 79.

15. Dickinson, "Those — dying then" (Fr 1581), in *Poems*, 582.

16. Henry David Thoreau, "Walking," in *Collected Essays and Poems*, ed. Elizabeth Hall Witherell (New York: Library of America, 2001), 251.

17. Henry David Thoreau, *The Maine Woods*, in *A Week on the Concord and Merrimack Rivers, Walden, The Maine Woods, Cape Cod* (New York: Library of America, 1985), 730.

18. Thoreau, *The Maine Woods*, 730–31.

19. Thoreau, *The Maine Woods*, 731.

20. Henry David Thoreau, "Night and Moonlight," *Atlantic Monthly*, November 1863, 579–83, https://archive.vcu.edu/english/engweb/transcendentalism/authors/thoreau/night-moon light.html.

21. Washington Irving, "The Legend of Sleepy Hollow," Project Gutenberg, https://www .gutenberg.org/files/41/41-h/41-h.htm.

22. Irving, "Sleepy Hollow."

23. Thomas Wentworth Higginson, *Army Life in a Black Regiment*, American Antiquarian Society, http://www.americanantiquarian.org/Freedmen/Manuscripts/higginson.html.

24. Dickinson, L330a, in *Letters*, 461.

25. Ruefle, "Poetry and the Moon," 14.

26. Ruefle, "Poetry and the Moon," 27.

27. Dickinson, "Wild nights — Wild nights!" (Fr 269), in *Poems*, 120.

28. Dana Phillips, *The Truth of Ecology: Nature, Culture, and Literature in America* (Oxford: Oxford University Press, 2003), 212.

29. Thoreau, *The Maine Woods*, 732.

30. Howell G. M. Edwards, "Will-o'-the-Wisp: An Ancient Mystery with Extremophile Origins?," *Philosophical Transactions of the Royal Society A: Mathematical, Physical, and Engineering Sciences*, December 13, 2014, http://rsta.royalsocietypublishing.org/content/372/2030/20140206.

31. Vargues, "Flashes in the Twilight."

Brian Teare, "The Earth Is Full of Men"

1. Ralph Waldo Emerson, "The Poet," in *Selections from Ralph Waldo Emerson*, ed. Stephen E. Whichler (New York: Houghton Mifflin, 1957), 224.

2. Emerson, "The Poet," 232.

3. Tommy Pico, *Nature Poem* (Portland, OR: Tin House Books, 2017), 37.

4. Emerson, "The Poet," 231.

5. Pico, *Nature Poem*, 50.

6. Pico, *Nature Poem*, 62.

7. Pico, *Nature Poem*, 16.

8. Pico, *Nature Poem*, 55.

9. Pico, *Nature Poem*, 24.

10. Pico, *Nature Poem*, 30.

11. Pico, *Nature Poem*, 32.

12. Pico, *Nature Poem*, 2.

13. Pico, *Nature Poem*, 43.

14. Pico, *Nature Poem*, 60.

15. William Cullen Bryant, *The Letters of William Cullen Bryant, Volume II, 1836–1849*, ed. William Cullen Bryant II and Thomas G. Voss (New York: Fordham University Press, 1977), 359.

16. Bryant, *Letters*, 338.

17. William Cullen Bryant, "The Prairies," Poetry Foundation, https://www.poetryfoundation .org/poems/55341/the-prairies.

18. Bryant, "The Prairies."

19. Laura Dassow Walls, *Seeing New Worlds: Henry David Thoreau and Nineteenth-Century Natural Science* (Madison: University of Wisconsin Press, 1995), 21.

20. Walls, *Seeing New Worlds*, 21.

21. Pico, *Nature Poem*, 2.

22. Pico, *Nature Poem*, 50.

23. Pico, *Nature Poem*, 56.

24. Pico, *Nature Poem*, 2.

25. Pico, *Nature Poem*, 15.

26. Pico, *Nature Poem*, 22.

27. Pico, *Nature Poem*, 62.

28. Pico, *Nature Poem*, 5.

29. Pico, *Nature Poem*, 55.

30. Pico, *Nature Poem*, 43.

31. Charles Capper, *Margaret Fuller: An American Romantic Life, Volume II: The Public Years* (Oxford: Oxford University Press, 2007), 124.

32. Capper, *Margaret Fuller*, 125.

33. Margaret Fuller, *Summer on the Lakes, in 1843*, in *The Portable Margaret Fuller*, ed. Mary Kelly (New York: Penguin Books, 1994), 173.

34. Fuller, *Summer*, 182.

35. Fuller, *Summer*, 189.

36. Fuller, *Summer*, 100.

37. Margaret Fuller, *The Letters of Margaret Fuller, Volume III, 1842–1844*, ed. Robert N. Hudspeth (Ithaca, NY: Cornell University Press, 1984), 134.

38. Fuller, *Summer*, 100.

39. Fuller, *Letters*, 132.

40. Roderick Beaton, "From Ancient to Modern: Byron, Shelley, and the Idea of Greece," *Athens Dialogues* 1 (2010): 1–22, http://athensdialogues.chs.harvard.edu/cgi-bin/WebObjects /athensdialogues.woa/wa/dist?dis=17.

41. Fuller, *Summer*, 100–01.

42. Capper, *Margaret Fuller*, 146.

43. Fuller, *Summer*, 101.

44. Fuller, *Summer*, 103–04.

45. Fuller, *Summer*, 104.

46. Fuller, *Summer*, 101.

47. Fuller, *Summer*, 102.

48. Capper, *Margaret Fuller*, 127.

49. Joshua Bellin, "Native American Rights," in *The Oxford Handbook of Transcendentalism*, ed. Joel Myerson, Sandra Harbert Petrulionis, and Laura Dassow Walls (Oxford: Oxford University Press, 2010), 198–99.

50. Pico, *Nature Poem*, 22.

51. Pico, *Nature Poem*, 65.

52. Pico, *Nature Poem*, 62.

53. Pico, *Nature Poem*, 67.

54. Pico, *Nature Poem*, 72.

55. Pico, *Nature Poem*, 72.

56. Pico, *Nature Poem*, 71.

57. Pico, *Nature Poem*, 73.

58. Pico, *Nature Poem*, 71.

59. Emerson, "The Poet," 227.

60. Fuller, *Summer*, 101.

61. Pico, *Nature Poem*, 74.

M. NourbeSe Philip, "Making Black Cake in Combustible Spaces"

1. All sections in italics come from the following text: M. NourbeSe Philip, "Burn Sugar," in *Imagining Women*, ed. Rhea Tregebov (Toronto: Women's Press, 1988).

2. I use the word "demotic" to describe the vernaculars of the Caribbean. Other writers, including Kamau Brathwaite, use the expression "nation language" to talk of the same linguistic practice.

3. M. NourbeSe Philip, "The Absence of Writing or How I Almost Became a Spy," in *She Tries Her Tongue; Her Silence Softly Breaks* (Middletown, CT: Wesleyan University Press, 2014), 76–91.

4. Davia Nelson and Nikki Silva, "62: Black Cake, Emily Dickinson's Hidden Kitchen," January 10, 2017, in *The Kitchen Sisters Present*, produced by PRX, podcast, MP3 audio, 00:32:39, https://www.kitchensisters.org/2017/01/10/episode-62-black-cake-emily-dickinsons-hidden-kitchen/.

5. Emilie Hardman of Harvard's Houghton Library, quoted in Nelson and Silva, "62: Black Cake."

6. Aife Murray, *Maid as Muse* (Lebanon: University of New Hampshire Press, 2009).

7. Murray, *Maid as Muse*, 24.

8. Murray, *Maid as Muse*, 15.

9. Murray, *Maid as Muse*, 15.

10. Hardman, quoted in Nelson and Silva, "62: Black Cake."

11. The philosopher's stone was thought to ensure enlightenment and immortality. It could turn base metals into gold. The alchemical process became a central metaphor in Carl Jung's therapeutic process of individuation.

12. Gaston Bachelard, *On Poetic Imagination and Reverie*, trans. C. Gaudin (Indianapolis: Bobbs-Merrill, 1971).

13. See Edouard Glissant, *The Poetics of Relations*, trans. Betsy Wing (Ann Arbor: University of Michigan Press, 1997).

Leila Wilson, "'The Tinge Awakes': Reading Whitman and Others in Trouble"

1. Walt Whitman, "Crossing Brooklyn Ferry," in *The Portable Walt Whitman*, ed. Michael Warner (New York: Penguin, 2004), 133.

2. Whitman, "Crossing Brooklyn Ferry," 133–34.

3. Oliver Sacks, *Migraine* (New York: Vintage, 1999), 278.

4. Whitman, "Crossing Brooklyn Ferry," 132.

5. Walt Whitman, "Song of Myself," in *The Portable Walt Whitman*, 65.

6. Whitman, "Song of Myself," 77.

7. Joyelle McSweeney, "What Is the Necropastoral?," *Harriet* (blog), Poetry Foundation, April 29, 2014, https://www.poetryfoundation.org/harriet/2014/04/what-is-the-necropastoral.

8. Walt Whitman, "This Compost," in *The Portable Walt Whitman,* 129.

9. Whitman, "Song of Myself," 3.

10. Donna J. Haraway, *Staying with the Trouble: Making Kin in the Chthulucene* (Durham, NC: Duke University Press, 2016), 58.

11. Haraway, *Staying with the Trouble,* 7.

12. Haraway, *Staying with the Trouble,* 4.

13. Haraway, *Staying with the Trouble,* 118.

14. Whitman, "Song of Myself," 66.

15. Walt Whitman, "Democratic Vistas," in *The Portable Walt Whitman,* 456.

16. Whitman, "Democratic Vistas," 456.

17. Whitman, "Democratic Vistas," 457.

18. Whitman, "Democratic Vistas," 456.

19. Haraway, *Staying with the Trouble,* 4.

20. Unless noted otherwise, all quotations in this section are taken from Carl Phillips, "After the Afterlife," in *Silverchest* (New York: Farrar, Straus and Giroux, 2014), 13.

21. Walt Whitman, "Unseen Buds," in *The Portable Walt Whitman*, 314.

22. Phillips, "After the Afterlife," 13.

23. Ken Chen, "What's the Matter with Poetry?," *New Republic*, June 23, 2016, https://www.newrepublic.com/article/134504/whats-matter-poetry.

24. Haraway, *Staying with the Trouble,* 3.

25. Unless noted otherwise, all quotations in this section are taken from Christina Davis, "Concord," in *An Ethic* (Callicoon, NY: Nightboat Books, 2013).

26. Whitman, "Crossing Brooklyn Ferry," 133.

27. Davis, "Concord," 43.

28. Richard McGuire, *Here* (New York: Pantheon, 2014). There are no chapters or page numbers in this 304-page book.

29. John Ruskin, *The Complete Works*, ed. E. T. Cook and Alexander Wedderburn (London: Allen, 1903), 4:81.

30. Whitman, "Crossing Brooklyn Ferry," 132.

31. Walt Whitman, "Song of the Open Road," in *The Portable Walt Whitman,* 140.

32. Walt Whitman, letter to William D. O'Connor, October 7, 1882, Walt Whitman Archive, gen. eds. Ed Folsom and Kenneth M. Price, https://www.whitmanarchive.org/.

33. Whitman, letter to William D. O'Connor.

34. Unless noted otherwise, all quotations in this section are taken from Saskia Hamilton, "Flatlands," in *Corridor* (Minneapolis: Graywolf Press, 2014), 15.

35. Haraway, *Staying with the Trouble*, 133.

36. Hamilton, "Flatlands," 15.

37. Walt Whitman, "A Backward Glance o'er Travel'd Roads," in *The Portable Walt Whitman*, 389.

38. Jorge Luis Borges, "Walt Whitman: Man and Myth," *Critical Inquiry* 1, no. 4 (1975): 707–18, http://www.jstor.org/stable/1342843.

39. Haraway, *Staying with the Trouble*, 4.

40. Unless noted otherwise, all quotations in this section are taken from Claudia Rankine, *Citizen: An American Lyric* (Minneapolis: Graywolf Press, 2014), 149.

41. Unless noted otherwise, all quotations in this section are taken from Walt Whitman, "Specimen Days," in *The Portable Walt Whitman*, 467.

42. Whitman, "Song of Myself," 65.

43. Whitman, "Specimen Days," 467.

44. Walt Whitman, *Notebooks and Unpublished Prose Manuscripts*, ed. Edward F. Grier (New York: New York University Press, 1984), 4:1313.

45. Walt Whitman, epitaph, Walt Whitman Mausoleum, Harleigh Cemetary, Camden, New Jersey.

46. Haraway, *Staying with the Trouble*, 4.

47. Urban Death Project, "What's Wrong with Our Current Funeral Practices?," http://www.urbandeathproject.org/.

48. Haraway, *Staying with the Trouble*, 4.

49. Urban Death Project, "What's Wrong."

50. Whitman, "This Compost," 130.

BIBLIOGRAPHY

Foreword by Fred Moten: "Approximity (in the Life, Her Attempt to Bring the Life of Her Mother Close"

Baldwin, James. *The Fire Next Time*. New York: Vintage, 1992.

Barad, Karen. *Meeting the Universe Halfway: Quantum Physics and the Entanglement of Matter and Meaning*. Durham, NC: Duke University Press, 2007.

Clark, T. J. "World of Faces: Face to Face with Rembrandt." *London Review of Books* 36, no. 3 (December 2014): 16–18.

Jacobs, Harriet. *Incidents in the Life of a Slave Girl*. New York: Penguin, 2000.

Long Soldier, Layli. *Whereas*. Minneapolis: Graywolf Press, 2017.

Mackey, Nathaniel. *Bedouin Hornbook*. Los Angeles: Sun and Moon Classics, 2000.

Patterson, Orlando. *Slavery and Social Death; A Comparative Study*. Cambridge, MA: Harvard University Press, 1982.

Prescod, Margaret. "Sojourner Truth Radio: A Tribute to L.A. Skid Row Activist Kevin Michael Key." July 27, 2017. https://soundcloud.com/sojournertruthradio/a-tribute-to-la-skid-row-activist-kevin-michael-key.

White, Simone. *Dear Angel of Death*. New York: Ugly Duckling Presse, 2018.

Williamson, Terrion. *Scandalize Her Name: Black Feminist Practice and the Making of Black Social Life*. New York: Fordham University Press, 2016.

Woods, Suné. *Falling to Get Here*. 2015. Video.

Zitkala-Ša. *American Indian Stories, Legends, and Other Writings*. New York: Penguin, 2003.

Introduction by Kristen Case and Alexandra Manglis: "Unsettling Proximities"

Emerson, Ralph Waldo. *The Essential Writings of Ralph Waldo Emerson*. Edited by Brooks Atkinson. New York: Modern Library, 2000.

Haraway, Donna J. *Staying with the Trouble: Making Kin in the Chthulucene*. Durham, NC: Duke University Press, 2016.

Harney, Stefano, and Fred Moten. *The Undercommons: Fugitive Planning and Black Study*. Brooklyn: Minor Compositions, 2013.

Parks, Cecily. *O'Nights*. Farmington, ME: Alice James, 2015.

Philip, M. NourbeSe. "Burn Sugar." In *Imagining Women*, edited by Rhea Tregebov. Toronto: Women's Press, 1988.

Sharpe, Christina. *In the Wake: On Blackness and Being*. Durham, NC: Duke University Press, 2016.

Dan Beachy-Quick: "Thinking as Burial Practice: Exhuming a Poetic Epistemology in Thoreau, Dickinson, and Emerson"

Dickinson, Emily. *The Poems of Emily Dickinson: Variorum Edition*. Edited by Ralph W. Franklin. Cambridge, MA: Harvard University Press, 1983.

Emerson, Ralph Waldo. *The Essential Writings of Ralph Waldo Emerson*. Edited by Brooks Atkinson. New York: Modern Library, 2000.

Thoreau, Henry David. *Walden*. Boston: Beacon Press, 2004.

Wittgenstein, Ludwig. *Tractatus Logico-Philosophicus*. Translated by C. K. Ogden. Mineola, NY: Dover, 1999.

José Felipe Alvergue, "Feeling the Riot: Fugitivity, Lyric, and Enduring Failure"

Appelbaum, David. *Voice*. Albany: State University of New York Press, 1990.

Bedient, Calvin. "Against Conceptualism: Defending the Poetry of Affect." *Boston Review*, July 24, 2013. http://bostonreview.net/poetry/against-conceptualism.

Cable, George W. *The Negro Question*. New York: Scribner, 1903.

Cacho, Lisa Marie. *Social Death: Racialized Rightlessness and the Crimalization of the Unprotected*. New York: New York University Press, 2012.

Cavarero, Adriana. *For More Than One Voice: Towards a Philosophy of Vocal Expression*. Translated by Paul A. Kottman. Stanford, CA: Stanford University Press, 2005.

DeFrantz, Thomas, and Anita Gonzalez, eds. *Black Performance Theory*. Durham, NC: Duke University Press, 2014.

Harney, Stefano, and Fred Moten. *The Undercommons: Fugitive Planning and Black Study*. Brooklyn: Minor Compositions, 2013.

Mbembe, Achille. *On the Postcolony*. Berkeley: University of California Press, 2001.

McKittrick, Katherine. *Demonic Grounds: Black Women and the Cartographies of Struggle*. Minneapolis: University of Minnesota Press, 2006.

Mouffe, Chantal. *The Democratic Paradox*. London: Verso, 2000.

Nancy, Jean-Luc. *The Muses*. Translated by Peggy Kamuf. Stanford, CA: Stanford University Press, 1994.

Reed, Anthony. *Freedom Time: The Poetics and Politics of Black Experimental Writing*. Baltimore: Johns Hopkins University Press, 2014.

Sedgwick, Eve Kosofsky. *Touching Feeling: Affect, Pedagogy, Performance*. Durham, NC: Duke University Press, 2003.

Tank and the Bangas. "RollerCoasters." Spotify track 3 on *Think Tank*. Independent, 2013.

Warren, Calvin. "Black Nihilism and the Politics of Hope." 2015. https://illwilleditions
.noblogs.org/files/2015/09/Warren-Black-Nihilism-the-Politics-of-Hope-READ.pdf.

Wells, Ida B. *The Reason Why the Colored American Is Not in the Columbian Exhibition: The
Afro American Contribution to Columbian Literature*. Chicago: Ida B. Wells, 1893. Reprint
edition edited by Robert W. Rydell. Urbana: University of Illinois Press, 1999.

Whitman, Albery Allson. *The Rape of Florida* (1884). Miami: Mnemosyne Publishing, 1969.

Stefania Heim, "Essay in Fragments, A Pile of Limbs: Walt Whitman's Body in the Book"

Andrewes, Lancelot. *Sermons of the Nativity and of Repentance and Fasting*. Oxford: James
Parker, 1878.

Cha, Theresa Hak Kyung. *Dictee*. Berkeley: University of California Press, 2009.

Derrida, Jacques. *Sovereignties in Question: The Poetics of Paul Celan*. Edited by Thomas Dutoit
and Outi Pasanen. New York: Fordham University Press, 2005.

Dickinson, Emily. *The Complete Poems of Emily Dickinson*. Edited by Thomas H. Johnson.
New York: Little, Brown, 1961.

Eby, Harold Edwin. *A Concordance of Walt Whitman's Leaves of Grass and Selected Prose
Writings*. Seattle: University of Washington Press, 1949.

Heyde, Charles L., to Louisa Whitman. December 1868. Autograph letter, three pages, signed.
Walt Whitman Papers. David M. Rubenstein Rare Book and Manuscript Library, Duke
University.

Kaplan, Justin. *Walt Whitman: A Life*. New York: Simon and Schuster, 1980.

Miller, Brian Craig. *Empty Sleeves: Amputation in the Civil War South*. Athens: University of
Georgia Press, 2015.

Whitman, Walt. *Complete Poetry and Collected Prose*. New York: Library of America, 1982.

———. *The Correspondence, Volume 1: 1842–1867*. Edited by Edwin Haviland Miller. New York:
New York University Press, 1961.

———. *The Correspondence, Volume 3: 1876–1885*. Edited by Edwin Haviland Miller. New York:
New York University Press, 1964.

———. "Song of Myself" from *Leaves of Grass*. Autograph manuscript and printed pages, printer's
copy for portions of 1881–1882 edition. Walt Whitman Papers. David M. Rubenstein Rare
Book and Manuscript Library, Duke University.

———. *Memoranda During the War*. Edited by Peter Coviello. Oxford: Oxford University Press,
2004.

Karen Weiser, "Touching Horror: Poe, Race, and Gun Violence"

Baldwin, James. "The Artist's Struggle for Integrity." Speech recorded at the Community Church,
New York City. Broadcast on WBAI radio on November 29, 1962. https://soundcloud.com
/brainpicker/james-baldwin-the-artists-struggle-for-integrity-full-lecture.

Brennan, Teresa. *The Transmission of Affect*. Cambridge: Cambridge University Press, 2004.

Brooks, Gwendolyn. *The Bean Eaters*. Whitefish, MT: Literary Licensing, 1960.

Faherty, Duncan. "'Legitimate Sources' and 'Legitimate Results': Surveying the Social Terror of 'Usher' and 'Ligeia.'" In *Approaches to Teaching Poe's Prose and Poetry*, edited by Jeffrey Andrew Weinstock and Tony Magistrale, 39–47. New York: MLA, 2008.

Felski, Rita. *The Limits of Critique*. Chicago: University of Chicago Press, 2015.

Howe, Susan. *The Birth-Mark: Unsettling the Wilderness in American Literary History*. Middletown, CT: Wesleyan University Press, 1993.

Hunt, Erica. "Risk Signature." *Bomb Magazine*, January 1, 1997. https://bombmagazine.org /articles/three-poems-77/.

Kristeva, Julia. *Powers of Horror: An Essay of Abjection*. Translated by Leon Roudiez. New York: Columbia University Press, 1982.

Latour, Bruno. "Why Has Critique Run Out of Steam? From Matters of Fact to Matters of Concern." *Critical Inquiry* 30, no. 2 (Winter 2004): 225–48.

Lorde, Audre. *Sister Outsider: Essays and Speeches by Audre Lorde*. Berkeley: Crossing Press, 2007.

Morrison, Toni. *Playing in the Dark: Whiteness and the Literary Imagination*. Cambridge, MA: Harvard University Press, 1992.

Nigatu, Heben, and Tracy Clayton. "83: Incognegro (with Jordan Peele)." *Another Round* podcast, WNYC, March 1, 2017. MP3 audio, 00:56:31. https://www.acast.com/anotherround /episode-83-incognegro-with-jordan-peele.

Phillips, Adam. *Missing Out: In Praise of the Unlived Life*. New York: Picador, 2013.

Poe, Edgar Allan. "The Facts in the Case of M. Valdemar." *American Review*, December 1845.

———. *The Narrative of Arthur Gordon Pym*. New York: Harper and Brothers, 1838. https:// www.eapoe.org/works/tales/pymb18.htm.

———. Letter to Thomas W. White, April 30, 1835. Edgar Allan Poe Society of Baltimore website. https://www.eapoe.org/works/letters/p3504300.htm.

Quinn, Arthur Hobson. *Edgar Allan Poe: A Critical Biography*. New York: Appleton-Century, 1941.

Rankine, Claudia. *Citizen: An American Lyric*. Minneapolis: Graywolf Press, 2014.

———. "The Condition of Black Life Is One of Mourning." *New York Times*, June 22, 2015. https://www.nytimes.com/2015/06/22/magazine/the-condition-of-black-life-is-one-of -mourning.html.

Sedgwick, Eve Kosofsky. *Touching Feeling: Affect, Pedagogy, Performativity*. Durham, NC: Duke University Press, 2003.

Schulman, Sarah. "Open Casket." *ArtsEverywhere* (blog), April 12, 2017. http://artseverywhere .ca/2017/04/12/open-casket/.

Stevens, Wallace. *Collected Poetry and Prose*. New York: Library of America, 1997.

Walls, Seth Colter. "Reviving the Ghostly Sounds of Maryanne Amarcher." *New York Times*, May 19, 2017. https://www.nytimes.com/2017/05/19/arts/music/reviving-the-ghostly -sounds-of-maryanne-amacher.html.

Whalen, Terence. *Edgar Allan Poe and the Masses: The Political Economy of Literature in Antebellum America*. Princeton: Princeton University Press, 1999.

Wittgenstein, Ludwig. *Tractatus Logico-Philosophicus*. Translated by D. G. Pears and B. F. McGuinness. Atlantic Highlands, NJ: Humanities Press International, 1992.

Benjamin Friedlander, "Homage to Bayard Taylor"

Agamben, Giorgio. *The Sacrament of Language: An Archaeology of the Oath*. Translated by Adam Kotsko. Stanford, CA: Stanford University Press, 2011.

Bernstein, Michael André. *Foregone Conclusions: Against Apocalyptic History*. Berkeley: University of California Press, 1994.

Carpenter, Edward. *Days with Walt Whitman*. New York: Macmillan, 1906.

Castiglia, Christopher, and Christopher Looby. "Come Again? New Approaches to Sexuality in Nineteenth-Century U.S. Literature." *ESQ* 55, no. 3–4 (2009): 195–209.

Conwell, Russell H. *The Life, Travels, and Literary Career of Bayard Taylor*. Boston: B. B. Russell, 1879.

Corley, Liam. *Bayard Taylor: Determined Dreamer of America's Rise, 1825–1878*. Lewisburg, PA: Bucknell University Press, 2014.

Coviello, Peter. *Tomorrow's Parties: Sex and the Untimely in Nineteenth-Century America*. New York: New York University Press, 2013.

Fradenburg, Louise, and Carla Freccero, eds. *Premodern Sexualities*. New York: Routledge, 1996.

G. H. B. [George Henry Boker]. Preface to *The Poetical Works of Bayard Taylor*, iii–iv. Boston: Houghton, Osgood, 1880.

von Goethe, Johann Wolfgang. *Faust: A Tragedy*. Translated by Bayard Taylor. Boston: Houghton Mifflin, 1870.

Hallock, John W. M. *The American Byron: Homosexuality and the Fall of Fitz-Greene Halleck*. Madison: University of Wisconsin Press, 2000.

Hansen-Taylor, Marie, and Horace Scudder, eds. *Life and Letters of Bayard Taylor*. 2 vols. Boston: Houghton Mifflin, 1885.

Katz, Jonathan Ned. *Love Stories: Sex between Men before Homosexuality*. Chicago: University of Chicago Press, 2001.

Looby, Christopher. "The Literariness of Sexuality: Or, How to Do the (Literary) History of (American) Sexuality." *American Literary History* 25, no. 4 (Winter 2013): 841–54.

Martin, Robert K. *The Homosexual Tradition in American Poetry*. Austin: University of Texas Press, 1979.

Nealon, Christopher. *Foundlings: Lesbian and Gay Historical Emotion before Stonewall*. Durham, NC: Duke University Press, 2001.

Nissen, Axel. *Manly Love: Romantic Friendship in American Fiction*. Chicago: University of Chicago Press, 2009.

Taylor, Bayard. "American vs. English Criticism." *New York Daily Tribune*, April 12, 1876.

———. *A Book of Romances, Lyrics, and Songs*. Boston: Ticknor, Reed, and Fields, 1852.

———. *The Echo Club and Other Literary Diversions*. Boston: James R. Osgood, 1876.

———. "In Re Walt Whitman." *New York Daily Tribune*, March 28, 1876.

———. *John Godfrey's Fortunes*. New York: G. P. Putnam; Hurd and Houghton, 1864.

———. *Joseph and His Friend: A Story of Pennsylvania*. New York: G. P. Putnam and Sons, 1870.

———. *The National Ode*. Boston: William F. Gill, 1877.

———. *The Poems of Bayard Taylor*. Boston: Ticknor and Fields, 1865.

———. *Poems of Home and Travel*. Boston: Ticknor and Fields, 1856.

———. *Poems of the Orient*. Boston: Ticknor and Fields, 1855.

———. *The Poetical Works of Bayard Taylor*. Household Edition. Boston: Houghton, Osgood, 1880.

———. *The Poetical Works of Bayard Taylor*. Household Edition. Boston: Houghton Mifflin, 1902.

———. *Selected Letters*. Edited by Paul C. Wermuth. Lewisburg, PA: Bucknell University Press, 1997.

Taylor, Marie Hansen. *On Two Continents: Memories of Half a Century*. New York: Doubleday, Page, 1905.

Theocritus. *The Greek Bucolic Poets*. Translated by J. M. Edmonds. New York: Macmillan, 1912.

Traubel, Horace. *With Walt Whitman in Camden*. 3 vols. 1906–1914. New York: Rowman and Littlefield, 1961.

Whitman, Walt. *Notebooks and Unpublished Prose Manuscripts*. Edited by Edward F. Grier. 6 vols. New York: New York University Press, 1984.

Joshua Bennett, "Revising *The Waste Land*: Black Antipastoral & The End of the World"

Agamben, Giorgio. *The Open: Man and Animal*. Stanford, CA: Stanford University Press, 2004.

Baraka, Amiri, dir. *The New-Ark*. 1968. Newark, NJ: Amiri Baraka, 2014. DVD.

Brown, Chip. "Kea's Improbable Ark." *Chicago Tribune*, April 22, 1987. http://articles.chicago tribune.com/1987-04-22/features/8701300910_1_kea-tawana-red-pine-central-ward.

Césaire, Aimé. *Notebook of a Return to the Native Land*. Middletown, CT: Wesleyan University Press, 2001.

Cullen, Countee. *The Lost Zoo*. Illustrated by Joseph Low. Westchester, IL: Follett, 1969.

———. "Yet Do I Marvel." In *The Black Poets*, edited by Dudley Randall, 100. New York: Bantam, 1971.

Dayan, Colin. *The Law Is a White Dog: How Legal Rituals Make and Unmake Persons*. Princeton, NJ: Princeton University Press, 2011.

Dunbar, Paul Laurence. "We Wear the Mask." In *Lyrics of Lowly Life*, 167. New York: Dodd, Mead, 1898.

Dungy, Camille T., ed. *Black Nature: Four Centuries of African American Nature Poetry*. Athens: University of Georgia Press, 2009.

Ellison, Ralph. *Invisible Man*. New York: Penguin, 2014.

Hartman, Saidiya V. *Lose Your Mother: A Journey Along the Atlantic Slave Route*. New York: Farrar, Straus and Giroux, 2008.

Horkheimer, Max, and Theodor W. Adorno. *Dialectic of Enlightenment*. Edited by Gunzelin Noeri. Translated by Edmund Jephcott. Stanford, CA: Stanford University Press, 2002.

Jordan, June. "On a New Year's Eve." In *Directed by Desire: The Collected Poems of June Jordan*, 206. Port Townsend, WA: Copper Canyon Press, 2007.

Kishik, David. *The Power of Life: Agamben and the Coming Politics, Volume 2*. Stanford, CA: Stanford University Press, 2012.

Monáe, Janelle, Big Boi, and Saul Williams, writers. "Dance or Die." *The ArchAndroid*. New York: Bad Boy Records, 2010, compact disc.

Moraga, Cherríe, and Gloria Anzaldúa, eds. *This Bridge Called My Back: Writings by Radical Women of Color*. Albany: State University of New York Press, 2015.

Morrison, Toni. *Beloved*. Philadelphia: Chelsea House, 1987.

———. *Song of Solomon*. New York: Vintage, 2004.

Ngai, Sianne. *Ugly Feelings*. Cambridge, MA: Harvard University Press, 2009.

Rankine, Claudia. *Citizen: An American Lyric*. Minneapolis: Graywolf Press, 2014.

Sexton, Jared. "Afro-Pessimism: The Unclear Word." *Rhizomes: Cultural Studies in Emerging Knowledge* 29 (2016). doi.org/10.20415/rhiz/029.e02.

Sharpe, Christina. *In the Wake: On Blackness and Being*. Durham, NC: Duke University Press, 2016.

Vergara, Camilo. "Why Newark's Ark Should Be Saved." *New York Times*, April 26, 1987. http://www.nytimes.com/1987/04/26/nyregion/new-jersey-opinion-why-newark-s-ark-should-be-saved.html.

Whitfield, James Monroe. "The Misanthropist." Poetry Foundation. https://www.poetry foundation.org/poems/52478/the-misanthropist.

Williams, Phillip B. "Mastery." *Paris Review* 223 (Winter 2017). https://www.theparisreview .org/poetry/7093/mastery-phillip-b-williams.

———. *Thief in the Interior*. Farmington, ME: Alice James Books, 2016.

Wynter, Sylvia. "Unsettling the Coloniality of Being/Power/Truth/Freedom: Towards the Human, After Man, Its Overrepresentation—An Argument." *CR: The New Centennial Review* 3, no. 3 (2003): 257–337.

Cole Swensen, "Henry Ossawa Tanner: Night Over Night"

Marley, Anna O., ed. *Henry Ossawa Tanner: Modern Spirit*. Berkeley: University of California Press, 2012.

Mathews, Marcia M. *Henry Ossawa Tanner: American Artist*. Chicago: University of Chicago Press, 1969.

Tanner, Henry Ossawa. *Abraham's Oak*. 1905. Smithsonian American Art Museum, Washington, DC.

———. *Algiers, Old Buildings Near Ka-hak*. c. 1912. Collection of Lewis Tanner Moore.

——— *Christ and his Disciples on Their Way to Bethany*. c. 1902–03. Musée d'Orsay, Paris, France.

———. *The Disciples See Christ Walking on the Water*. c. 1907. Des Moines Art Center, Des Moines, Iowa.

———. *Entrance to the Casbah*. 1912. Art Museum of Greater Lafayette, Lafayette, Indiana.

———. *Étaples Fisher Folk*. 1923. High Museum of Art, Atlanta, Georgia.

——. *Fishermen's Return*. 1926. Harmon and Harriet Kelley Foundation for the Arts, San Antonio, Texas.

——. *Gateway Tangier*. c. 1910. Smithsonian American Art Museum, Washington, DC.

——. *The Good Shepherd*. 1902–03. Zimmerli Art Museum, Rutgers University, New Brunswick, New Jersey.

——. *The Jews' Wailing Place*. c. 1897. Museum of the Rhode Island School of Design, Providence, Rhode Island.

——. *The Miraculous Haul of Fishes*. c. 1913–14. National Academy Museum, New York, New York.

——. *Moonlight, Walls of Tangiers*. c. 1913–14. Los Angeles County Museum of Art, Los Angeles, California.

——. *A Mosque in Cairo*. 1897. Collection of William M. Lewis Jr. and Carol Sutton Lewis.

——. *Nicodemus*. 1899. Pennsylvania Academy of the Fine Arts, Philadelphia, Pennsylvania.

——. *Nicodemus Visiting Jesus*. 1927. Collection of Raymond J. McGuire, New York, New York.

—— *Palace of Justice, Tangier*. c. 1912–13. Smithsonian American Art Museum, Washington, DC.

——. *Return at Night from the Market*. c. 1912. Clark Atlanta University Art Collection, Atlanta, Georgia.

——. *Le Touquet*. c. 1910. Des Moines Art Center, Des Moines, Iowa.

——. *A View of Palestine*. 1898–99. Frances Lehman Loeb Art Center, Vassar College, Poughkeepsie, New York.

Cecily Parks, "Nights and Lights in Nineteenth-Century American Poetics"

Bourne, Hermon. *Flores Poetici, The Florist's Manual: Designed as an Introduction to Vegetable Physiology and Systematic Botany for Cultivators of Flowers*. Boston: Munroe and Francis, 1833. https://babel.hathitrust.org/cgi/pt?id=nyp.33433006561470.

Davies, Terence, dir. *A Quiet Passion*. Chicago: Music Box Films, 2017. DVD.

Dickinson, Emily. *The Letters of Emily Dickinson*. Edited by Thomas H. Johnson and Theodora Ward. Cambridge, MA: Belknap Press of Harvard University Press, 1986.

——. *The Poems of Emily Dickinson: Reading Edition*. Edited by R. W. Franklin. Cambridge, MA: Belknap Press of Harvard University Press, 2005.

Edwards, Howell G. M. "Will-o'-the-Wisp: An Ancient Mystery with Extremophile Origins?" *Philosophical Transactions of the Royal Society A: Mathematical, Physical, and Engineering Sciences*. December 13, 2014. http://rsta.royalsocietypublishing.org/content/372/2030/20140206.

Farr, Judith. *The Gardens of Emily Dickinson*. Cambridge, MA: Harvard University Press, 2005.

Irving, Washington. "The Legend of Sleepy Hollow." Project Gutenberg. https://www.gutenberg.org/files/41/41-h/41-h.htm.

Kilcup, Karen. *Fallen Forests: Emotion, Embodiment, and Ethics in American Women's Environmental Writing, 1781–1924*. Athens: University of Georgia Press, 2013.

Macfarlane, Robert. *Landmarks*. New York: Penguin Books, 2015.

Phillips, Dana. *The Truth of Ecology: Nature, Culture, and Literature in America*. Oxford: Oxford University Press, 2003.

Ruefle, Mary. "Poetry and the Moon." In *Madness, Rack, and Honey*, 10–29. Seattle: Wave Books, 2012.

Stewart, Susan. *Poetry and the Fate of the Senses*. Chicago: University of Chicago Press, 2002.

Thoreau, Henry David. *The Journal of Henry David Thoreau, 1837–1861*. Edited by Damion Searls. New York: New York Review Books Classics, 2009.

——. *The Maine Woods*. In *A Week on the Concord and Merrimack Rivers, Walden, The Maine Woods, Cape Cod*. Edited by Robert F. Sayre. New York: Library of America, 1985.

Vargues, Lisa. "Flashes in the Twilight." *Science Talk: Exploring the Science of Plants, from the Field to the Lab* (blog). New York Botanical Garden. December 30, 2013. https://www.nybg.org/blogs/science-talk/2013/12/flashes-in-the-twilight/.

Brian Teare, "The Earth Is Full of Men"

Beaton, Roderick. "From Ancient to Modern: Byron, Shelley, and the Idea of Greece." *Athens Dialogues* 1 (2010): 1–22. http://argos.chs.harvard.edu/cgi-bin/WebObjects/ athensdialogues .woa/wa/dist?dis=17.

Bellin, Joshua. "Native American Rights." In *The Oxford Handbook of Transcendentalism*, edited by Joel Myerson, Sandra Harbert Petrulionis, and Laura Dassow Walls, 198–209. Oxford: Oxford University Press, 2010.

Bryant, William Cullen. *The Letters of William Cullen Bryant, Volume I, 1809–1836*. Edited by William Cullen Bryant II and Thomas G. Voss. New York: Fordham University Press, 1975.

——. *The Letters of William Cullen Bryant, Volume II, 1836–1849*. Edited by William Cullen Bryant II and Thomas G. Voss. New York: Fordham University Press, 1977.

——. "The Prairies." Poetry Foundation. https://www.poetryfoundation.org/poems/55341 /the-prairies.

——. *The Prose Writings of William Cullen Bryant, Volume II*. Edited by Parke Godwin. New York: Russell and Russell, 1964.

Capper, Charles. *Margaret Fuller: An American Romantic Life, Volume II: The Public Years*. Oxford: Oxford University Press, 2007.

Emerson, Ralph Waldo. "The Poet." In *Selections from Ralph Waldo Emerson*, edited by Stephen E. Whichler, 222–41. New York: Houghton Mifflin, 1957.

Fuller, Margaret. *Summer on the Lakes, in 1843*. In *The Portable Margaret Fuller*, edited by Mary Kelly, 69–227. New York: Penguin Books, 1994.

——. *The Letters of Margaret Fuller, Volume III, 1842–1844*. Edited by Robert N. Hudspeth. Ithaca, NY: Cornell University Press, 1984.

Muller, Gilbert H. *William Cullen Bryant: Author of America*. Albany: State University of New York Press, 2008.

Pico, Tommy. *Nature Poem*. Portland, OR: Tin House Books, 2017.

Walls, Laura Dassow. *Seeing New Worlds: Henry David Thoreau and Nineteenth-Century Natural Science*. Madison: University of Wisconsin Press, 1995.

M. NourbeSe Philip, "Making Black Cake in Combustible Spaces"

Bachelard, Gaston. *On Poetic Imagination and Reverie*. Translated by C. Gaudin. Indianapolis: Bobbs-Merrill, 1971.

Murray, Aífe. *Maid as Muse*. Lebanon: University of New Hampshire Press, 2009.

Nelson, Davia, and Nikki Silva. "62: Black Cake, Emily Dickinson's Hidden Kitchen." *The Kitchen Sisters Present*, PRX. January 10, 2017. MP3 audio, 00:32:39. https://www.kitchensisters .org/2017/01/10/episode-62-black-cake-emily-dickinsons-hidden-kitchen/.

Philip, M. NourbeSe. "Burn Sugar." In *Imagining Women*, edited by Rhea Tregebov. Toronto: Women's Press, 1988.

———. *She Tries Her Tongue; Her Silence Softly Breaks*. Middletown, CT: Wesleyan University Press, 2014.

Leila Wilson, "'The Tinge Awakes': Reading Whitman and Others in Trouble"

Borges, Jorge Luis. "Walt Whitman: Man and Myth." *Critical Inquiry* 1, no. 4 (1975): 707–18. https://www.jstor.org/stable/1342843.

Chen, Ken. "What's the Matter with Poetry?" *New Republic*, June 23, 2016. https://www .newrepublic.com/article/134504/whats-matter-poetry.

Davis, Christina. *An Ethic*. Callicoon, NY: Nightboat Books, 2013.

Hamilton, Saskia. *Corridor*. Minneapolis: Graywolf Press, 2014.

Haraway, Donna J. *Staying with the Trouble: Making Kin in the Chthulucene*. Durham, NC: Duke University Press, 2016.

McGuire, Richard. *Here*. New York: Pantheon, 2014.

McSweeney, Joyelle. "What Is the Necropastoral?" *Harriet* (blog), April 29, 2014. Poetry Foundation. https://www.poetryfoundation.org/harriet/2014/04/what-is-the-necropastoral.

Phillips, Carl. *Silverchest*. New York: Farrar, Straus and Giroux, 2014.

Rankine, Claudia. *Citizen: An American Lyric*. Minneapolis: Graywolf Press, 2014.

Ruskin, John. *The Complete Works, Volume IV*. Edited by E. T. Cook and Alexander Wedderburn. London: Allen, 1903.

Sacks, Oliver. *Migraine*. New York: Vintage, 1999.

Urban Death Project. "What's Wrong with Our Current Funeral Practices?" http://www .urbandeathproject.org/.

Whitman, Walt. Epitaph. Walt Whitman Mausoleum, Harleigh Cemetary, Camden, NJ.

———. Letter to William D. O'Connor. October 7, 1882. Walt Whitman Archive. General editors Ed Folsom and Kenneth M. Price. https://www.whitmanarchive.org/.

———. *Notebooks and Unpublished Prose Manuscripts, Volume IV*. Edited by Edward F. Grier. New York: New York University Press, 1984.

———. *The Portable Walt Whitman*. Edited by Michael Warner. New York: Penguin, 2004.

IMAGE CREDITS

José Felipe Alvergue, "Feeling the Riot: Fugitivity, Lyric, and Enduring Failure"

Cannon Balls from Fort Gadsden State Historic Site—Sumatra, FL, photograph, Florida Photographic Collection, FPS01364.

Frontispiece to Joan Blaeu's *Atlas Maior*, 1665, courtesy of Dartmouth College Library.

Juvenile Convicts at Work in the Fields, c. 1903, photograph, Library of Congress, Prints & Photographs Division, Detroit Publishing Company Collection [reproduction number, e.g., LCD410865].

Plan of Fort Gadsden, 1818, reprint from the *Florida Historical Quarterly* 16 (July 1937).

Thomas Ball, *Emancipation Group*, 1873, white Italian marble, 45 1/2 x 27 9/16 x 21 1/4 in., Chazen Museum of Art, University of Wisconsin-Madison, gift of Dr. Warren E. Gilson, 1976.

Steve Helber, *Protester Arrested Flame Thrower*, 2017, photograph, Associated Press.

Stefania Heim, "Essay in Fragments, A Pile of Limbs: Walt Whitman's Body in the Book"

The images in this essay—"Song of Myself" from *Leaves of Grass* (autograph manuscript and printed pages, printer's copy for portions of 1881–1882 edition), from the Walt Whitman Papers—are printed with the permission of the David M. Rubenstein Rare Book and Manuscript Library, Duke University.

Special thanks to David Pavelich for his memorable introduction to the Walt Whitman Papers and Arianne Hartsell-Gundy of Duke University Libraries.

Joshua Bennett, "Revising *The Waste Land:* Black Antipastoral & The End of the World"

Robert Foster, photograph of Kea Tawana, *Ark*, 1987, Spaces Archives.

M. NourbeSe Philip, "Making Black Cake in Combustible Spaces"

Emily Dickinson, *[Recipe for] Black Cake*, Houghton Library, Harvard University, MS Am 1118.7.

EDITORS

Orestis Lambrou

ALEXANDRA MANGLIS is a writer, editor, and cofounder of the experimental poetry magazine *Wave Composition*. Her work has appeared in *The Millions*, the *Times Literary Supplement*, the *Los Angeles Review of Books*, and *Strange Horizons*. She is a graduate of the Clarion West Writers Workshop and holds a DPhil in English from the University of Oxford. She lives in Nicosia, Cyprus.

KRISTEN CASE is a poet, editor, and scholar. She is the author of *American Pragmatism and Poetic Practice: Crosscurrents from Emerson to Susan Howe*. Her first collection of poems, *Little Arias*, won the Maine Literary Award for Poetry in 2016, and her second collection, *Principles of Economics*, won the 2018 Gatewood Prize. She is also coeditor of *Thoreau at 200: Essays and Reassessments* and director of *Thoreau's Kalendar: A Digital Archive of the Phenological Manuscripts of Henry David Thoreau*. She teaches at the University of Maine at Farmington, where she is director of the New Commons Project.

Jaime Ranger

CONTRIBUTORS

JOSÉ FELIPE ALVERGUE is the author of the poetry collections *gist : rift : drift : bloom* and *precis*. A graduate of both the CalArts Writing and Buffalo Poetics programs, Alvergue teaches contemporary literature and transnationalism at the University of Wisconsin-Eau Claire.

DAN BEACHY-QUICK is a poet and essayist. His most recently published book is *Of Silence and Song*. He teaches in the MFA creative writing program at Colorado State University.

JOSHUA BENNETT is the author of *The Sobbing School*, which was a National Poetry Series selection and a finalist for an NAACP Image Award in Poetry. His writing has appeared in *The Nation*, the *New York Times*, the *Paris Review*, and *Poetry*, and he has recited original work at venues such as the Sundance Film Festival, the NAACP Image Awards, and President Obama's Evening of Poetry and Music at the White House. He teaches English and creative writing at Dartmouth College.

BENJAMIN FRIEDLANDER is the author of many books, including *Simulcast: Four Experiments in Criticism*, *One Hundred Etudes*, and, as editor, Robert Creeley's *Selected Poems, 1945–2005*. He teaches American literature and poetics at the University of Maine.

STEFANIA HEIM is the author of the poetry collections *A Table That Goes On for Miles* and *HOUR BOOK*, which was selected by Jennifer Moxley as winner of the Sawtooth Prize. Her published translations include Giorgio de Chirico's *Geometry of*

Shadows, and her essays and scholarship on American poetry have appeared in venues including *Jacket2*, *Journal of Narrative Theory*, *Textual Practice*, and Lost & Found: The CUNY Poetics Document Initiative. She teaches at Western Washington University.

FRED MOTEN is a poet and scholar who teaches in the department of performance studies at New York University. The author of numerous works of poetry and non-fiction, Moten's latest work is *consent not to be a single being*. Moten has received a Guggenheim Fellowship and the Stephen E. Henderson Award for Outstanding Achievement in Poetry from the African American Literature and Culture Society, among other awards.

JOAN NAVIYUK KANE is Inupiaq with family from King Island (Ugiuvak) and Mary's Igloo, Alaska. She was raised in and attended public school in Anchorage, Alaska, where she currently raises her sons as a single mother. A 2018 Guggenheim Fellow in Poetry, Kane is also the author of the essay collection *A Few Lines in the Manifest* and several books and chapbooks of poetry including *The Cormorant Hunter's Wife*, *Hyperboreal*, *The Straits*, *Milk Black Carbon*, and *Sublingual*.

CECILY PARKS is the author of the poetry collections *Field Folly Snow* and *O'Nights*, and editor of the anthology *The Echoing Green: Poems of Fields, Meadows, and Grasses*. Her poems have appeared in the *New Republic*, the *New Yorker*, *Tin House*, and elsewhere. The recipient of a Pushcart Prize, Parks teaches in the MFA program at Texas State University.

M. NOURBESE PHILIP is the author of the poetry collections *Thorns*, *Salmon Courage*, *She Tries Her Tongue; Her Silence Softly Breaks*, and *Zong!* Her critical work includes *Frontiers: Essays and Writings on Racism and Culture*, *Showing Grit: Showboating North of the 44th Parallel*, *CARIBANA: African Roots and Continuities—Race, Space and the Poetics of Moving*, and *Genealogy of Resistance and Other Essays*. She has also published two novels, *Harriet's Daughter* and *Looking for Livingstone: An Odyssey of Silence*. Her numerous honors and awards include fellowships from the Guggenheim Foundation, the Rockefeller Foundation, and the MacDowell Colony.

COLE SWENSEN is the author of seventeen volumes of poetry, most recently *On Walking On*. She is also the author of a collection of critical essays, *Noise That Stays Noise*. And she has translated over twenty volumes of French poetry and prose, with a focus on art criticism. She coedited the 2009 Norton anthology *American Hybrid* and is the founding editor of La Presse, which publishes contemporary French poetry in translation. She teaches at Brown University.

BRIAN TEARE is the author of six books, including *Doomstead Days*; *Companion Grasses,* which was a finalist for the Kingsley Tufts Award; and *The Empty Form Goes All the Way to Heaven*. Teare's honors include a Lambda Literary Award and fellowships from the NEA, the Pew Foundation, the American Antiquarian Society, and the MacDowell Colony. He is an associate professor at Temple University, lives in South Philadelphia, and makes books by hand for his micropress, Albion Books.

KAREN WEISER is the author of two poetry collections, *Or, The Ambiguities* and *To Light Out*. She has a forthcoming essay on Edgar Allan Poe, Erasmus Darwin, and scientific poems in *Poe Studies*, as well as poems in a forthcoming number of *Critical Quarterly*. She earned her PhD in English from the CUNY Graduate Center, and is currently in training in psychoanalysis at ICP in New York City, where she works as a therapist.

LEILA WILSON is the author of *The Hundred Grasses*, a finalist for the 2014 Kate Tufts Discovery Award. A recipient of honors from the Academy of American Poets and the Poetry Foundation, Wilson runs the Writing Center and teaches creative writing and literature at the School of the Art Institute in Chicago.

Founded as a nonprofit organization in 1980, Milkweed Editions is an independent publisher. Our mission is to identify, nurture and publish transformative literature, and build an engaged community around it.

milkweed.org

Interior design by Janet Evans-Scanlon
Typeset in Minion Pro

Designed by Robert Slimbach, Minion is inspired
by late Renaissance-era type and intended
for body text and extended reading.